T0334792

EDUCATION TRANSFORMATION IN MUSLIM SOCIETIES

ADVANCING EDUCATION IN MUSLIM SOCIETIES

BOOK SERIES

Editor Ilham Nasser

EDUCATION TRANSFORMATION IN MUSLIM SOCIETIES

A Discourse of Hope

—ɯ—

EDITED BY
ILHAM NASSER

INDIANA UNIVERSITY PRESS AND
INTERNATIONAL INSTITUTE OF ISLAMIC THOUGHT

This book is a joint publication of

Indiana University Press
Office of Scholarly Publishing
Herman B Wells Library 350
1320 East 10th Street
Bloomington, Indiana 47405 USA

iupress.org

and

The International Institute of Islamic Thought
500 Grove Street, Suite 2020
Herndon, VA 20170
iiit.org

Manufactured in the United States of America

First printing 2022

Library of Congress Cataloging-in-Publication Data

Names: Nasser, Ilham, [date] author. | International Institute of Islamic Thought.
Title: Education transformation in Muslim societies : a discourse of hope / Ilham Nasser.
Identifiers: LCCN 2022026882 (print) | LCCN 2022026883 (ebook) | ISBN 9780253063793 (hardcover) | ISBN 9780253063809 (pdf)
Subjects: LCSH: Muslims—Education. | Islamic education. | Educational change.
Classification: LCC LC903 .N387 2022 (print) | LCC LC903 (ebook) | DDC 371.077—dc23/eng/20220718
LC record available at https://lccn.loc.gov/2022026882
LC ebook record available at https://lccn.loc.gov/2022026883

CONTENTS

ACKNOWLEDGMENTS

I EXTEND MY DEEPEST GRATITUDE to all the contributing authors and their students for their work and patience as we undertook this first book in the series on Advancing Education in Muslim Societies published by the International Institute of Islamic Thought and Indiana University Press. This book is the first product of a collaborative agreement between an academic institution and a research nonprofit organization. Special thanks to our editorial team at IIIT and the team at Indiana University Press. Finally, thanks to Shiraz Khan and Batool Al-Shaar for editing and formatting this book. This book is dedicated to my mother who passed away during the preparation of this book.

PREFACE

THE ADVANCING EDUCATION IN MUSLIM Societies (AEMS) is an initiative of the International Institute of Islamic Thought (IIIT). For the past few years, the IIIT has invested in empirical research, to add to many years of theoretical scholarship and to contribute to the agenda of reform in Muslim societies. Along with that, two additional methods of dissemination came to life: (1) The *Journal of Education in Muslim Societies* and (2) The AEMS book series with a focus on in-depth investigations, reflections, and analysis of educational themes pertinent to Muslim societies and communities.

AEMS is an aspiration and a long-term goal of the IIIT.[1] It is part of a larger effort to reform education in general and to share the lessons learned with others, especially in the Global South, or what international agencies call "lower income countries" (Adamson et al., 2016). AEMS also responds to the global reform effort that goes against the current approach to education as an "ideological package" of reform ideas (Carnoy & Rhoten, 2002). This includes, for example, the Global Education Reform Movement (GERM) of privatization, standardized testing, accountability, and school choice.

The GERM's rationale is based on economic investments in the private and corporate sectors of education, and the resulting reforms are typically driven by top-down policies and imports from developed countries (Adamson et al., 2016). For example, Chile imported the neoliberal (free market) model of education developed in the United States to improve education through competition and school choice (Castro-Hidalgo & Gomez-Alvarez, 2016). Such scenarios, however, have often been criticized for how school choice disproportionately benefits wealthier communities, as opposed to those living in poverty.[2]

A closer historical examination of reform efforts' timelines, specific to Muslim societies, is important but is beyond the scope of this book. Nevertheless, it is important to acknowledge the contributions of many Muslim scholars, such as those in Egypt and other countries who called for reform of education in general and more specifically Islamic education (Gesink, 2006). The further examination of the impact of the GERM on Muslim societies and the ways international aid is determined is also an important component of reform that may provide the historical, geopolitical, and social contexts for advancing education.

More specifically to the organization and its efforts to contribute to the dialogue, the IIIT has been both an agent to achieve and promote the goals of reform and a leading academic and research institution charged with renewing Islamic thought through the integration of knowledge (IOK) in the social sciences. The IIIT made an intentional refocus on the AEMS as a core framework that guides the theoretical, empirical, and organizational aspects of the institute. The initiative closes the circle of more than thirty-five years of theoretical work to the applied research and thereby shares the knowledge widely and acquires a voice in the discussion on reform initiatives and the IOK. AEMS comes as a "theoretical discourse as well as to generate data-driven research that represents the highest levels of intellectual integrity" (Alwani & Nasser, 2019, p. 30). The book series comes as a critical component to advance this vision.

RATIONALE

Reform of education in its broadest sense requires forces coming together to improve education systems as well as educational policies and leadership. It also necessitates long-term planning and flexible designs, including the involvement of multiple stakeholders to impact policies, curriculum, and teaching practices. With full awareness of the enormous tasks that a reform agenda entails, AEMS views education as a platform for addressing the status quo and the larger geopolitical environments to explore ways in which education can play a role in infusing values and empowering individuals and groups to pursue those as part of their personal development. Hope, in this case, is a research construct as well as a value that grounds the empirical research plans of AEMS and contributes to its future orientation.

Finally, AEMS contributes to educational thinking that is authentic and culturally appropriate. In contexts such as Muslim societies of today, where religion is central to the state, a thorough and sensitive approach is critical. For example, schooling typically includes Islamic studies as a distinct subject within or as an integrated part of school curriculum, indicating its centrality to education and importance to local communities and what they deem important (Nasser et al., 2019). Thus, it is as important to equip Muslim youths with tools and skills founded in faith and religion to respond to modern pressures. This edited book contributes to the dialogue on ways to answer the question of how to prepare youth in Muslim communities for the twenty-first century. This is done by providing examples of and a closer look at educational initiatives that have promise in their authenticity and focus on change. It serves a critical role in making stakeholders such as teachers, families, and policymakers aware of the whole-person approach by enriching the brain as well as the spirit and instilling hope into the teaching and learning spaces of educational institutions.

The goals of AEMS are what inspired this book. The following are the main objectives of the initiative.

- Contribute to the IOK intellectual discourse and its interface with academic disciplines in Muslim societies' educational systems. The initial interface with academic disciplines and educational systems will be through the adoption of the Universal Quranic Values approach.
- Provide evidence-based knowledge on advancing education in Muslim societies. Eventually, it will be expanded into other possible ways to interface the IOK's theoretical framework with the empirical aspects of AEMS.
- Recommend policies that engage governments, nongovernmental organizations, and universities, among others, in ways to transform education systems and advance people's well-being so they can participate proactively in building their societies and a civilization of peace and prosperity for all.
- Advocate for a developmental approach that is relevant to Muslim youths, schools, universities, families, and communities at large.
- Contribute to preparing a new generation of Muslim intellectuals, educators, and academics for research and teaching careers engaged with AEMS's major initiatives.
- Forge a universal intellectual discourse on the IOK and its Universal Quranic Values as a paradigm (Alwani & Nasser, 2019, p. 32).

A BOOK ON HOPE IN EDUCATION

This edited book responds in many ways to the need to shift the educational discourse in Muslim societies from a deficit to a strength-based orientation where youth and their prior knowledge, emotions, and faith are integrated. Learning from authentic experiences and innovations that are grounded in local realities may serve Muslim societies well and provide new and future knowledge to a larger audience of educational experts, policymakers, and government officials, among others. This is especially relevant to counter the heavy reliance on measuring impact based on rankings and performance on international assessments, where only a few of the Muslim majority societies make it. Even those who do, however, are usually at the bottom of the ranking. For example, on an overall best countries rating list, United Arab Emirates (UAE), Qatar, and Saudi Arabia appeared on the list of best countries in overall education (2019), but they only ranked 23, 31, and 32, respectively.[3] Furthermore, these assessments provide a partial evaluation of educational attainment because of their focus on achievement and not necessarily on the education of the whole person.

This volume contributes to a larger body of knowledge gathered on innovative and unique educational programs and research from various contexts around the globe. Quite a few books address Islamic education with a focus on Islamic sources of thought, theory, and practice, whereas this book expands on and provides an in-depth examination from multiple educational lenses utilizing Islamic education, in some cases, and teaching and learning contexts in pre-K through higher education in others. The book examines initiatives relevant to and inspired by local academics and practitioners in the field of education. It invites the larger education community to engage in dialogue and collaborative critical analysis of the future of education to serve the next generations around the globe.

As the first volume in this series, this book achieves the following goals:

1. Highlight asset/strength-based educational approaches by presenting initiatives in Muslim contexts where religion and religious education are used to instill hope.
2. Identify indicators and conditions needed to implement successful educational interventions and document those as they are expressed in curriculum, pedagogy, policy, and educational settings (the formal and nonformal).
3. Examine system-wide case studies that promote promising agendas with a focus on future generations.

4. Provide resources for educators looking for innovative methods to reform education.
5. Bring out the voices of researchers in Muslim contexts, especially educators.

This book argues for a hopeful education that is transformative, active, and innovative. It does not preach for hope in its most naive way but rather is a call to action and a critical examination of what works and what does not, only to change the status quo. Of course, this process is best guided by influential others in a person's life.

This book is divided into five parts and ten chapters, with contributors providing diverse perspectives and insights based on fields of expertise to reach a wide audience in the education world and beyond. The first part lays out the framework and the relevant theories and research on the topic of hope in education. The first chapter presents a general overview of the literature on hope and provides a framework for transformative learning to examine and operationalize hope in different educational contexts. The chapter explores the multiple definitions of hope and clarifies that hope in this edited volume is not defined in only one way or by one methodology and discipline. It also highlights that hope is not about optimism but is about adopting an orientation that is grounded in proactive living and achieving one's best potential.

Chapter 2, by Nuraan Davids, addresses Muslim education and ways it can encompass hope as one of the messages of Islam. The author takes us into an exploration of the South African context and Muslim schools to show how hope may be a vehicle for a better trajectory in education. Drawing on the seminal ideas espoused by Freire and hooks, the author argues that if Muslim education is to address divisions and marginalization both within and beyond its communities, then such an education cannot be remiss of hopefulness. To this end, the chapter offers a reimagined account of Muslim education—one that looks at hope as transcending human ruptures and dissonances, and that advances a cosmopolitan, human connection and resonance.

The second part of the book highlights higher-education contexts of learning. The four chapters (3–6) provide insights, questions, and reflections from different social and cultural contexts and environments. In chapter 3, Mualla Selçuk describes her work with student-teachers in a religious education program in Turkey using the multiple names of God to build their core values and beliefs and to find meaning in humanity. She focuses on one name of God: Al-Fattah (الفتاح) to guide the students into self-reflections based on her conceptual clarity model (CCM) and connects that with the aspiration for hope. Based on this pedagogical experiment, Selçuk asserts that hope requires three qualities: flexibility, imagination, and innovation. She ends with reiterating the messages of hope to the future generation of learners who can create change through social responsibility and a deeper understanding of the names of Allah (God) and their faith. One of the main messages of chapter 3 is that hope is a disposition and a stance, and it is necessary for Muslim education. Hope empowers teachers of religious education to be messengers and decision-makers, elevating the role of teachers to that of educators who impact the lives of their communities.

Chapter 4 discusses programs and case studies in higher education focused on students' learning journeys and, more specifically, on those of Muslim women and the empowerment of their gender identities in a Malaysian context. The chapter points out the hegemony of globalization, fear of change, and the function of working for hope as a solution. Suhailah Hussien highlights the importance of transformative pedagogy as a methodology to initiate dialogue among students on issues of identity, gender, and culture. She led students through in-depth discussions as female and Muslim educators at a university in Malaysia.

Chapters 5 and 6 highlight programs focused on reform through teachers' professional development. They draw from two case studies in Palestine and Egypt focusing on in-service teachers: one that was led by the government of Egypt and the other by an international nongovernmental organization in Palestine. Both chapters make recommendations on innovative methods and models that may ensure quality and take into consideration the local contexts. Both chapters also highlight the utilization of research and program evaluations as ways to document impact and provide evidence-based solutions to educational problems such as teacher qualifications and professional growth.

Chapter 5 is a participatory empirical study evaluating a model of professional development in Palestine (the West Bank and Gaza). It looks closely at a program targeting early-childhood teachers who went through intensive professional development training that lasted for a complete academic year. The study examines teachers' scores on a classroom climate checklist to explore the classroom environments of teachers who participated in the professional development program. The authors of this chapter recommend methods to empower teachers as agents of change and hope. They also describe a field-tested program for professional development—an issue that has been disputed, especially its effectiveness at transforming the teaching profession and empowering teachers.

Chapter 6 discusses teacher development efforts and professional growth programs taking a top-down approach from Egypt. It examines the schooling culture as a factor in school reform and highlights the importance of teachers' buy-in, input, and understanding of reform agenda (when reform is imposed), while also planning learning that shows promise and inspires transformation. The author documents teachers' responses to one of the reform programs grounded in the implementation of the multiple intelligences approach to learning and teachers' understanding of this approach as it is implemented in traditional learning contexts.

The fourth part of the book includes three chapters that take a close look at hope in schooling in K–12 environments. Chapter 7 sets the stage in K–12 by presenting a model that invites young students to think about the future in hopeful and positive ways. The model presented may be adapted to Islamic schooling contexts and applies to various social and political contexts. The chapter presents a model of hope education that engages students in an appreciative inquiry cycle to promote a future orientation that is positive and might be a catalyst for change in many societies and contexts.

Chapters 8 and 9 examine Islamic schools in the United States. Chapter 8 provides a close look at Islamic living, spaces, and schooling in North America and juxtaposes them with the modern secular lives of students in the United States. In-depth interviews present the views of teachers, administrators, and parents on the balancing act of Islamic education and secular education, and the interface of both with technology as it relates to students and their learning. Chapter 9 takes a closer look at a specific curriculum of an Islamic school and the ways these educators implement a transformative and hopeful curriculum and pedagogy models. The chapter takes a close look at materials, routines, and pedagogy, and how these incorporate hope and universal values. The uniqueness of this chapter is that it focuses on religious education as a model for student-centered pedagogy and religious identity formation for Muslim students in the United States.

In the fifth and final part, authors Shelley Wong and Tyrone Pits contribute final reflections as two Christian scholars of color in the United States. In chapter 10, they use an interfaith lens to find commonalities and lessons learned among the various contributions of this volume. They provide a critical analysis and synthesis to this edited volume utilizing their experiences and scholastic work to identify the powers at play in recent realities (whether educational or political) as well as identifying alliances and forces of hope for Muslims and non-Muslims. The chapter reviews the ideas and underpinning theories of the hope literature in a way that summarizes the messages of the edited volume.

The authors bring theoretical concepts as well as the research on hope to the forefront of this book in a way that appeals to a large audience of educators, policymakers, and concerned citizens of the world. It leaves us with further research questions and ideas necessary to deepen the understanding of the discourse of hope as it relates to Muslim societies and the Global South.

REFERENCES

Adamson, F., Åstrand, B., & Darling-Hammond, L. (Eds.). (2016). *Global education reform: How privatization and public investment influence education outcomes.* Routledge.

Alwani, A., & Nasser, I. (2019). IIIT's advancing education in Muslim societies initiative. *Islamic Horizons,* 30–32.

Carnoy, M., & Rhoten, D. (2002). What does globalization mean for educational change? A comparative approach (guest editorial essay). *Comparative Education Review, 46*(1), 1–9.

Castro-Hidalgo, A., & Gomez-Alvarez, L. (2016). Chile: A long-term neoliberal experiment and its impact on the quality and equity of education, 16–49. In F. Adamson, B. Åstrand, & L. Darling-Hammond (Eds.), *Global education reform: How privatization and public investment influence education outcomes.* Routledge.

Gesink, I. F. (2006). Islamic reformation: A history of *madrasa* reform and legal change in Egypt. *Comparative Education Review, 50*(3), 325–345.

Nasser, I., Miller-Idriss, C., & Alwani, A. (2019). Reconceptualizing education transformation in Muslim societies: The human development approach. *Journal of Education in Muslim Societies, 1*(1), 3–25.

NOTES

1. For further information on AEMS, see www.iiit.org.

2. Excerpts of this section were published in "Mapping the Terrain of Education," *Report of IIIT,* 2018–19.

3. Overall best countries rating, USNews.com, https://www.usnews.com/news/best-countries/overall-rankings.

PART I

EDUCATION, HOPE, AND MUSLIM SOCIETIES

ONE

ADVANCING EDUCATION IN MUSLIM SOCIETIES THROUGH A DISCOURSE OF HOPE

An Introduction

ILHAM NASSER

A young and proud fourteen-year-old Arab teenager sat in front of me while her mind and eyes were focused elsewhere. She had spent more than an hour glued to her phone without interacting with anyone. I looked at her and attempted to start a conversation, hoping to get her to open up and speak about her career goals in life. "What are your aspirations for the future?" I asked. She looked up and replied, "To immigrate and live in the West!" I asked why, and she responded firmly, "To have a future of happiness."

INTRODUCTION

In significantly distressing situations, virtues such as dignity and creativity are often quickly crushed. A people's positive and shared visions of themselves and the future of their society become lost, victim to the weight of the reality around them. This depressing situation marks life as experienced by many Muslim people and Muslim societies across the world. As a result, today we are witnessing that without a sound and unifying vision, nations "cast off restraint" and focus on survival, with cultures and societies simply existing to "survive and not thrive" (Teeffelen, 2007, p. 17). This is especially true since 2020, when the whole world was hit with the COVID-19 pandemic. The necessity of staying in survival mode feeds into the psyche of Muslim youth, especially when a general feeling of skepticism and helplessness hangs heavily in the air, in addition to a perceived collective sense of hopelessness and disappointment. In some cases, Muslim youth see immigration as the only way out, a means to escape the bitter realities of their local existence and the wider socioeconomic conditions of their societies. As they search for a better life and future, their despair-based perspective becomes outwardly centered, with a focus not on investing in their community but on escaping its grip, as they see it, and leaving it all behind. Skalli (2004) claims that Muslim youth are "in revolt against their own sense of powerlessness in the face of all the global forces that threaten their religious and cultural identity" (pp. 43–44). The globalization of our world and the hegemony of global trends pose even greater challenges for Muslim youth trying to adapt and remain hopeful. Countering this discourse of negativity and powerlessness is the hope education offers—the inspiration behind this edited volume. It is believed that hope can serve as an antidote to despair, functioning as a strong, psychologically protective factor for adolescents facing adverse conditions (Valle et al., 2006).

Thus, in the face of economic, political, health, and educational declines, it is vital that Muslim societies adopt agendas of hope—proactive and innovative, sweeping widely across the many sectors of society—to break the cycle of depression that lack of progress brings and to galvanize energy for finding viable solutions. Education, in this context, becomes an ideal public forum for instilling hope, rallying people, and challenging uncertainty. Education is often considered a safe space to promote and legitimize certain policies and approaches, and hope is both a concept and a measure that can be easily promoted with no one raising objections against it. Translating hope into practical steps and programs in the educational sphere is, however, a much harder enterprise and, in many cases, one too challenging to operationalize. A key reason for this is that educational transformation is a long-term process and rarely shows immediate gains, and where quick fixes usually do not work (Lewis & Young, 2015). The Egyptian public educational system (see chapter 6 on Egypt reform efforts) is a case in point; evidence indicates that despite significant funding by international agencies, investment has not paid off, and the situation has become so dire that many students resort to private tutors for their education. Those who cannot afford private instruction suffer education of substandard quality (El-Bilawi & Nasser, 2017), and income disparity is thus reflected in education disparity. This has been an ongoing struggle in many Muslim societies.

What is true of Egypt is also true of other Muslim societies. Despite financial investments by international development agencies, educational systems have not seen adequate and prolonged funding in countries that need it most. Pakistan, for example, receives a large amount of aid for infrastructure and curriculum reform, but it is not adequate to the task. The net impact on the Pakistani educational system is so small that people cannot see these programs offering hope for success (International Crisis Group, 2014). According to Ball

(2008), this may be due in some cases to the narrowing down of the goals of education. He concludes that "the social and economic purposes of education have been collapsed into a single, overriding emphasis on policymaking for economic competitiveness and an increasing neglect or sidelining (other than in rhetoric) of the social and spiritual purposes of education" (pp. 11–12). In the current political and economic environments in Muslim societies such as in the Middle East, it seems fitting to pay attention to education as a vehicle to advance hope and to encourage a positive future orientation. It is also equally important to change the public discourse from one of helplessness and despair to one of future-oriented growth and activity. Improving early-childhood education and increasing enrollment for girls and young women are some areas of learning where Muslim societies have made progress, but these cases are not well documented and have failed to produce measurable long-term gains. assessing effective educational initiatives and frameworks and analyzing reasons behind their success may provide a catalyst for positive educational outcomes and better targeted funding. Investing in education and highlighting promising initiatives may also send out a message of hope and encouragement for future generations as well as for educators.

The United Nations' Sustainable Development Goals 2030 (SDGs) emphasize education as a major achievable aspiration. This should motivate governments and funding organizations to prioritize education and use it as a mechanism for hopeful change that is embedded in advocacy for human dignity, social cohesion, and justice. The United Nations Educational, Scientific and Cultural Organization (UNESCO) tried to operationalize these goals by implementing a "Happy Schools" curriculum that sought to address the well-being of learners as a top agenda item in global policy (UNESCO, 2016, p. 10). The authors of the UNESCO report suggest that well-being correlates positively with better learning by sharing evidence from the work of The International Positive Education Network (IPEN, https://www.ipen-network.com/). We also have seen examples of governments paying attention to and promoting the well-being of citizens, as when the United Arab Emirates (UAE) launched a ministry of happiness and positivity[1] and Bhutan declared itself to be a happy country.[2]

Socioemotional education has been increasingly recognized as a promoter of well-being, especially as a critical component in achieving academic success (Durlak et al., 2011; Elias & Arnold, 2006) and has been linked to success in higher education (Chemers et al., 2001) as well as in professional lives (Heckman & Kautz, 2012). According to Chemers et al. (2001), hope, considered to be an indicator of wellbeing, highly correlates with academic self-efficacy and academic achievement in college students. Unfortunately, in the last decade and in many contexts, schools have been placing greater emphasis on literacy and math skills as the bases for curricula and assessment (McMurrer, 2008), using standardized testing in elementary and secondary education (Heckman & Kautz, 2012; Labaree, 2014), while ignoring the overall well-being of students and promoting initiatives in socioemotional development. This is despite a growing body of empirical research that suggests that socioemotional education improves grades and overall avoidance of unsafe behaviors by equipping students with skills that help them navigate their school experiences holistically (Durlak et al., 2011; Zins et al., 2004). Hope, as discussed in this book, is an important catalyst for an integrated education system that encourages well-being as an important element of overall educational achievement and productivity.

Based on a review of previous literature and multiple definitions of the term, we define *hope* as an orientation to pursue innovation and critical thinking as well as to promote creativity and initiative. This definition is not inclusive, but it provides a starting point, as one of the objectives of this volume is to present and examine diverse views on hope and to present multidisciplinary approaches to its understanding and implementation. Nevertheless, we attempt to give hope more weight in transformation because we recognize its potential and the need for its critical inclusion in education in Muslim societies. Of course, this approach may differ from the way others examine hope, and as such a brief review of representative definitions may explain our choices. According to *Webster's Dictionary*, we use the term *hope* in everyday speech to refer to "1) trust or reliance; 2) desire accompanied with expectation of obtaining what is desired or belief that it is obtainable" (Benton, 1971, p. 1089). Hope has meaning beyond academics, including cultural, spiritual, social, and philosophical orientations and perspectives (Krafft, 2018). In some approaches, there is the tendency to use hope to glorify the past and/or to accept the unknown while also expressing optimism. Weingarten (2010) argues that hope is not about an ideal concept or perfection; rather, it encompasses the dreams, visions, wishes, and values of people. In other words, hope is grounded and real, and it focuses on what is possible. It also has deep cultural connotations and can be a catalyst for bringing people together in a shared space. Following the tragic events of 9/11 and the subsequent war on terror in the United States, for example, the message communicated widely and increasingly was one of hope for a better future to counteract the mood of fear and anxiety. In troubling times, it is important to keep open the space of interconnectedness, a place where hope lies (see chapter 10).

Others, such as Zournazi (2002), define hope as the pursuit of societal justice and as a virtue that has implications in politics, economies, and societies.

Freire (1997) and Snyder et al. (2005) describe hope as an expectation for things to change for the better, and Simon (1992) reiterates this further by emphasizing that "hope is a commitment to responsibility" (p. 4). According to Freire, humans seek hope in order not to despair; it is hope that acts as the "necessary impetus in the context of our unfinishedness" (1972, p. 64,). In this volume, multiple authors refer to Freire's work, aware of the complex nature of hope and its multifaceted aspects, while using Freire's methods of reflection and dialogue to advance transformation. Most notable is that they articulate a definition of hope that is multidimensional, active, and future oriented as well as inclusive because hope should not be limited to one view, one orientation, and one faith. On the contrary, the objective in this introduction to hope literature and approaches is to widen definitions, examine scholarship, and provide space for exploration of an Islamic teaching perspective as well as an interfaith and international one.

Historically, the concept of hope has been interwoven with classical traditions and cultural rituals, some rooted in Greek mythology, such as the story of Pandora's box, in which hope is the only comfort remaining for humanity once the box has been opened and all its evils have been released into the world (as told by Snyder & Lopez [2007]). Leaders such as Mahatma Gandhi have found hope in their belief in the intrinsic goodness of human nature. Gandhi's message, his pedagogy of hope, was to educate people on alternatives to violence, to offer them real possibilities for transformation. He hoped that they would respond positively (Grey, 2007, p. 15). In some religious doctrines, such as in Christianity, hope is a "divine virtue, with God as the first source and the final target of hope" (Krafft, 2018, p. 3).

In Islam, hope is rooted in doing good deeds and finding meaning beyond a materialistic life. It has cognitive as well as affective meanings that are embedded in the belief in spiritual transcendence, which is also true of other major religions (Krafft, chapter 7). The Quran is filled with phrases that acknowledge human experiences and the ease of falling into despair. Both the Quran and the teachings of the Prophet Muhammad invite people to put their faith in God and rely on Him for relief when facing hardship and challenges. Verse 2:155 of the Quran illustrates the idea very clearly, stating: "Be sure we shall test you with something of fear and hunger, some loss in goods or lives or the fruits of your toil but give glad tidings to those who patiently persevere."[3] Hope is to be sought throughout life, with people placing their trust in God and living their lives on a moral and ethical basis, as good human beings.

Several of the authors in this volume elaborate more on the Islamic roots of hope and explain that the Arabic translation of hope in religious scripts is *raja*

(الرجاء), which is an important inward element behind worship in Islam. It refers to hope that proceeds from God consciousness, *taqwa*, and the love of God. The word *raja* appears frequently in the Quran and the Sunnah, and *raja* is considered one of the greatest manifestations of the heart. Although amal is the Arabic word for hope, *raja* is understood to capture a wider range of meanings. *Raja* is often defined as "opposite to despair" (see chapters 2, 3, and 4). It is an idea that very clearly adds the intentional and purposeful dimensions to hope. This also illustrates that hope (*amal*) is static, while wishing and working toward a better future (*Raja*) is more proactive and long term (in Arabic, a formal difference between the two terms is that a*mal* can be plural, i.e., *amaal*).

Hope as a research construct is complex and operationalized in multiple ways. Major theorists in positive psychology such as Snyder et al. (1991) have defined hope as having positive expectations toward the future. Additionally, it involves "having positive expectations, anchored by future goals, and possessing perceived 'will' and 'ways' for reaching these goals, even when faced with obstacles" (Alverson, 2014, p. 10). Snyder et al. (2002) also defined hope as a dynamic motivational and cognitive power toward reaching one's goals. Snyder (2002) came up with a widely used theory of hope and measures of hope, which stemmed from his definition of the concept as "the sum of perceived capabilities to produce routes to desired goals, along with the perceived motivation to use those routes" (p. 8). According to Snyder's theory, there are two elements to hope: a will and a way. Snyder (1995) refers to these as a pathway and agency and asserts that both are needed to produce high hope. Snyder's theory emphasizes the importance of cognitive as well as motivational engagements to achieve hope. These predictions have been studied and are well documented in a variety of contexts, and according to Feldman and Kubota (2015), Snyder's is among the most thoroughly researched and conceptualized theories on hope.

Krafft (chapter 7), however, argues that Snyder's theory has limitations because of its emphasis on the cognitive and motivational aspects of hope. As Krafft states: "In Snyder's theory hope is conceptualized as an iterative cognitive process. The emotional and the existential-transcendental dimensions play a subordinate or no role at all" (chapter 7). Further, along with other authors in this volume (see chapters 2–6), Krafft emphasizes the importance of empowerment and action in hope and a future orientation to education. This similar understanding stems from different roots, such as in-depth reading and understanding of the Quranic message for transformation (chapters 3–4), or hope stemming from Islamic schooling (see chapters 8 and 9).

To attest to the complexity of the term, Webb (2012) claims that there are "twenty-six theories of hope and fifty-four definitions" (p. 398). When asked what hope is, all will agree on its importance, but an array of disciplines will claim its definition, including psychology, philosophy, theology, and the cognitive sciences, to name a few. Webb suggests that "hope is best understood as a socially mediated human capacity with varying affective, cognitive, and behavioral dimensions" (p. 398). Webb (2012) outlines five modes of hope that are relevant not only to psychology, which is the focus of this volume, but to the philosophy and theology of hope. These are "patient, critical, sound, resolute, and transformative" modes (p. 398). Patient hope is future oriented and positive and appreciates the pathway to a better life and an unplanned objective, while critical hope is centered on a future that is unpredictable and new. According to Giroux (2001), critical hope is about moving forward with a future orientation and an eye for what is missing. In this case, the role of the educator is to open spaces for possibilities and to take responsibility "to show the way" (Webb, 2012, p. 404).

Sound hope is a mode of hope that is calculated and planned to avoid disappointments and too much risk. It is the focus on possible losses versus gains. Webb's fourth mode of hope (2012) is resolute hope. Resolute hope is self-regulated and oriented toward the achievement of goals through willpower and self-empowerment, a perspective that helps the educator level the hope playing field and foster high hope in students. This view is supported by the work of Snyder (2002), who highlights the importance of providing high-hope versus low-hope learning environments (p. 250) and the role teachers play to motivate high-hope students. According to Webb, the last mode is the transformative one, which goes beyond the individual setting goals and moves toward his changing reality to pursue hope. It is the advocacy and mobilization for a better way of being (see chapter 4 for more on transformative hope in higher education). Transformative hope is political and action-oriented. Freire's (1972) concept of *conscientization* is the discourse of transformative hope. It is the belief that we have the strength despite obstacles and hurdles to change the world and education (p. 81).

There are several constructs related to hope that are important for such a discourse. These include, for example, the willingness to learn and a sense of well-being (Lazarus, 2006). Dufrane and LeClair (1984) and Frank (1968) articulated the critical role of hope in instigating therapeutic change and other types of action. Snyder's work also brought attention to the importance of hope for constructs such as optimism and self-efficacy that are goal oriented and cognitive. Further, Snyder et al. (1991) suggested an important element of hope, which is the perception of successful agency to achieve one's goals. According to them, "the agency component refers to a sense of successful determination in meeting goals in the past, present, and future" (pp. 570–571).

The roles educators play in instilling a pedagogy of hope have been further elaborated by philosophers and transformative educators mentioned earlier. All agree, though, that awareness of the power mismatch between teachers and students is a first step toward teaching in a nonoppressive way, in which the teacher initiates and reciprocates in dialogue and criticality with the student. Students in this scenario come to realize their humanity and, as a result, become critical citizens with the potential to effect change in themselves and their own communities (hooks, 2003). According to hooks, the classroom context, when used creatively, may generate hope. The K–12 curricula, higher-education case studies, and pedagogy reflections described in this volume elaborate further on this process.

Tamashiro's (2018) transformative education model proposes that a stage of discomfort precedes transformation. The learner experiences a dilemma and engages in reflections and reconstructions to reach transformation, but this transformation cannot occur without hope. This volume attempts to disrupt and renew faith in education and its power to transform. Table 1.1 describes the typical process that may be applied in a learning situation.

The model ignites this willingness and ability to transform, but it is not a specific program. Rather, it intends to provide a framework in which to read this

Table 1.1. A Transformative Learning Process

Stage 1	**Disorienting dilemma:** A situation that perplexes a person and poses a situation that requires action. The classroom in schools or higher-education institutions can provide a safe environment to struggle with a dilemma.
Stage 2	**Questioning and deconstruction:** The way forward to addressing a dilemma must involve a process of questioning that will result in strengthening existing views and tendencies or replacing them with new ones, hence the deconstruction followed by the reframing and restructuring.
Stage 3	**Reframing and restructuring:** This is a reflective process with a mentor in a teaching and learning situation, such as is discussed in this volume.
Stage 4	**Shift in consciousness:** This is the beginning of forming a new way of thinking that is based on a strong foundation and in-depth contemplation.

Note. Adapted from Tamashiro, R. (2018). Planetary consciousness, witnessing the inhuman, and transformative learning: Insights from peace pilgrimage oral histories and autoethnographies. *Religions, 9*(5), 148.

volume. Various chapters introduce educational models for interacting with students to instill a positive future orientation among the next generations. After all, hope in schooling has been connected to academic achievement, life satisfaction, and flourishing. Hope flourishes in environments that are supportive and provide social relations that are positive (Eraslan-Capan, 2016), and the opposite is true regarding hopelessness. In Eraslan-Capan's study (2016), it was found that among university students, strong negative correlations existed between hopelessness and social connectedness and flourishing (p. 936). In addition, hope is suggested to mediate between a sense of purpose and life satisfaction (Bronk et al., 2009). This confirms Snyder's (2002) assertion that students who are high on hope will find multiple pathways to achieve their goals and be motivated to realize them. This is the place and these are the mechanisms whereby teachers and higher-education instructors can be intentional with their learners.

In Muslim societies, this approach to instilling hope has a grounding in Islamic teaching and verses, but it also has a basis in the cultural contexts and traditions of many Muslim majority societies, including those described in this volume. Contributing authors have expressed their own ways of addressing hope within various Muslim contexts utilizing writings from other religions and approaches, including those prevalent in critical Western literature. It is important to mention that the authors of this edited book are also not naive enough to think that "hope" is the only path to reform of education and the transformation of societies. The idea here is to examine hope as part of an integrated system considering diverse approaches and research findings in relation to the learning environment and the broader cultural context, to highlight what is hopeful in Muslim societies, and to discuss ways we can manage, coordinate, and further hope and foster what is in effect a critical factor for the well-being of Muslim youth and society.

At the time of the final editorial work on this volume, the whole world is experiencing unprecedented conditions of isolation and fear because of the COVID-19 pandemic. Millions of students are out of school, and economies around the world are struggling with high unemployment (United Nations, 2020). The situation in low-income communities and among ethnic minorities and refugees is alarming (Inter-agency Network for Education in Emergencies [INEE], 2020) and will require global campaigns and many years to repair. The world is in despair and chaos (the full impact of the pandemic is yet to be learned, including increased violence and discrimination against marginalized groups) and is desperately in need of mandates and an agenda for a hopeful future that is planned and systemic. This book is of tremendous value in its ability to set this new agenda of transformation and better living for the future, partly because the work is multidimensional and multidisciplinary and appeals to a large audience. Further, hope in education is both contextualized and localized so it contains a global (or global to local) approach to education and a transformative agenda that stems from a close examination of theories, pedagogies, and philosophies. The chapters that follow describe programs, strategies, and case studies to expand on the ideas described and highlighted in this introduction.

REFERENCES

Alverson, J. R. (2014). *A model of hopelessness, belongingness, engagement, and academic achievement* [A dissertation submitted to the Department of Research Studies in Educational Psychology]. University of Alabama.

Ball, S. (2008). *The education debate: Policy and politics in the twenty-first century.* Policy.

Benton, W. (1971). *Webster's third new international dictionary of the English language, unabridged.* G & C Merriam.

Bronk, K. C., Hill, P. L., Lapsley, D. K., Talib, T. L., & Finch, H. (2009). Purpose, hope, and life satisfaction in three age groups. *The Journal of Positive Psychology, 4*(6), 500–510.

Chemers, M. M., Hu, L.-t., & Garcia, B. F. (2001). Academic self-efficacy and first year college student performance and adjustment. *Journal of Educational Psychology, 93*(1), 55–64. https://doi.org/10.1037/0022-0663.93.1.55

Dufrane, K., & LeClair, S. W. (1984). Using hope in the counseling process. *Counseling and Values, 29*(1), 32–41.

Durlak, J. A., Weissberg, R. P., Dymnicki, A. B., Taylor, R. D., & Schellinger, K. (2011). The impact of enhancing students' social and emotional learning: A meta-analysis of school-based universal interventions. *Child Development, 82*, 405–432.

El-Bilawi, N. H., & Nasser, I. (2017). Teachers' professional development as a pathway for educational reform in Egypt. *International and Multidisciplinary Perspectives, 18*(2), 147–160.

Elias, M. J., & Arnold, H. A. (Eds.). (2006). *The educator's guide to emotional intelligence and academic achievement: Social-emotional learning in the classroom.* Corwin.

Eraslan-Capan, B. (2016). Social connectedness and flourishing: The mediating role of hopelessness. *Universal Journal of Educational Research, 4*(5), 933–940. https://doi.org/10.13189/ujer.2016.040501

Feldman, D. B., & Kubota, M. (2015). Hope, self-efficacy, optimism, and academic achievement: Distinguishing constructs and levels of specificity in predicting college grade-point average. *Learning and Individual Differences, 37,* 210–216. https://doi.org/10.1016/j.lindif.2014.11.022

Frank, J. D. (1968). The role of hope in psychotherapy. *International Journal of Psychiatry, 5,* 383–395.

Freire, P. (1972). *Pedagogy of the oppressed.* Penguin.

Giroux, H. A. (2001). Cultural studies as performative politics. *Cultural Studies ↔ Critical Methodologies, 1*(1), 5–23. https://doi.org/10.1177/153270860100100102

Grey, M. (2007). Deep breath—Taking a deep breath: Spiritual resources for a pedagogy of hope. In T. V. Teeffelen (Ed.), *Challenging the wall: Toward a pedagogy of hope* (pp. 12–16). Arab Educational Institute. www.aeicenter.org

Heckman, J. J., & Kautz, T. (2012). Hard evidence on soft skills. *Labour Economics, 19*(4), 451–464.

hooks, B. (2003). *Teaching community: A pedagogy of hope.* Routledge.

International Crisis Group. (2014). *Education reform in Pakistan, crisis group Asia report no. 257.* International Crisis Group.

Inter-agency Network for Education in Emergencies. (2020). *Prioritize, Protect, and Plan for Education: INEE advocacy messages for during and after the COVID-19 pandemic.* https://inee.org/covid-19/advocacy#question

Krafft, C. (2018). Is school the best route to skills? Returns to vocational school and vocational skills in Egypt. *The Journal of Development Studies, 54*(7), 1100–1120.

Labaree, D. (2014). Consuming the public school. *Educational Theory, 61*(4), 381–394.

Lewis, W. D., & Young, T. (2015). Educational policy implementation revisited. *Educational Policy, 29*(1), 3–17.

Lazarus, R. S. (2006). Emotions and interpersonal relationships: Toward a person-centered conceptualization of emotions and coping. *Journal of Personality, 74,* 9–46. https://doi.org/10.1111/j.1467-6494.2005.00368.x

McMurrer, J. (2008). *NCLB year 5: Instructional time in elementary schools: A closer look at changes for specific subjects.* Center on Education Policy.

Skalli, L. (2004). Loving Muslim women with a vengeance: The West, women, and fundamentalism. In J. L. Kincheloe & S. R. Steinberg (Eds.), *The miseducation of the West: How schools and the media distort our understanding of the Islamic World* (pp. 43–57). Praeger.

Snyder, C. (1995). Conceptualizing, measuring, and nurturing hope. *Journal of Counseling and Development, 73*(3), 355–360.

Snyder, C. R. (2002). Hope theory: Rainbows in the mind. *Psychological Inquiry, 13,* 249–275.

Snyder, C. R., Cheavens, J. S., & Michael, S. T. (2005). Hope theory: History and elaborated model. In J. A. Eliott (Ed.), *Interdisciplinary perspectives on hope* (pp. 101–118). Nova Science.

Snyder, C. R., Harris, C., Anderson, J. R., Holleran, S. A., Irving, L. M., Sigmon, S., & Harney, P. (1991). The will and the ways: Development and validation of an individual differences measure of hope. *Journal of Personality & Social Psychology, 60*(4), 570–585.

Snyder, C. R., & Lopez, S. J. (2007). *Positive psychology: The scientific and practical explorations of human strengths.* Sage.

Snyder, C. R., Shorey, H. S., Cheavens, J., Pulvers, K. M., Adams, V. H., & Wiklund, C. (2002). Hope and academic success in college. *Journal of Educational Psychology, 94*(4), 820–826.

Tamashiro, R. (2018). Planetary consciousness, witnessing the inhuman, and transformative learning: Insights from peace pilgrimage oral histories and autoethnographies. *Religions, 9*(5), 148.

Teeffelen, T. V. (2007). *Challenging the wall: Toward a pedagogy of hope.* Arab Educational Institute. www.aeicenter.org

United Nations. (2020). *Responding to COVID-19 and recovering better: A compilation by UN DESA.* https://www.un.org/development/desa/en/wp-content/uploads/2020/07/PB-Compilation-final.pdf

United Nations Educational, Scientific and Cultural Organization. (2016). *Happy schools, A framework for learner well-being in the Asia-Pacific.* Author.

Valle, M. F., Huebner, S., & Suldo, S. M. (2006). An analysis of hope as a psychological strength. *Journal of School Psychology, 44*, 393–406.

Webb, D. (2012). Pedagogies of hope. *Studies in philosophy of education, 32*(4), 397–414.

Weingarten, K. (2010). Reasonable hope: Construct, clinical applications, and supports. *Family Process, 49*(1), 5–25.

Zins, J. E., Weissberg, R. P., Wang, M. C., & Walberg, H. J. (Eds.). (2004). *Building academic success on social and emotional learning: What does the research say?* Teachers College Press.

Zournazi, M. (2002). *Hope: New philosophies for change.* Routledge.

NOTES

1. "Happiness," the United Arab Emirates Government Portal, https://government.ae/en/about-the-uae/the-uae-government/government-of-future/happiness.

2. Andrew Buncombe, "Is Bhutan the Happiest Place in the World?" *Independent,* https://www.independent.co.uk/life-style/health-and-families/healthy-living/is-bhutan-the-happiest-place-in-the-world-6288053.html.

3. Several chapters in this edited volume elaborate on this.

TRANSCENDING HUMAN RUPTURES THROUGH A HOPEFUL MUSLIM EDUCATION

NURAAN DAVIDS

INTRODUCTION

Theologically, across monotheistic faiths, hope serves not only as an affirmation of belief but also as a confirmation of belief in the transcendental. For Muslims, hope finds expression in frequent utterances in the unquestionability of God's will; that is, while humans have hope, God knows and does best. As in faith, hope in education symbolizes an expectation and a desire, an unwavering belief that a positive outcome is not only possible but realizable. In this sense, hope has the potential of enhancing and nurturing the pedagogical encounter. Normatively, Muslim education can be understood to be constituted and framed by three discernable yet interrelated epistemological and ethical practices; namely, *tarbiyyah* (derived from the Arabic root *rabā*, meaning "to make or let grow," "to nurture, to raise or rear up," or "to educate or teach a child"). In the context of education, the term refers to pedagogy and instruction, and in the sense of Islamic education, it refers to nurturing and educating children in the beliefs, values, and principles of Islam. *Ta'līm* (derived from the Arabic word *'ilm*, *ta'līm*) denotes knowledge and learning, or the instruction and training of the mind and the transmission of knowledge. In the Islamic context, it encompasses both revealed and nonrevealed knowledge. *Ta'dīb* (derived from the Arabic root *aduba*, which includes the meanings of being well-mannered, educated, and cultured) can be said to encompass both *tarbiyyah* and *ta'līm* (Davids & Waghid, 2016; Waghid, 2011). As such, first, when Muslims are socialized into the tenets and traditions in and about Islam they are taught individually and socially to be the self in relation to others; that is, that Islam, while divinely inspired, is made manifest in social engagements and interactions. Second, *ta'līm* for Muslims is associated with doing things in community; that is, engaging in deliberation about matters in society that interest them. Third, through *ta'dīb*, which underscores the basis of Muslim education, Muslims are taught that through belief, prayer, charity, fasting, pilgrimage, and the exercise of morality, their actions ought to be responsive to societal demands.

What is not immediately evident from these epistemologies, however, is how hope might serve not only to enhance Muslim education but also to cultivate it in relation to a cosmopolitan Muslim education; that is, an education that extends into pluralist forms of existence, serving, in the words of Freire (1998), as "an indispensable seasoning in our human, historical experience" (p. 69). This chapter draws on the ideas of bell hooks and specifically her text *Teaching Community: A Pedagogy of Hope* (2003), which, of course, is an invocation of Freire's (2000) *Pedagogy of Hope*. Of particular interest is hooks's conceptualization of education as "rooted in hopefulness"; that is, the capacity of education to transcend self-interest, so the interconnectedness with others might be harnessed. The chapter, therefore, commences by providing an overview of the three epistemological practices of *tarbiyyah, ta'līm,* and *ta'dīb.* Drawing on Freire and hooks, the chapter continues by arguing that if Muslim education is to address divisions and marginalization both within and beyond its communities, then such an education cannot be remiss of hopefulness. To this end, the chapter offers a reimagined account of Muslim education—one that looks at hope as transcending human ruptures and dissonances, and instead advances a cosmopolitan, human connection and resonance.

Epistemologies of Muslim Education

Foundational to Muslim education, and hence to Islam, are the two source codes of the Quran and the Sunnah (customs and practices based on the example of the Prophet Muhammad [SAAS], from his actions, words, and tacit approvals or disapprovals). It is a primary source in Islam alongside and complementing the Quran. As Ramadan (2001) explains, the Quran, together with the Sunnah, defines the points of reference for all Muslim spheres of life—the individual, the social, the economic, and the political (p. 78). The Quran holds many descriptions and associations, such as "the Book" (*al-kitāb*); the writings "descended" from the sky during the "Blessed Night"; "the Warning" (*al-dhikr*); "the Discrimination" or the "discriminating proof" (*al-furqān*); that is, the revelation (Arkoun, 1994, p. 30). In turn, Nasr (2010) clarifies that while the

Quran is referred to as "the gathering" of all bona fide knowledge, the "mother of all books," and "the guidance," its literal meaning is "the recitation" (p. 130). Commonly, the Quran is accepted as a source of guidance for humanity (*hudā al-nās*). Because the Quran speaks generally about universal concepts, the specificity of conduct and behavior is found in the lived example of Prophet Muhammad (Sunnah) (Al-Hasan et al., 2013, p. 11). Muslims, therefore, consider the Sunnah as critical to the sustenance of their faith, the preservation of their identity, and all their moral and social conduct.

In clarifying what Muslim education entails and how it is internalized, it is necessary to focus on how the Quran presents itself. Abu Zayd (2004), for example, suggests that it is important to shift beyond looking at the Quran as only a text and to also explore it as a discourse or discourses (p. 11). He explains that while it is indisputable that the Quran is the "speech of God," the discourse structure of the Quran reveals a multiplicity of voices—brought about through the responsive nature of the Quran to events, battles, and appeals (Abu Zayd, 2004, p. 19). The Quran, states Abu Zayd, is not in itself a book of law; rather, "[l]egal stipulations are expressed in discourse style, which reveals a context of engagement with human needs in specific time, which, in turn, opens up the appropriation of the 'meaning' intended into every paradigm of meaning" (2004, p. 37). One cannot find the meaning of a religion in the text, argues Abu Zayd (2010), "but in the interaction between the text and the historical process, in the interaction between the believer(s)/the communities with their holy texts" (p. 286). This view discounts the idea of the Quran as a monolithic text of laws unrelated to the flexibility of varying contexts. This view is also confirmed in the evocation of the first revelation of "Recite! (or Read!) in the name of your Lord and Cherisher" (Quran, 96:1), as directed at the Prophet Muhammad (Davids & Waghid, 2016). Abu Zayd (2010) reminds us that the primary objective of the revelations was to convert the then inhabitants of the Arabian Peninsula from polytheism to a belief in one God (p. 281). From a historical perspective, therefore, the Quran responded to contexts, events, and behavior.

Although initially directed at the Prophet, Muslims accept the command to "Read!" as equally directed at them. Reading and pursuing knowledge are understood as fundamental to belief in and practice of Islam. To read, however, is not limited to mere recitation and acceptance of words. In the Quran, Muslims are asked to think, to reflect, and to contemplate about themselves, about God, about creation, and about themselves in relation to the world in which they find themselves: "Why do they not reflect on themselves?" (Quran, 30:8); "Will they not then ponder on the Qur'an?" (Quran, 4:82). Because of the insistence that reading be accompanied by critical engagement and self-reflection, the Quran distinguishes between "those who know" and "who reflect" from those who are heedless people.

First, *'ilm* (knowledge; science) in Islam is not divided into conceptions or categories of sacred and secular. Second, knowledge in Islam draws from two distinct knowledge forms, namely, *ulum al-aqli* (speculative, rational, or intellectual sciences) and *ulum al-naqli* (religious or traditional sciences), as encapsulated in the primary sources of the Quran and *ahādīth* (reports describing the words, actions, or habits of the Prophet Muhammad). It is the second primary source of guidance for Muslims after the Quran; these two sources are not mutually exclusive. That is, while different, these two forms of knowledge coexist and are brought together through reason. The harmonious unity of the two kinds of knowledge, states al-Attas (1977), has always been emphasized and maintained: "no single branch of knowledge ought to be pursued indefinitely exclusively of others, for that would result in disharmony, which would affect the unity of knowledge, and render its validity questionable" (p. 204). Muslims are instructed to read, reflect, and make sense of revealed knowledge, as enunciated in the Quran, to gain understanding. In doing so, Muslims bring their own identities to the text; they read with complex histories and constructions of social and cultural conventions, thereby rendering all knowledge as value based.

Muslim education, which embodies both *aqlī* (nonrevealed) and *naqlī* (revealed) knowledge, is generally understood and categorized in relation to three intertwined epistemologies: *tarbiyyah*, *ta'līm*, and *ta'dīb* (Al-Attas, 1977; Nasr, 2010; Waghid, 2011). *Ta'līm*, explains Waghid (2011), refers to both teaching and seeking knowledge, where meanings are shared and deliberated on the basis that something new might originate. In this regard, spaces and opportunities for discussion and debate become a necessary feature of teaching and learning. *Ta'dīb*, according to Wan Daud (2009), centers on the social dimension of human behavior; that is, to act with moral conduct, in all spheres of life, and in all social and personal relationships. In turn, *tarbiyyah*, says Waghid (2011), is a process of socializing people into an inherited body of knowledge; that is, producing people who can think and act in accordance with knowledge as it is both transmitted and constructed vis-à-vis legitimate sources of knowledge. For example, Muslims are often taught to memorize various portions of the Quran and *ahādīth* and then concurrently internalize its teachings that would then be reflected in their conduct in society—conduct often associated with virtues of good character and morality, which demand acting respectfully and decently in society. Hence, *tarbiyyah* aims to engender a virtuous person; that is, a person with profound morality and civility. Second, *ta'līm* for Muslims is associated with thinking, reflecting on knowledge and practices, and doing things in community, so that knowledge has bearing on the interests of society.

In sum, what Muslim education seeks to embody and espouse is, on the one hand, knowledge of the source codes (that is, the Quran and the Sunnah); reflection on this knowledge; and hence reflection on the self in relation to others, society, and God. As such, Muslims are expected to be attentive and responsive not only to their identities and responsibilities as Muslims but also to how this identity and responsibility ought to manifest in relation to God's creation—so that what they know, and who they are as Muslims, are of benefit to God's creation. For this reason, Al-Attas (2005) maintains that the objective of seeking knowledge and education is to produce a good person; that is, one who has *adab* (etiquette). In the context of Islamic behavior, it refers to having good etiquette, manners, or decorum in accordance with Islamic morality (p. 22). Similarly, Nasr (2010) contends that Muslim education does not separate the training of the mind from that of the soul: "it never considered the transmission of knowledge or its possession to be legitimate without the possession of appropriate moral and spiritual qualities" (p. 131).

The imperative, therefore, of Muslim education is to bring into being an individual who strives toward human excellence—one who embodies *khalīfatullāh fī al-ard* (the qualities of trusteeship) by honoring his or her responsibilities to God's creation. Since trust cannot be attained without knowledge and understanding, conceptions and practices of *khalīfatullāh fī al-ard* are necessarily informed by education. In this sense, "to be educated is the realization that what one knows is because of, about, and for the sake of Allah [God]. This means, that unless knowledge leads to awareness of oneself as being always in relation to Allah and His creation (which includes all others), one cannot lay claim to being educated" (Davids & Waghid, 2016, p. 44).

Now that I have provided some discussion on what informs Muslim education, how it is espoused, and what it hopes to achieve within individuals, and hence society, I will continue by considering Muslim education as a hopeful encounter. I will commence this discussion by first exploring the concept of hope, as espoused by Paulo Freire.

MUSLIM EDUCATION IN SOUTH AFRICA: A PROOF OF HOPEFULNESS

It is negligent to read Freire's *Pedagogy of the Oppressed* (first published in 1968) or his *Pedagogy of Hope* (first published in 1992) without taking cognizance of the strong influence of his faith, Christianity. As a result, his work is as influential on liberation theology as it is on educational philosophy (Kirylo, 2017). Liberation theology, explains Kirylo (2011), suggests that faith corresponds to real historical circumstances; more specifically, a history, which is from the perspective of the marginalized and the poor (p. 185). In his faith Freire (1997) found hope—hope through which it is possible to undermine oppression and inequality (p. 104). That is, despite oppression and its accompanying hardships, faith provides a resort to hope, which cannot be oppressed and marginalized. To Freire (1997), a more humane and just society can be realized through an awareness of self (conscientization) and others, engaging in deliberative dialogue for purposes of transformation, and becoming deeply committed to the struggle for social justice. He describes hope as something spiritual "shared between teachers and students. The hope that we can learn together, teach together, be curiously impatient together, produce something together, and resist together the obstacles that prevent the flowering of our joy" (Freire, 1998, p. 69).

Like spirituality, contends Freire (1998), hope is "natural, possible, and [a] necessary impetus in the context of our 'unfinishedness'" (p. 69). The entire point of teaching, learning, and pursuing knowledge is because of a recognition of the "unfinishedness" of our lives; we do not know, and hence we pursue that which is yet to be known and experienced. Hope, therefore, following Freire (1998), is an indispensable seasoning in our human and historical experience. Without it, instead of history, we would have pure determinism. Hope, Freire (1998) maintains, is social; it exists within all individuals and is a part of all social relations. The more an individual engages in these social relations with hope, the more he or she can change it. Such an individual is unafraid of change and is unafraid of confronting that which needs change.

The point about a Freirean understanding of hope is that it speaks to being open to new ideas and new ways of thinking, confronting that which is harmful and silencing, and acting with justice (Davids & Waghid, 2019). In this sense, hope, says Freire (2000), "is rooted in men's [and women's] incompletion, from which they move out in constant search—a search which can be carried out only in communion with others," acting and reflecting on the world to change it (p. 72). Apparent from the three epistemologies of *tarbiyyah*, *ta'līm*, and *ta'dīb*, is that Muslim identity is not limited to a confessional stance. Rather, the idea of *khalīfatullāh fī al-ard* confirms not only an inherent responsibility to God by serving creation but also a pursuit of human excellence so that the trusteeship might be enacted. This trusteeship is defined and informed by a recognition and acceptance to act with justice and righteousness: "Be just; that is nearer to righteousness" (Quran, 5:8). To act with justice and to pursue excellence within the self and within others are manifestations of both belief and hope.

Conceptually and practically, belief and hope are mutually contingent; the one cannot exist without the other. In Islam, to have hope is a manifestation of belief: "Do people think they will not be tested because they say, we have faith?" (Quran, 29:2). The Quran is replete with verses, inviting Muslims to believe and have hope in the mercy of God. In turn, God expresses the potentiality of humanity to overcome the dystopias and hardships of life in this world: "Surely there is in the person of Allah's messenger an excellent example for you—for every person who has hope in Allah and the hereafter and who remembers Allah" (Quran, 33:21); "So whoever would hope for the meeting with his Lord—let him do righteous work and not associate in the worship of his Lord anyone" (Quran, 18:110).

Following the above, one gets a sense of the prominence of hope as a spiritual dimension and manifestation. One also gets a sense of the necessity of hope in times of despair, marginalization, and oppression—as if difficulty exists so that humanity might turn to hope. Muslim education in South Africa, for example, survived only because of the hope that lived in the slaves and political prisoners who arrived at the Cape from the Indonesian archipelago and South and Southeast Asia, from 1658 onward (Mohamed, 2002). They were forcefully displaced from their homes. Some, including Abdullah Kadi Abdus Salaam or Tuan Guru (Mister Teacher), a prince from Tidore, were imprisoned on Robben Island; the latter for thirteen years. In turn, Muslims were prohibited from practicing their faith and had to do so clandestinely, fearful of being found out. Despite the obvious hardships of forced migrations and exiles—first under Dutch and then British rule—Islam managed to flourish. Tuan Guru's book *Fiqka Kitaab*, on Islamic jurisprudence, completed in 1781 and written in Malay and Portuguese, became the main source of reference for the Cape Muslim community (Lübbe, 1986). After being released from Robben Island, Tuan Guru established the first masjid (mosque), which was a place of ritual prostration (for prayer to God); hence, a place of worship for Muslims and a madrassa (school). The term generally denotes any type of educational institution, secular or religious (of any religion and education level). In the West, it refers to a Muslim educational institute for the instruction of Islam. The Auwal Masjid in Dorp Street, Cape Town, established in 1798, is still in vibrant existence today.

The same hope that allowed Islam to take root in South Africa was perpetuated with greater determination during apartheid, as implemented in 1948. As during colonialism, where the Dutch Reformed Church was the only recognized and acceptable form of religion, apartheid South Africa propagated the values of Christian National Education. Based on an Afrikaner form of Calvinistic principles, Christian National Education ensured not only the marriage between the state and church but also that Christian values permeated every aspect of education in public schools. In response to a climate in which neither public state schools nor Christian mission schools accommodated or acknowledged the religious beliefs and practices of Muslim children, Dr. Abdullah Abdurrahman established in 1913 the first state-aided Muslim school in Cape Town. The school, known as Rahmaniyeh Institute, focused on infusing "secular" schooling with basic Islamic teachings. On the one hand, schools like Rahmaniyeh employed Muslim teachers who could not find posts in Christian-dominated schools. On the other hand, they provided schooling for Muslim children whose parents were concerned about the dominant Christian ethos in both state and missionary schools (Tayob et al., 2011).

Through the steadfastness and works of the Indonesian slaves Shaykh Yusuf, from Macassar, who was exiled to the Cape in 1694, and Abdullah Kadi Abdus Salaam, or Tuan Guru, and later Dr. Abdullah Abdurrahman, Islam not only served the purpose of individual preservation; it also served as a buffer against oppressive and dehumanizing conditions—first under colonialism and then apartheid. In this sense, the propagation of Islam, via the establishments of mosques, madrassas, and Muslim-based schools not only ensured the cultivation of a religious identity and its ensuing communities; it also provided Muslims with a discourse that could withstand the practices of marginalization, oppression, exclusion, and humiliation, which are all at the core of conceptions of colonialism and apartheid. One of the unintended consequences of both colonialism and apartheid is that in forcing Muslims to live and practice their faith on the periphery of society, fertile grounds for the preservation of this faith were created. It would be fair, therefore, to argue that the very isolation imposed on Muslims because of their perceived otherness was used by Muslims to construct parallel sets of communities, and their identities and practices became enactments of resistance.

It is remarkable to note how Muslim women in European liberal democracies continue to use their identities as hijab-clad (often translated as *veil*; it can refer to any head or body covering worn by Muslim women that conforms with Islamic standards of modesty and morality) as a form of resistance against attempts of regulation, prescription, and oppression. The point is that practices of identities can by themselves serve as sites of resistance. In turn, in showing resistance against dehumanizing structures, hope takes shape and lives in the very existence of these identities and communities. Furthermore, that Islam managed to emerge because of the forced migration of slaves and political prisoners is a testament to human perseverance of hope in the mercy of God. Muslims are taught via the Quran and through the Sunnah that a loss of hope is akin to a loss of faith: "Do not lose heart nor fall into despair! You shall triumph if you are believers" (Quran, 3:139); "So, verily, with every difficulty, there is relief: Verily with every difficulty there is relief" (Quran, 94:5–7). Muslims, therefore, are immersed and socialized (*tarbiyyah*) into an inherited knowledge and worldview of an inherent hope and mercy—as made visible through the immense conflicts and pain of each of the prophets.

The point about being educated is not limited to gaining knowledge. To be educated, states al-Attas (1977), is to recognize and acknowledge "the proper places of things, in the order of creation, such that it leads to the recognition and acknowledgement of God in the order of being and existence" (p. 11). Apparent from al-Attas's (1977) elucidation is the idea of recognition of the position of the self or individual in relation to God and the rest of the creation; that is, there is a connection between the individual and the order of creation. This connection is made visible in the manifestation of *khalīfatullāh fī al-ard* and, in turn, can only be realized when an individual links what he or she knows (knowledge) with practice. Unless the acquisition of knowledge includes a moral purpose that activates the one who acquires it, it cannot be called education (Al-Attas, 2005).

I have shown how hope resides within the epistemologies of Muslim education. I have drawn attention not only to the need for education to serve the purpose of the pursuit of knowledge but also to the idea that any knowledge ought to serve the good of the self, and of the self in relation to others, and, hence, God. In addition, I have provided some insights into the emergence of Islam and Muslim education in a South African context, drawing attention to the underlying premise, which motivated the propagation of Islam not only as a faith identity but also as a response to repeated climates of injustice. In this regard, Muslim education is constitutive of hope in terms of both content and practice. In the next half of the chapter, I will consider Muslim education in relation to a cosmopolitan Muslim education; that is, an education that extends into pluralist forms of existence, serving, in the words of Freire (1998), as "an indispensable seasoning in our human, historical experience" (p. 69). Against the backdrop of a South African context, I will argue that if Muslim education is to address divisions and marginalization both within and beyond its communities, then such an education cannot be remiss of hopefulness. A reimagined Muslim education looks at hope as transcending human ruptures and dissonances, and advances a cosmopolitan, human connection and resonance.

MUSLIM EDUCATION IN DEMOCRATIC SOUTH AFRICA

As discussed in this chapter, much of the motivation for and emphasis in Muslim education in South Africa has been on resisting climates of political and social hostility, thanks first to colonialism and followed by apartheid. During the time of colonialism, the works of Shaykh Yusuf, Tuan Guru, and later Shaykh Abu Bakr Effendi set the foundation and tone of the type of Muslim education in South Africa. While Tuan Guru's mosque-based madrassas focused primarily on Quranic recitation and memorization, Shaykh Abu Bakr's Arabic-Afrikaans text *Bayan al-Din (The Elucidation of Religion)* provided the basis for more scholarly and sophisticated approaches to Islamic theology, jurisprudence, and history, as well as the establishment of seminaries and community colleges (Hoel, 2016). According to Hoel (2016), the two strands of madrassa education—children's Quranic literacy and higher Islamic seminaries—can be said to be the forerunners of what came to be known as madrassas in contemporary and democratic South Africa.

The onset of a postapartheid democratic South Africa has seen an unintended consequence of a surge in the number of private Muslim schools. Unlike madrassas, which function after school hours, Muslim schools accommodate both the state curriculum and Muslim education. Tayob et al. (2011) reports that statistics collected at the end of 2006 show that although the number of independent Muslim schools (seventy-four) formed a small percentage of the total number of independent schools (5.74%), that number was significantly higher than the proportion of Muslims in the population (2%) (p. 43). Despite the assurances that come with a democracy, which include freedom of religious expression, Muslim communities across South Africa have seen the need to disengage from public schools and retreat into their own spaces. There are complex reasons for this withdrawal. On one hand is the perception of poor quality of education due to a combination of high teacher-learner ratios and inadequate resources (Du Toit, 2004). On the other is the mistrust in public schools to accommodate the religious needs of Muslim children—a similar argument maintained during apartheid South Africa.

For this reason, Tayob et al. (2011) contend that the spike in the number of Muslim schools is a mere continuation of a long process through which Muslim communities attempt to provide Islamic and secular education to their adherents (p. 42). Given the constitutional space to practice their religion unhindered, asserts Vawda (2017), many Muslims in South Africa began to focus on "values of piety and morality, rather than continue to engage in the larger public debates about recognition of cultural differences and the relevance of Islam in times of continued inequality, nation-building, reconciliation, reconstruction, and development" (p. 34). To Vawda (2017), the focus on intrinsic normative driven standards of expected behavior derived from religion, rather than public engagement, represents a shift toward a normality of inward-looking Islam (p. 34). In line with this inward-looking aspect is the reality that Muslim schools in postapartheid South Africa have retained the same racial and cultural exclusivity as that enforced during apartheid; that is, these schools have not desegregated in terms of racial and cultural demographics. This is due to intersecting factors of residential clustering, school fees, and issues of language.

In terms of content and structure, Muslim schools, which are formally registered with and subsidized by the National Department of Basic Education in South Africa, are required to implement the national curriculum, known as the Curriculum Assessment Policy Statements (CAPS). In addition to teaching the core subjects, as prescribed by the CAPS, the curricula of Muslim schools generally also include Quran, Arabic, and Islamic studies. The ongoing concern with Muslim schools, however, is their overreliance on memorization and rote learning, which Waghid (2018) describes as "compliant transmission education" (p. 108). In this sense, while due attention might be given to *tarbiyyah* and *ta'dīb*, questions need to be asked about the prevalence of *ta'līm* and deliberative thinking. Questions also need to be asked about how children in Muslim schools come to understand themselves in relation to others and the differences between them when they are likely to only encounter one kind of learner and one kind of teacher.

Teacher appointments at Muslim schools seem to be a continuation of the patterns adopted during colonialism and apartheid. Historically, Muslim teachers who could not find employment in Christian mission schools found posts in the Muslim mission schools. Fataar (2003) reports that many teachers employed in postapartheid Muslim schools are recently qualified teacher education graduates who are unable to find jobs in a shrunken teacher employment market in public schools (pp. 1–2). How prepared are Muslim children to engage with those who are different from them, whether in terms of race, religion, or culture? If Muslim schools, following Vawda (2017), are inward-looking, then how prepared are learners at these schools for the diverse and pluralist society in which they find themselves? In turn, if the practices of teaching and learning are reliant on "compliant transmission education" (Waghid, 2018), then the questions need to be asked about the capacity for autonomous thinking and critical reasoning.

Although Muslims and Muslim education are allowed similar freedoms as those afforded to all other citizens and religious communities, democratic

South Africa is not without its social injustices, marginalization, and exclusion. The advent of democracy has been accompanied by new and unexpected challenges for Muslims, such as how to consider and position themselves in relation to an incredibly diverse and multiplex society. The unintended shrouding of colonialism and apartheid is no longer available, and Muslim education now has the challenge of shifting from an inward focus to one that prepares Muslims to live with and have regard for differences. In addition, the new democratic landscape has also meant an openness of diversity, which calls for more coherent self-understandings of faith and identity, so that Muslims can find points of resonance, which are necessary for peaceful coexistence.

In sum, South Africa's new democracy presents a particularly hopeful opportunity for Muslims to bring their identities, narratives, and beliefs to the forefront. Through a reimagined Muslim education, Muslims can assume a new social and political locality; it is possible for the shaping of a new narrative, one that transitions from a discourse of resistance to a discourse of *shūrā* (consultation)—a principle rooted in the Quran, which calls on the Muslim community to consult with one another in their affairs. In continuing, therefore, what type of Muslim education is necessary for the countenance of exclusionary practices and the cultivation of spaces for human connection and mutual accountability; that is, an education that speaks to and enhances peaceful coexistence in democracy? How might hope assist Muslim education in advancing the democratic project?

MUSLIM EDUCATION AS TRANSCENDENTAL

The Quran reminds Muslims that God is nearer to them than their jugular veins (Quran, 50:16). As such, the transcendental nature of God does not imply a literal distance; God is within reach. In turn, human beings by understanding of God's closeness and active involvement in all affairs have both the resilience and hope to transcend the injustices and hardships of this world. God is not remote, aloof, or disinterested in the affairs of his creation but is with humanity every step of the way. However, human beings are only able to cultivate hope once they have internalized what it means to be educated; that is, recognizing the interconnectedness of being humans. The recognition of a common humanity implies a recognition of when that humanity is compromised and of whether to act or speak out against that compromise.

When Muslims are socialized into the tenets of Islam, they are initiated into a heritage of knowledge, which facilitates and confirms their identity in relation to an *ummah* (global Muslim community). Within an Islamic context, it designates a fundamental concept used to express the collective or unity of Muslims. Commonly, the term *ummah* is understood to refer to Muslim communities—a type of communal identity that implies safety, love, and belonging. Denny (1975) explains that in terms of Quranic exegeses, the term *ummah* is used in sixty-two different forms (p. 43). According to Denny (1975), the definitive passages in which the term *ummah* appears to refer exclusively to the Muslims are found in the Madinan period—that is, the time after the Prophet Muhammad had migrated to the city of Madinah. Denny (1975) notes that the concept of *ummah* evolves "from a general one, applying to non-Arab groups, too, toward a more exclusive one which is limited to the Muslim community" (p. 36). In this sense, *ummah* adopts multihermeneutical enunciations, which speak to religious, social, political, and ethical expressions. *Ummah* can refer to an individual as part of a community, as well as a universal community.

"O mankind! We created you from a single (pair) of a male and a female, and made you into nations and tribes, that ye may know each other (not that ye may despise each other). Verily the most honored of you in the sight of Allah is (he who is) the most righteous of you. And Allah has full knowledge and is well acquainted (with all things)" (Quran, 49:13). From this verse, it becomes evident that differences among people are not intentional but exist so that human beings might learn to know the other, and so they might recognize their internal connections and accountability to and with one another. Human coexistence, therefore, is encouraged based on *ta'āruf* (to get to know one another). It has acquired significance as an Islamic concept/principle, with its basis in verse 49:13. Despite having been created with differences and similarities, the task of humans is to attain knowledge of one another. And in so doing, humans are urged to mutually respect one another on the grounds of their virtuous actions (Davids & Waghid, 2016).

The Quran describes a group that has mutual regard and respect and that practices moderation as an *ummatan wasatan* (justly balanced community). A Quranic reference (2:143) to the Muslim community connotes the idea that God has provided the guidance needed for believers to exemplify a just and moderate community: "And thus have We willed you to be a community of the middle way [that is, justly balanced], so that [with your lives] you might bear witness to the truth before all mankind" (Quran, 2:143). The categorization of *ummatan wasatan*, explains Denny (1975, p. 54), came into effect at a time when the Muslim religious community reached its most developed stage. In other words, when the Muslim community reached its religious and spiritual maturity, and when its adherents coexisted peacefully with the Jewish and Christian communities.

If engaging with others in mutual respect, recognition, and responsibility is what confirms the collective identity of community (*ummah*), then the type of education necessary for the sustenance of such a community must advance a cosmopolitan discourse, whereby hope can transcend human ruptures and dissonance. Of course, conceptions of *ummah* are entirely commensurate with conceptions of cosmopolitanism, in that both imply the idea of a single community based on a shared morality. By implication, advancing a cosmopolitan discourse implies a mutually agreed-on set of values, based on a commonly shared humanity—intent on contesting dystopias. The influence of Freire's (2000) elucidation of hope resonates loudly in hooks's (2003) explication of hope, to move beyond critique and cynicism. Like Freire, hooks (2003) frames her understanding of hope as something that can transcend political oppression and suffering and, hence, practices of marginalization and exclusion.

Following hooks (2003), teaching should never be a vehicle that entrenches or creates oppression, marginalization, or exclusion. To hooks (2003), teaching with hope implies the cultivation of a sense of community, a "feeling of connection and closeness with the world beyond the academy" and "enables us to confront feelings of loss and restore our sense of connection" (p. xv). The idea of a restoration of connection through a confrontation of feelings of loss is especially pertinent in a South African context, where Muslims continue to experience deep and unspoken uneasiness with the society in which they live. Many Muslims have struggled to define themselves politically and ideologically. One possible explanation for this, explains Nadvi (2008), is the racial, ethnic, and cultural conditioning under apartheid which resulted in Islam developing largely within a conservative context, dominated by the rudiments of religious practice. As a result, many Muslims began to focus on "values of piety and morality, rather than continue to engage in the larger public debates about recognition of cultural differences and the relevance of Islam in times of continued inequality, nation building, reconciliation, reconstruction and development" (Vawda, 2017, p. 34). The construction of boundaries, and its implication of isolation, is quite contrary to the objective of Muslim education, which is to fulfill the responsibilities of *khalīfatullāh fī al-ard* in relation to all of God's creation.

One of the first considerations for Muslim education, therefore, is to reconsider and reshape the current constructions of Muslim schools. In this regard, attention ought to be given to whom the teachers and the learners are, and how ideas of community and community practices are understood and implemented. It cannot be that Muslim schools, which exist in a pluralist and diverse society, are not reflective of that society. As highlighted in this chapter, Islamic conceptions of *ummah* are not limited to a religious marker of Islam. The Quran is abundantly clear in its reference to the creation of tribes and, hence, differences, with the expressed purpose of knowing about the other (see Quran, 49:13). In turn, knowing about the other implies a recognition of a common humanity that connects all humanity as an *ummah*.

Freire's (1998) argument of hope as a "necessary impetus in the context of our unfinishedness" (p. 69) connects with Hansen's (2011) depiction of cosmopolitanism as a "reflective openness to the new fused with reflective loyalty to the known" (p. 7). To Hansen (2011), as is the case with Freire (1998) and hooks (2003), teaching and learning involve making claims to surprise and discovery, as well as frustration and discomfort, all aspects of the new; that is, being open reflectively to the new and unknown. The point, therefore, of education is to cultivate learning as a form of "coming into the world" (Hansen, 2011, p. 113). In the case of Muslim education, learners are socialized (*tarbiyyah*) into a loyalty of heritage, as embodied in the Quran and the Sunnah.

By adopting ways of being and acting, they connect themselves to a preexisting framework and to ways of being and acting. However, education cannot be limited to that which is already known and familiar, and certainly contexts evolve and change, so that preexisting norms would need to be reconsidered. To reflect on one's loyalty does not mean abandoning religious heritage and norms. Rather, following Hansen (2011), reflective loyalty to the known means that what one knows is not treated as final; rather, one is willing to listen to others with a desire to understand the other and thus consolidate what one knows. To Hansen (2011), a cosmopolitan teacher has the "ability to traverse the space between the far and the near, the general and the particular, the universal and the neighbourhood" (p. 70). If learners are to come into a world of plurality, with the idea of being open to engaging from the perspectives of others, then the epistemology of *ta'dīb* must be understood as implicitly embedded in *ta'līm* and deliberative thinking. In other words, just action is shown when teachers and learners alike are prepared to challenge taken-for-granted norms of gender inequality, for example, and are prepared to reconsider understandings and practices through an ethical lens of critical engagement with the source codes, rather than passively accepting existing norms. By being open to renewed understandings, the *ummah* can expand in relation to accommodating dissenting views and different ways of thinking and being. In this regard, a reimagined consideration of *ummah* holds the capacity for deeper human connection and attunement with others and their lived experiences, thereby ensuring mutual engagement.

Finally, the contexts of Muslim education in South Africa have shifted dramatically from those of colonialism, followed by apartheid, and, more recently, to that of democracy. While the contexts of colonialism and apartheid necessarily implied the oppression, exclusion, and marginalization of Muslims, democratic South Africa provides an abode of peace (*dār al-sulh*); that is, although in the minority, Muslims enjoy religious freedom and a space for peaceful coexistence. The urgency and motivation for an isolated and contained expression of Muslim identity and practices no longer exist. As such, the role and responsibility of Muslim education must shift to renewed pathways of hope and human connections. Following hooks (2003), hope provides a means for Muslim education to move beyond critique and cynicism. Hope, she continues, "empowers us to continue our work for justice even as the forces of injustice may gain greater power for a time" (hooks, 2003, p. xiv).

Hooks (2003) emphasizes the importance of self-awareness and interconnections with people as practices of hope that must be nurtured through reflective listening, deep contemplation, and mindfulness. Her idea of hope involves offering a resistance to gender inequity as well as racial and economic inequality. Hooks (2003) posits that cultivating our full humanity is connected to transcending our self-interests and harnessing our interconnectedness with other humans. Hooks's (2003) argument for moving together, or in mutual engagement, implies a form of deliberation but also recognizes the "unfinishedness" (Freire, 1998, p. 69) of this world. The concept of the unfinishedness of this world holds deep significance in the epistemologies of *tarbiyyah, ta'līm*, and *ta'dīb*, and speaks to the transcendental potential of education.

Human excellence, as made visible through just action, according to al-Fārābī, is equated with the realization of supreme happiness (*al-sa'ādat al-quswā*) with God in the hereafter, which is dependent on the achievement of happiness in the present life (*al-sa'ādat al-dunyā*) (Bakar, 1992, p. 107). Al-Fārābī links the achievement of happiness in both the present and afterlife to the acquisition of virtues, which is explained as the states of the soul by which a person does good deeds, where *good* refers to surrendering to God (being Muslim) and the aspiration of moral excellence (Bakar, 1992). Drawing on al-Fārābī, human excellence unfolds because of humans' intellect engaging with knowledge and wisdom, which can result in a deeper understanding of God, the transcendental (unseen), and the material (visible) realms (Bakar, 1992). Further, when humans' theoretical intellect (through knowledge and wisdom) is expanded, they can make better sense of themselves and what impacts them in this world (Davids & Waghid, 2016).

The recognition of the self as being in relation to God implicitly holds that all human action in relation to all spheres and interactions must be guided by *adab* (etiquette). To be guided by just action is to draw on and to engage with hope in the other's humanity. The response of the other is therefore immaterial. What matters is that the moral imperative of Muslims is driven by hope in the other. Muslim education in South Africa has the opportunity—politically and socially—to not only shift the domain of Muslim teaching and learning but to shift in relation to embracing a maximalist conception of community (*ummah*). If Muslim education is to continue the legacy of hopefulness, which ensured its fruition in highly hostile and antagonistic ideological contexts, then it must extend and socialize its own hope. For this to happen, Muslim education in democratic South Africa needs to critically engage with what is understood by being a Muslim, not as difference, but as what ethically connects Muslims to all others.

I started this chapter with a recognition of the theological centrality of hope across the three monotheistic faiths. And, of course, hope is by no means the exclusive possession of religious ideologies. Hope, as Freire (1998) contends, is "natural, possible, and [a] necessary impetus in the context of our unfinishedness" (p. 69). One of the key successes of both colonialism and apartheid has been the isolation of communities and, hence, otherness. What connects all South Africans who believe in the hope signaled through a democracy is their common humanity and their capacity to act responsibly in relation to all others. Muslim education is not only entirely commensurate with the values of a democracy; through its epistemologies and its conceptions of community, it also has the foundations to be receptive to openness, as implied within hope. The first step in achieving this is in recognizing that Muslim education is not the preserve of Muslims; rather, it is the preserve of a community (*ummah*), which has in common a shared value of humanity.

REFERENCES

Abu Zayd, N. (2004). *Rethinking the Qur'an: Towards humanistic hermeneutics.* Humanistics University Press.

Abu Zayd, N. (2010). The Qur'an, Islam and Muhammad. *Philosophy & Social Criticism, 36,* 281–294.

Al-Attas, M. N. (1977). The concept of education in Islam [Keynote address]. First World Conference in Muslim Education. Makkatul Mu'azzamah.

Al-Attas, M. N. (2005). Islam and secularism. *Journal of Islamic Philosophy, 1,* 11–43.

Al-Hasan, A., Faridahwati, M. S., & Kamil, M. I. (2013). Ethics and ethical theories from an Islamic perspective. *International Journal of Islamic Thought, 4*, 1–13.

Arkoun, M. (1994). *Rethinking Islam: Common questions, uncommon answers* (Robert D. Lee, Trans.). Westview.

Bakar, O. (1992). *Classification of knowledge in Islam: A study in Islamic philosophies of science.* Institute for Policy Research.

Davids, N., & Waghid, Y. (2016). *Ethical dimensions of Muslim education.* Palgrave Macmillan.

Davids, N., & Waghid, Y. (2019). *Teaching and learning as a pedagogic pilgrimage: Cultivating faith, hope and imagination.* Routledge.

Denny, F. M. (1975). The meaning of "ummah" in the Qur'ān. *History of Religions, 15*(1), 34–70.

Du Toit, J. (2004). *Independent schooling in post-apartheid South Africa: Quantitative overview.* HSRC.

Fataar, A. (2003). Muslim community schools in Cape Town: Exemplifying adaptation to the democratic landscape. *Annual Review of Islam in South Africa, 6*, 1–7.

Freire, P. (1997). *Pedagogy of hope: Reliving pedagogy of the oppressed.* Continuum.

Freire, P. (1998). *Pedagogy of freedom: Ethics, democracy, and civic courage.* Rowman & Littlefield.

Freire, P. (2000). *Pedagogy of the oppressed.* Continuum.

Hansen, D. T. (2011). *The teacher and the world: A study of cosmopolitanism as education.* Routledge.

Hoel, N. (2016). Exploring women's *madrasahs* in South Africa: Implications for the construction of Muslim personhood and religious literacy. *Religious Education, 111*(1), 30–48.

hooks, b. (2003). *Teaching community: A pedagogy of hope.* Routledge.

Kirylo, J. D. (2011). *Paulo Freire: The man from Recife.* Peter Lang.

Kirylo, J. D. (2017). *Paulo Freire: His faith, spirituality, and theology.* Sense.

Lübbe, H. (1986). Scientific practice and responsibility. In M. C. Doeser & J. N. Kraay (Eds.), *Facts and values, volume 19.* Martinus Nijhoff Philosophy Library. Springer.

Mohamed, Y. (2002). Islamic education in South Africa. *ISIM Newsletter 9* (2): 30.

Nadvi, L. (2008). South African Muslims and Political Engagement in a Globalising Context. *South African Historical Journal, 60*(4), 618–636.

Nasr, S. H. (2010). *Islam in the modern world: Challenged by the West, threatened by fundamentalism, keeping faith with tradition.* HarperOne.

Ramadan, T. (2001). *Islam, the West and the challenges of modernity.* Islamic Foundation.

Tayob, A., Niehaus, I., & Weisse, W. (2011). Introduction. In A. Tayob, I. Niehaus, & W. Weisse (Eds.), *Muslim schools and education in Europe and South Africa* (pp. 7–14). Waxmann.

Vawda, S. (2017). Migration and Muslim identities: Malawians and Senegalese Muslims in Durban, South Africa. *Journal for the Study of Religion, 30*(2), 32–74.

Waghid, Y. (2011). *Conceptions of Islamic education: Pedagogical framings.* Peter Lang.

Waghid, Y. (2018). Reconceptualising madrasah education: Towards a radicalised imaginary. In M. Abu Bakar (Ed.), *Rethinking Madrasah education in a globalised world* (pp. 105–117). Routledge.

Wan Daud, M. W. (2009). Al-Attas' concept of ta'dib as true and comprehensive education in Islam. https://seekersguidance.org/articles/general-artices/al-attas -concept-of-tadib-as-true-and-comprehensive-education-in-islam-wan-mohd -nor-wan-daud/

PART II

CONTEXTS OF HOPE IN HIGHER EDUCATION

THREE

—ᚾᚾ—

THE POWER OF HOPE AND TRANSFORMATIVE TEACHING

How to Frame an Educational Vision by Means of the Most Beautiful Names of Allah (*al-Asma' al-Husna*)

MUALLA SELÇUK

THE IMPORTANCE OF HOPE AND the teaching of hope cannot be overestimated, yet its significance is easy to ignore. For me, teaching hope also holds personal meaning and underscores the fact that even one person can make a lasting difference in someone's life. Reflecting on my own life and academic journey as I was preparing to write this chapter, I realized that for me, the person who made that lasting difference was my mother. She taught me from my early childhood what it was to be a person of hope both in daily life and in changing and challenging circumstances.

My mother grew up at a time when girls did not go to school because it went against prevailing religious and cultural beliefs. She quit during third grade in primary school in accordance with her father's decision. Never losing her love and passion for learning, however, she ended up waiting impatiently for me to come home from school so I could tell her what I had learned that day and take joy from this. And thus would I come to realize the value of learning and of generating and keeping the avenues of hope alive. My mother remained like a student her entire life . . . open and willing to learn from everyone and anyone. When we came home from school, her question would not be the usual "How was your day?" but instead "What did you learn today?" I was very keen on giving her a complete account, unlike my siblings, and would regale in detail my successes, failures, frustrations, and interactions with fellow pupils. She would listen with an open heart, paying close attention to my feelings of anxiety about what had been achieved and my worries about what might be done, and so on. And I remember some of her reactions: "Stop focusing on those things that offend you—they only weaken you. Take stock of all that you learned at school today." "Stop blaming others, your friends, your teachers, you cannot go around being what other people think of you and become a good student." "You must control your emotions—you do not have to get angry—just slow down and tell me." "You are always valuable to me." In other words, she conveyed a positive outlook and constructive advice.

I think most parents try to instill some level of hope and resilience in their children, but for me, the one piece of advice that resonates most, shapes my life consistently, and provides a sense of hope even in the most challenging of times is this: Always remember every difficulty is a test and an opportunity. From time to time, I think about how to differentiate between them. That is, which is the test, and which is the opportunity? As a child, I knew to some extent what *test* meant, at least from the tests we had in school, but how to see the opportunity part when faced with difficulty was not so easy. How shall I get there from here, and how will I know that I have arrived? I liked going over what I had learned each day on the way home and thinking how I would relate it to my mother (and I still do!). How was I to express my feelings so that my mother could understand me? It was easy to tell her of grades and test results but much harder to see wherein the opportunity aspect lay when I was being rejected and not appreciated. Then one day I asked her how to find opportunities in the difficulties I faced. She replied, "Darling just listen to your inner voice, God will help you." My mother used to say "*Ya Fattah*" as many times as needed to bring order to any chaotic situations the family faced in life or to give thanks in grateful moments. Al-Fattah (الفتّاح) is one of the many beautiful names of God, meaning the Opener, the Reliever. It references the judge by whose guidance everything obscure is manifested. Muslims have ninety-nine names for God, known as ʾasmāʾu llāhi l-ḥusnā. They all praise and dignify God. What remains strongest in my memory are the many times I have used the name *Ya Fattah*, as my mother taught me.

This knowledge and practice began to filter in more powerfully as I grew older and began studies at a faculty of theology. One day, as I was reciting verses 94:5–6 of *Surat al-Sharh*: "and, behold, with every hardship comes ease: verily, with every hardship comes ease!" I was struck by the words and impressed by their import. My mother's words came back to me with clarity, and I saw therein the pattern of difficulty, test, and opportunity that she had constantly directed me to understand and apply.

In the years that followed, I studied these ninety-nine names of God in more detail, reflecting on the attributes of the Merciful, the Peace, the Great, the Provider, the Truth, the Glorious, the First, the Last, the Enricher, the Light, the Guide, the Friend, and more. I analyzed them in terms of humankind's existential relationship with God. I studied the story of the prophet Abraham, honored with the title "friend of God," a man of faith and courage who used his heart and reason to reject the idols of his people and seek the infinite and beloved Creator, struggling to the extent that he was willing to face death for his beliefs. And I mastered the life of Prophet Muhammad as a lifelong educator, the best example for Muslims to emulate in all aspects of life, and a mercy to humankind. His words and deeds powerfully enunciated the concept of *Tawhid* (the Oneness of God), which flows through the length and breadth of our senses and life. I found meaning in the words and imagery of Rumi's profound poem *The Guest House*, which powerfully describes the human being embracing whomever and whatever comes as a guide from beyond and a teacher to be welcomed, and our emotions, whether good or bad, as visitors to learn lessons from.

Over time, as a scholar and a researcher of Islam in education, I have developed a teaching philosophy aligned with this theology. It has taught me the importance of framing a new vision of reality: to not be crushed by life as we live it, to not play the victim, and to not impose my expectations on my surroundings. Instead I try to welcome experiences positively in the belief that there are new things in store for us all. I know it is not always possible to think as such in every situation, for, after all, we are mere human beings with attendant weaknesses, wanting a quick fix, impatient, having compulsive needs, needing to control, wanting power, wanting to win, full of fears and anxiety, prone to prejudice, and falling into pride when all is well and into distress when things do not go as expected (*Hud*, 11:9–11, 17; *al-Isra'*, 17:83).

These realities reveal themselves in our teaching endeavors as well. While I see many teachers enter schools with a strong passion for teaching and the drive and energy to succeed, in the end, and in my experience, only some manage to survive and flourish, while others, unfortunately, do not. Why is this the case? Teaching is without a doubt a hard and taxing profession on several levels. Most find it hard to cope with the rapidly changing worlds of schools and classrooms and to resist the challenges to their sense of well-being that may be imposed by policy, pupils, parents, the workplace, and other internal and external authorities. Yet what is it that keeps those teachers that manage to stay the course believing in what they do, and maintaining within themselves the ethic that they can make a difference in the lives of those they teach?

In my opinion, identity and worldview play a significant role in how a teacher functions in the broader context of the learning environment and how they choose to educate the children and individuals in front of them, connecting and interacting effectively to impart knowledge. This means that the desire to contribute to growth in knowledge, while commendable, is by itself not enough; there are further qualities demanded of the role. One of these is to be true to oneself, presenting this authenticity confidently to students as part of the learning transaction. However, being sure of one's worldview, while fundamental to one's role as an educator, is not enough. One might have clear objectives, and a clear objective of the exercise, but to be effective, these need to be married to the idea of teaching as an activity. This is more a philosophy of education, as teaching is more than a profession. A teacher educates primarily through their behavior, by their very being. Teaching methods—new techniques and approaches and so on—may be fine in and of themselves, but they do not necessarily make an effective teacher. The true teacher is one who uses their skills to move beyond the realm of instruction to that of the transformation. In addition, as the work of teachers becomes ever more complex and thus more demanding, nurturing and generating the hope needed to overcome the many challenges that will inevitably arise while keeping the ethic of imparting knowledge continually in focus (to see tests as opportunities, to echo my mother) has become a more central issue among teachers themselves and all those who are truly committed to their work.

I aim to help those student-teachers involved in teaching religion to develop a strong worldview based on the core values of the Quran and Sunnah as well as on the life of the Prophet Muhammad. Any worldview rests on a foundation of premises, but when it is based on strong ethical and theological foundations, it gives a profound sense of worth and purpose to all our endeavors and, in the case of education, a critical sense of responsibility toward those whom we are teaching and an idea of how best to teach them. Understanding what it means to be human and allowing this moral approach to seep into our teaching methodology will keep us focused on our true goals as educators and will bring out the best in our students.

I consistently pray that my students become and remain open to God's grace as they explore their own academic and life journey, and that they develop their critical faculties along channels that allow them to realize their own individuality and intellectual independence, and not fit themselves into forms determined by others, nor repeat the handed-out, prepackaged thoughts of others. I wish for them to develop a deep sense of God-consciousness and an awareness of their civic responsibilities and to bring these into all contexts of their lives, including the classroom. It is my hope that they will infuse all that they do with a balanced moral outlook, such that they can think and engage at a sophisticated level underscored by a mature theological understanding of things.

Can I claim success in having realized these objectives or in shaping personalities such as these in my classroom setting? I cannot say for sure, but what I do know is that in the sense that all teaching is a transactional enterprise, my students have become my coagents in the process of writing this chapter.[1]

IMAGINING A CURRICULUM BASED ON *AL-ASMA' AL-HUSNA*: WHEN GOD BECOMES THE CONTENT OF OUR TEACHING

Finding ways to help young people understand and apply the Quranic message to all aspects of their life has been the primary goal of teacher training at Ankara University's Religious Education Department, as well as at the Faculty of Divinity (of which I am a part). Our aim is to train teachers who will be reflective practitioners, which means those able to thoughtfully consider a text during its teaching and have an accurate and refined understanding of its content. We consider it essential that teachers be able to master this skill set so they have within them the potential to make a difference in understanding and knowledge.

We wish teachers to be active agents, recognizing that they have a major role to play as key decision-makers in the formation of curricula and a responsibility to not act as mere passive participants, faithfully following or implementing a curriculum planned and handed out to them. And, working with scholars of theory, research, teaching, and practice in the field of Islamic religious education curriculum development, we have become increasingly aware of the importance of the role of religious education teachers in this regard (Selçuk, 2013). In our opinion, teachers should have a strong conception of themselves in this capacity and a greater sense of their power to affect the curriculum. The reason for this is that, regarding the argument made earlier for teachers to have authenticity, a personal worldview, and clear objectives, this cannot be realized unless one assumes an active sense of responsibility toward what is being taught and how best to teach it. Consequently, as scholars of Islamic education at the faculty, we contend that the philosophy for religious education should not be separated from the philosophy of the curriculum.

The question at the heart of our philosophy and steering its course is simply this: What would be the potential impact of transforming our religious education system such that the educators we train are empowered with the ability and knowledge to engage fully with the message of the Quran in order to find guidance to crafting meaningful lives for themselves and their future students?

Studying the beautiful names of God could be one pivotal pathway to developing that spiritual connection and understanding of the Quranic text and our inner gnosis and spiritual wisdom as we engage with theological matters. God's attributes as reflected in His names—such as His great magnanimity, generosity, and mercy—if studied and actively cultivated will inspire in educators a higher ethic and behavioral norms that affirm hope and inspire those whom they teach to emulate them. That is, focusing on *al-Asma' al-Husna* as an area of research means the power to strengthen the existential relationship with God and thus help both the educator and the student to become the best person they can be. Research on *al-Asma' al-Husna* opens an avenue to get students engaged in discussions about God, thereby enhancing their understanding. The difficulty lies in how to teach these names and their meaning to the young.

I was therefore delighted to come across al-Ghazali's book *Al-Maqsad al-Asna Fi Sharh Ma'ani Asma' Allah Al-Husna* in the course of my studies. The book discusses the relationship between faith and conduct; its aim is mainly to explain the meaning and importance of the hadith "تخلقوا بأخلاق الله", to become moral with God's morality" and to focus on the wisdom of the Prophet Muhammad's words. Al-Ghazali, in his book, takes the words of the Prophet as a motivating idea: "Allah has such attributes and the one who holds on to one of them will go to heaven" (p. 72). According to al-Ghazali, we must be active agents regarding the names of God, going beyond simply superficially hearing them, learning their meaning, and memorizing them. Far more important and relevant is to understand their spiritual import and mold ourselves according to the qualities they call for, to attempt to perfect our imperfections, and to refine our soul and morality as best we can to mirror them.

The point in terms of education is that the meaning of God's message cannot be grasped fully by didactical ways. Considering the holistic nature of human beings, al-Ghazali draws attention to the cooperation of senses, mind, and revelation, and in doing so opens the way to integrate the worlds of mind, heart, life, and self, which leads educators to ask themselves the further question: "But what do you really understand?"

The following paragraphs offer further elaborations on the theological concepts and frames of reference we, as religious educators, have at our disposal today to understand the meaning of the beautiful names of God and their application to our faith and life. We will use the name Al-Fattah as an example.

A TEACHING MODEL

In this section, I outline a teacher training model for teaching religion that I have termed the Conceptual Clarity Model (CCM; see Figure 3.1).

Overview: Key Aspects and Aims of the Conceptual Clarity Model

As shown below, the model comprises five key phases: reflections on the current situation, exploring text and context relation, reflections on personal development, reflections for the common good, and, finally, integration of content with effective pedagogy.

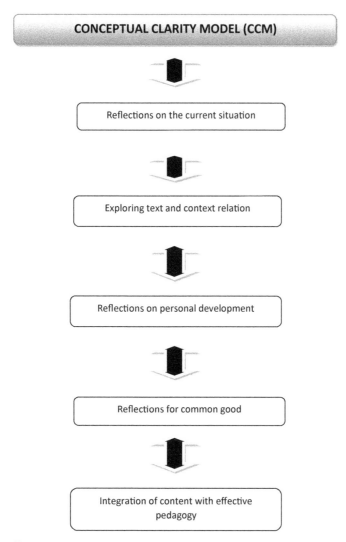

Figure 3.1

REFLECTIONS ON THE CURRENT SITUATION

Keeping in mind that not all students will have the same degree of knowledge, this is an initial exploratory phase, in which students are to uncover any existing knowledge they may have regarding the issue under consideration, to bring any relevant experiences of it to the table, to examine their common codes of conduct, and, finally, to reflect on their feelings and actions toward it. They are to explore common understanding and practices concerning the issue and provide evidence for their views, including what experiences promote their interpretations and behavior. In sum, this phase is an exercise in collating existing opinions and insights gained from the past, providing food for thought, and pushing students to move outside their comfort zone.

EXPLORING THE RELATIONSHIP BETWEEN TEXT AND CONTEXT

In this phase, students study the content and context of Quranic verses through a historical-critical analysis considering the time-space factor. The objective here is to encourage students to explore and comprehend the deeper spiritual meanings of the Quranic text and to develop an ability to discern those messages directed to its original listeners and to those of later times, up to and including modern generations. Faith teachers must develop contextual thinking in a discursive tradition; this has produced historically contingent categorizations of doctrines and practices. The historical-critical analysis is to be rooted around questions such as "What happened before and during the time of the Prophet? What did the Quran bring to the forefront? What developed in history? What are the essentials for today?" and many more.

The objectives in terms of developing paths of thinking and teaching skills are to comprehend that the context is both the background and the horizon; to gain a broader perspective on the ethos of Quranic knowledge, including its moral and intellectual grounding; and to be aware of the link between past, present, and future while communicating with the text.

REFLECTIONS ON PERSONAL DEVELOPMENT

In this phase, the student has the option to ask the question, "What does it all mean to me personally?" The role of the teacher in this capacity will be to develop the student's knowledge and understanding of (1) how they can enhance the role of religion in their personal development; (2) their comprehension of what the role of God's vicegerent means and implies; (3) the human condition, or to know oneself and what this means; and (4) the relationship between social or cultural behaviors and personal choices. Students should be concerned with grasping the human condition fully, to understand the interplay of human emotions, desires, feelings, values, and commitments that lead human beings to perceive themselves in the most favorable light while being critical of others. In other words, students should consider the importance of our ability to honestly appraise ourselves and accept the uncomfortable truth that we tend to judge ourselves according to our ideals and others according to their mistakes.

REFLECTIONS FOR THE COMMON GOOD

This phase is a search for a theology, which has a public language and develops the student's appreciation of and commitment to social ways of living. Skills in forming and maintaining positive relationships with others as well as civic responsibility need to be improved. Without delivering static "truths" or determined attitudes, teachers should encourage students through raising concern for societal welfare, social justice, and the rights and dignity of all people, as well as drawing attention to how ethical outlooks and equality are affected by cultural norms and practices.

INTEGRATION OF CONTENT WITH AN EFFECTIVE PEDAGOGY

In this phase, students' attention is drawn to the issue of maintaining integrity between faith and its principles and life. The teacher should guide students toward accepting the importance of appraising human beings justly, accurately, and holistically, with the understanding that each human being is a unique creature of God composed of many different experiences, traits, and backstories, which need to be considered in any opinion formation. Furthermore, teachers should impart to students an enriched understanding of the human experience and what it means to be fully human. The following questions may assist in ensuring that the information explored is relevant: What exactly does a Muslim believe? What is the primary force directing the mind and heart toward the Divine? What underlying commitments concerning faith, knowledge, and education are at work? Getting students to think at these spiritually deeper levels of comprehension and discernment will allow them to grow in what Islam calls *musalama* (مسالمة a peaceful relationship with God, with oneself, with others, and with creation).

Each of the five phases of this model is important. Depending on their aims and objectives, teachers may use one phase or a combination of several to develop students' comprehension, skills, knowledge, understanding, and attitudes regarding the topic under discussion.

CASE STUDY: The Classroom as a Place of Hope

In this section, I intend to discuss the beautiful name of God, Al-Fattah, and how it relates to the notion of hope to demonstrate an application of the CCM. It is important to note that the model is flexible and not to be taken as rigid blocks or to be followed in static form. Rather, through a series of questions to act as guidelines, it is to function as a safe and sometimes brave space to open and facilitate reflection. The questions can be drawn either from the model outlined above or from aspects relating to the teacher, student, and content dynamic of the educational setting.

In my experience, this model has turned out to be productive in developing student and teacher relationships with the Quran. What I present below is the product of collaborative work undertaken from the beginning of June 2018 to the end of December 2018 using the CCM as a tool. On the one hand, I intend to present the dynamics of students' understanding of hope, on the other to provide insight into what the framework embodies. While the primary focus is on the explanatory role of hope and the part this plays in the religious makeup of the Muslim thinking, behavior, and moral attitudes, it also aims to offer a relevant pedagogy for teaching and learning religion.

At the beginning of our study, each student was required to work on one of the steps of the model, make presentations of their research, and initiate discussion. The case study below is based on my students' presentations and discussions and on the collaborative work carried out throughout the project.

REFLECTIONS ON THE CURRENT SITUATION: *LEARNING IN THE PRESENCE OF THE OTHER*

The first step recommended by the model was to undertake a review of current material and map findings. We engaged in collaborative reading, reflection, and research across different disciplines and organized two workshops. Within the scope of these workshops, which explored the transformative power of hope, we invited two well-known scholars, one Christian and one Muslim, to our weekly meetings: Professor Martin Thurner[2] and Professor İsmail Hakkı Ünal.[3] We chose these particular distinguished scholars because both had written articles on hope for the *Dictionary of Encounter: Basic Terms of Christianity and Islam.*[4] These articles, which were written from the perspectives of the authors' religious faith and belief, became the starting point and inspiration for our workshops.[5] Dr. Thurner points out that the Bible considers the concept of hope as well as those of faith and love. According to Thurner, reflecting on the Bible reveals that a main factor that fosters hope is trust in God's word and promise and having sincere faith in him.

In Professor Ünal's view, a Muslim should live a life balanced between *khauf* (خوف, fear, despair, anxiety) and *raja'* (رجاء, wish, expectation). Maintaining a balance between these two states, he points out, prevents believers from being overly obsessed with or tied to fears or, at the opposite end, to be overly obsessed with optimism. According to the Quran and the Sunnah, being a Muslim demands self-understanding and taking responsibility for what kind of person one becomes. Although the traditional understanding of hope in Islamic resources focuses mostly on the context of the hereafter, a careful examination paves the way to an interpretation of hope within daily life situations. This leads to the question of whether Islamic religious education is ready to cultivate an understanding of this mindset of maintaining constant balance and to show what it means for the faithful in terms of generating hope.

The workshops helped us to clarify where we are and where we stand. Together with students, we explored the ever-present human tension between *khauf* and *raja'* as well as the restorative nature of faith and considered these as points of departure to move forward in our research. Tension is a necessary corollary of the human state, essentially in harmony with human nature because human beings in their nature are an entity left in tension. The Quran declares this state of being as a given of human existence, for "verily, we have created man into (a life of) pain, toil and trial" (*al-Balad*: 90:4).

After intense reading and discussions of both primary and secondary sources, we finally concluded that a basic trust in God and His love, mercy, and grace provides the person of faith with strong foundations to overcome the difficulties and challenges of life and equips them with the resolve to be active agents, always responsible and ready to respond to whatever they are faced with. This basic sense of trust is powerful and transformative, resulting in an inner peace and acceptance of the divine decree in cases that exceed an individual's limit. Likewise, descriptively, we suggested that hope could be understood as a practical, active, and relational component of our faith in God. Equipped with this outlook, we moved on to examine the religious texts and to open new avenues for the next steps of the CCM, as shown below.

EXPLORING THE RELATIONSHIP BETWEEN
TEXT AND CONTEXT: LOOKING AT LIFE
THROUGH THE MESSAGE OF THE TEXT

This stage of inquiry requires scholarly communication with the text and a deeper understanding of how to engage students with the core message of the Quran. In terms of epistemology, the general textual context should be borne in mind. The following verses elucidate the basic aims of the Quran:[6] "And spend (freely) in God's cause and let not your own hands throw you into destruction; and persevere in doing good: behold, God loves the doers of good" (al-Baqara: 2:195); "O humankind! Behold, We have created you all out of a male and a female, and have made you into nations and tribes, so that you might come to know one another. Verily, the noblest of you in the sight of God is the one who is most deeply conscious of Him. Behold, God is All-Knowing, All-Aware" (al-Hujurat: 49:13); "To a happy state shall indeed attain he who causes this (self) to grow in purity" (Ash Shams: 91:9).

The group decided to address two principal questions through the general worldview of the Quran: What does the Quran bring to the fore in terms of hope? What are the essentials for our understanding of hope in the context of the Quran?

One student who had spent many years teaching the Quran to young people reminded us that the following verses could provide insight on the notion of hope:[7] "God provides for him in a manner beyond all expectation; and for everyone who places his trust in God, He (alone) is enough. Verily, God always attains to His purpose: (and) indeed, unto everything has God appointed its (term and) measure" (at-Talaq: 65:3); "Now whoever surrenders his whole being unto God, and is a doer of good withal, has indeed taken hold of a support most unfailing: for with God rests the final outcome of all events" (Luqman: 31:22).

According to these verses, generating hope seems to be a critical factor for the believer. The Quran presents hope not as an option but rather as a requirement. Hope is vital in sustaining commitment and in managing tension. We understand this from the story of Joseph in the Quran, where his father, Jacob, states: "It is only to God that I complain of my deep grief and my sorrow: for I know, from God, something that you do not know. (Hence,) O my sons, go forth and try to obtain some tidings of Joseph and his brother; and do not lose hope of God's life-giving mercy: verily, none but people who deny the truth can ever lose hope of God's life-giving mercy" (Yusuf: 12:86–87).

We learn from the Quran that there is always a light of hope, even in situations that involve struggle and pain. Based on this Quranic insight, the students were able to reflect on the text and the context from a variety of angles. Here are some examples of their thinking that came up during the study:

> Hope simply symbolizes the soul's surrender to God. . . . Hope provides courage for overcoming the state of despair. . . . Hope is not a simple expectation but an active wait, full of faith and patience. . . . Hope creates a space for a true assessment. . . . If you are hopeless, you can't see the whole picture; what you see is missing something. . . . When I read the verses in

the Quran, I see that hope is not a historical matter, but it has a universal connotation. The verses associated with hope seem generally valid in the context of good behavior and sincere faith.

These reflections by students demonstrate a rich communication with the text and reflective interaction to elucidate the meaning of verses in connection to their perceptions of hope in different contexts. Indeed, developing the skills to reflect on the text, interpret it, and understand that it has multiple meanings requires both a sound understanding of the text and an ability to relate it to, for example, in daily life. It was found that students were able to successfully deepen and enrich their understanding of things through the lens of the Quranic worldview and describe the correlation between faith and life in a didactical way. A very important outcome of the classroom environment was the students' receptiveness to the stories in the Quran.

REFLECTIONS ON PERSONAL DEVELOPMENT:
WHAT DOES IT ALL MEAN TO YOU?

One of the goals of using the CCM in education could be helping each student in their personal quest for meaning. In our experience, as noted earlier, almost all the students demonstrated a clear enthusiasm for the exercise, and all enjoyed the collaborative work involved, repeatedly identifying questioning as a key skill and an effective tool in understanding the text. Students also did well in the transmission of knowledge from the relevant literature, whether religious or nonreligious. Unfortunately, they were less enthusiastic in their responses to the question of "What does it all mean to you?" For example, one of the students stated: "I have been working on hope for months, why then such a loss of hope? Why then is there a reason for this despair and fear of failure of not being able to find something interesting for our project?"

In setting out concepts central to the work and related to personal development, I had to raise and address many uncomfortable queries on my part as a religious educator: Why was religious education not successful enough when addressing the issue of the inner dimensions of life and faith? How, why, and where were we failing in our educational efforts to impart a greater knowledge of the human self? How were educators to develop the best in students if they had not connected with or realized the best within themselves? Of course, educators can mechanically learn about Islam and its many complexities during their teacher training programs and have firm faith in fundamental Islamic values and principles, but that does not mean that they have acquired the type of spiritual knowledge that comes from a deeper conscious reflection on the nature of God and matters of faith. As far as I can see, we need more inclusive practices in education that consider existential questions to help students gain deeper insights into the human reality and their inner selves and to learn how to view and measure their authenticity using Quranic terms effectively.

It is hoped that in the long run the CCM will serve as a platform that allows exploration of these types of existential questions and dimensions and helps students and educators interpret situations they personally encounter in ways that give them insight into their faith and spiritual development. I continued discussions along these lines with my students and started to challenge them: "You, as Muslim youth, believe in the ONE God, Allah. One of the good names of Allah is the name Al-Fattah, which has guided us since the beginning of our work. As a Muslim and a believer in the name of Al-Fattah, how does your faith help you explain the concept of hope?"

One student responded excitedly: "It helps to overcome uncertainty, thinking about the name Al-Fattah seems to provide a kind of expansion, space, and movement concerning new situations instead of keeping me focusing on success, failure, or fears." Another added: "Al-Fattah makes me feel relaxed, helps me retain my efforts to stabilize the situation and literally leads me to the flow."

Another student summed up the existing gap between knowledge *about* religion and learning *from* religion: "We live in an age where the relationships we have established with the world, ourselves, others, and the Creator are so widely transformed that religious education has the responsibility to propose new ways of thinking about these relations. Because in principle we accept the teachings of our faith, but we have difficulty in living with them in everyday life."

One of the students tried to describe the traditional definition of the meaning: "Al-Fattah, which is one of the beautiful names of God, literally means overcoming all difficulties and being helped in this process. Rich interpretations were made in Islamic tradition. For example, it is said that this beautiful name comes from the verb 'to conquer' (فتح, *feth*). *Feth* means to open that which is closed. There are many varieties of opening something that is closed. It could be material, such as opening a locked door. It can be immaterial, such as opening the soul by getting rid of pain and sorrow in the heart." Another student concurred wholeheartedly: "The most precious among these is to open the door of the soul."

More broadly speaking, the name Al-Fattah helped my students to spiritually comprehend the issue of hope and translate this meaning into action. It also provided them a space to reflect on the strong link between God, human beings, and the universe. Hope seemed to act as a kind of relief, powerfully channeling human emotion to a state of optimism, acting as a beacon and catalyst for renewed energies and viewpoints to overcome obstacles under the spirit of complete trust in God, his love, mercy, grace, and aid. The type of comprehension of hope that the name Al-Fattah inspires is one primarily connected to understanding, governing, and changing our perspective and viewpoint of reality, and putting this within the framework of our relationship with the Divine Transcendent, underscored by patience, perseverance, trust in his decree. Hope is a disposition and a stance, but it is also a dynamic process that needs to be sustained.

As a group, we came to realize that, more important than anything, hope existed as a powerful dormant potential if only we as Muslims could tap in to it. It was an amazing source of vitality and spiritual strength and a major component of the Islamic faith. Hope was not to be relegated to the subject of cold academic study but to be studied in terms of its spiritual potential and existential dimensions, regarding the human condition and the inner workings of human thinking patterns and souls. Hope had revealed itself as a tool and state of mind in response to despair and the search to find something new. Hope had lain a dormant reality, always there and ready to be discovered. It was the undercurrent of the collaborative student-teacher relationship that we had developed, always there while we listened, read, wrote, and reimagined together. Hope was not the *expectation* for something to happen or for a wish to come true but a *belief* that God is in control. It was a way of thinking that rested in an optimistic viewpoint, which gave us the knowledge that we could confidently overcome the difficulties of any situation we faced, including the one we had found ourselves in as educators and students. The "new" we were looking for was already in this open space, and it revealed itself with yet another important concept from the Quran: *al-Furqan* (الفرقان, the Criterion).

The final proposal in this step was thus to relate the concept of hope with the concept of *Furqan* to address the interplay of *khauf* (خوف) and *raja'* (رجاء) for our spiritual growth and development and how this relates to the constant state of tension that is the undercurrent of the human psychological state.

Definition of Furqan

The root meaning of the word *Furqan* is "to distinguish or separate." Muslims believe that the Quran has the authority to distinguish between things that are mixed together and to place them in appropriate categories. In this respect, the Quran is also named *al-Furqan*, or, the Criterion. The first verse of *Surat al-Furqan* reads: "Hallowed is He who from on high, step by step, has bestowed upon His servant the standard by which to discern the true from the false, so that to all the world it might be a warning." Thus, one of the features of the Quran is to clarify. The Quran has the authority to distinguish good and evil, the beautiful from the ugly, the righteous from the sinner, order from chaos, halal from haram, good deeds from bad ones, truth from falsehood, and light from dark by its feature of being a *Furqan*. So, the Quran aims to remove ambiguity and confusion by being a decisive factor for the heart, mind, and soul, providing a clear understanding and comprehension (*al-Anfal*: 8:29).

How do we bring and apply the Quranic criterion to our lives? By constantly and consistently applying the values and principles of the Quran in all that we do. Truth, justice, and the rights of people are not abstract concepts but have a basis in living action, dictating how we are to view given circumstances and act in each given situation. Furthermore, the way we translate these values to specific life experiences is also important and is to be aligned with the requirements of the criterion. The application must be holistic, considering the time-space factor and utilizing the tools and knowledge available; that is, science with wisdom without violating the spirit of the Quran or its values. In this respect, Muslims can benefit from the distinctive nature of the Quran without ignoring the spirit of the time they live in. Of course, we are likely to make mistakes or wrong choices sometimes, for our belief may be one thing but despite our best intentions our attitude or behavior in any given situation might not be fully aligned with the principles or values of the Quran. However, this does not decrease our humanity, for Muslims have the advantage of constantly measuring themselves against the *Furqan* and recognizing where they have slipped, and are given the scope to do *tawbah* and make amends quickly. Muslims are always given the opportunity, in other words, to realign themselves. For while Allah in the Quran has set the measure of behavior, he also states in the Quran that "verily, good deeds drive away evil deeds" (*Hud*: 11:114). Allah has set the measure of all things and is merciful and forgiving. In this respect, we can always make a fresh start in our life. Humankind's repentance, connected to God's love and forgiveness, is the weft and warp of our existence and revives us at any given point in time and in any given circumstance. In this sense, we are powerfully connected to hope. Educators should be aware that hope lies in God-consciousness and in generating this state of *taqwa*, or mindfulness of God. Evaluating and assessing students in light of this dynamic through questioning, reflection, and response will be an important part of their educational practice.

REFLECTIONS FOR THE COMMON GOOD: RESTORING
HOPE, SOCIAL JUSTICE, AND DIGNITY

When I asked my students whether their research on the relationship between Al-Fattah, the common good, or civic responsibility influenced their understanding of Islam and the way they live now and/or the life they intended to live in the future, their comments focused on one single Quranic concept: *Amal-Salih* (عمل صالح, Righteous Deeds). This resonated deeply with students, who saw a profound connection between hope and remaining passionately dedicated to building a more just and equitable society. In this regard, the Quran draws our attention to the meaning and purpose of life: "He who has created death as well as life, so that He might put you to a test and thus show which of you is best in conduct (*amal*), and (make you realize that) He alone is Almighty, truly forgiving" (*Al-Mulk*: 67:2).

The word *amal* (deed) in the verse refers to continuity. The Quran emphasizes the importance of action, or *amal*, but the word does not denote bodily, physical action only. It also refers to the inner dimension of action, meaning the action of the heart, the intellect, and other cognitive acts. All these actions can be expressed in the word *deed*. To this end, members of the group focused on the roles of teachers, parents, social and religious leaders, scientists, and many other decision-makers in the community and concluded that they can be important role models or mentors to generate hope. They discovered the importance of lifelong learning and the innovative aspect of hope while engaging with the Quranic text. They also confirmed that the moral quality of knowledge lies in how it can widen awareness and contribute to the common good of society—in other words, knowledge and belief tied to action results in dividends. This exercise helped them to improve their contextual thinking, which is much needed in religious education today.

With this understanding and having engaged with some good examples of school practices on generating hope presented in the media, students concluded that teachers have a social responsibility to promote an ethical, moral outlook both for the moral development of students and for the good of society. That responsibility is to teach virtues by enjoining the good and preventing people from falling into error (evil). To emphasize morality is not just a question of character alone but also of action. An educational system composed of teachers with a strong sense of social responsibility will be successful in instilling and spreading integrity, good values, and hope, with teachers acting as important role models for human behavior. It should be evident that fostering such a strong sense of morality embodies a shared vision of faith among teachers of religion: "But behold, as for those who say, 'Our Sustainer is God' and then steadfastly pursue the right way—on them do angels often descend, (saying) 'Fear not and grieve not, but receive the glad tiding of that paradise which has been promised to you!'" (*Fussilat*: 41:30; see also *Al-Kahf*: 110).

INTEGRATION OF CONTENT WITH AN EFFECTIVE PEDAGOGY: TOWARD A REFLECTIVE FAITH

So far, we have stressed the significance of a perspective that may continue to shape the professional lives of trainee religious teachers, helping them to be responsive to the varying challenges they will face and adding to their moral development. Teaching and learning do not end on graduation but are lifelong processes. As stated, those who develop empathy and the skills of reflection have a great capacity to generate a sense of hope, which in turn empowers the educational environment and their mode of teaching.

Because trainee religious educators, it is assumed, harbor a serious commitment to Islam, underscored by a sincere spiritual and moral perspective, the framework of learning outlined above allows them the scope to examine and develop this further. Ultimately, as they are able to reconcile issues relating to ideal values and realizing these in life, while taking into account the education crisis pervading society in general, they will be equipped to act as role models. They will be able to guide others both within and outside of educational settings, through aligning their behavior and actions with the values and principles outlined by Islam. In other words, they will be able to demonstrate how to realize Islamic values and morals in all dimensions of life. To put it succinctly, we need to practice what we preach. We know what to do, but too often we do not do it! While there is no easy route to moral leadership in the education sector, what follows is a conceptualization developed to foster collaboration between religious education and the social sciences.

Wearing the hat of a cognitively oriented scientist, I see three habits of mind in the practice of teaching that are worth examining for the development of the disposition of hope: flexibility, imagination, and innovation (Costa & Kallick, 2008; Selçuk, 1997). *Thinking flexibly* involves analyzing and sifting through multiple options to find the most appropriate solution. The plastic nature of the mind allows us to quickly and easily adapt to differing situations. Thus, confronted with age-old questions of right and wrong, teachers who have learned the habit of flexibility will realize that there are many alternative ways of dealing with the challenges that life throws at them, and they will find the best and most feasible solutions. *Imagining* is another habit of mind that is good to inculcate. An important avenue for generating hope, imagination allows scope for innovative thinking as well as for considering future possibilities to aid in overcoming dilemmas one may face. Encouraging imagination also functions as a pedagogical practice of hope; developing the capacity for imagination may also improve skills for generating and maintaining hope among students and in society (Green, 2016, p. 149). *Innovative thinking* suggests being open to new ideas, new situations, and new possibilities, and it can also be considered among the mental skills that sustain hope. Developing the habit of innovative thinking better prepares teachers to comprehend and handle the many varying challenges and circumstances of life that they will face. Life is difficult and unpredictable, and one must be open to taking risks as problems arise and circumstances change, but we can acquire a skill set and develop a habit of mind that will allow us to tolerate risk with more confidence. Being open-minded also requires taking certain risks. It must be stressed that unless educational environments place strong importance on the value of encountering difference, teachers will not be able to open themselves easily in facing them. These three major habits of the mind remain at the core of religious education: they shape perspectives, responses, and solutions in accordance with a spiritual and faith tradition, and they give learners critical tools to deal with the challenges that life brings to their door.

Religious education must primarily have in place a pedagogy that develops habits of mind that allow teachers to be creative and productive role models, to actively analyze, assess, and confidently address situations, circumstances, and challenges; and ultimately to pass these skills along to students as they help them to develop a moral outlook on life. Therefore, teacher training programs should take the findings of research on human development seriously and prioritize the questions of how people think. The members of our group also found value in the categories identified by Costa & Kallick (2008), and we concluded by pointing out the importance of some of these categories, such as persisting, managing impulsivity and thinking about thinking (metacognition), for our ongoing educational endeavors to flesh out the values of our faith in daily situations.

SUMMARY OBSERVATION AND FUTURE DIRECTIONS

This chapter has offered a unique cultural understanding of Islam. It has attempted to outline what is happening on the ground during teaching and learning practices in Islamic religious education. To a certain extent, this perspective can be considered a reflection in action, but it should not be considered either as absolutism or relativism. Rather, it is an attempt to evaluate the tradition using the CCM. This model seeks to help student-teachers develop skills of inquiry and communication, create personal meaning, search for the common good, value the importance of learning in encounters, and respect the variety of divine gifts we find in each other. The model aims to serve as a framework for the development and assessment of teaching and learning dispositions, all involving thinking, feeling, and doing.

In its simplest expression, this educational process is one of learning by doing. The methodology engages literature review; conceptual analysis of the Quran; and insights from two interfaith workshops with scholars, a community of students, and practitioners. Students learned by engaging with questions and problems in religious education and became participants in their own learning. The CCM, which emerged from my many years of teaching, enabled students to experience the processes of knowledge creation. I hope the case study described in this chapter demonstrates how integrating faith and life can create a new dialogue among educators on what it means to be in between our fears and our expectations.

I have attempted to show the value of empathy and hope as driving forces of life, as well as the potential of developing habits of mind based on reflective thinking and the ability to stand back and create a space to understand given situations based on shifting perspectives and orientations. Our research has illuminated understanding and hope through the beautiful name of God Al-Fattah (the Opener, the Reliever), and I add to that two more Quranic concepts: *Furqan* (the Criterion) and *Amal-i Salih* (Righteous Deeds) to act as guiding principles. Searching for *Furqan* and performing *Amal-i Salih* are two faithful responses of Muslims to the graciousness of Allah, who calls us to worship Him in Islam.

Teaching within the framework of CCM leads to inquiry-based research, and this is most appropriate for high-level forms of learning, such as analysis, evaluation, and synthesis. Therefore, I suggest the model as the basis of a transformative teacher training program. In addition to the theoretical knowledge they will gain from the program, future teachers will also develop communication skills and the ability to self-direct their learning. The values of Islam are already deeply held by student-teachers, but they need to find ways to foster their imagination and empower their intellectual development through critical thinking and literacy skills. This will in turn give hope for the future of Islamic religious education as we educate teachers to become authentic beings who are actively managing their life situations, even as they demonstrate the value of the knowledge they have acquired through their academic studies and commitments.

The time has come to share new ways of thinking and experiences to overcome the fear of failing in our responsibility toward future generations. Focusing on conceptual clarity as the key to unlocking the meaning within our tradition will give us the power to write a new story against the culture of pessimism and fear. But, of course, like all other human activities, this will always be partial and incomplete. Therefore, I urge those in charge of educational programs to encourage and seek innovative ways to teach and learn religious content and to invite students to find their voice as authentic subjects in relation to their faith. In reflecting on the life of the Prophet, for instance, those materials regarding our understanding of hope could be a further focus of research. When I announced this expectation toward the end of our study, a student showed up with a big smile on his face and read a poem from his recent research on poetry. This was one of the poems that Prophet Muhammad (Peace be upon Him) most enjoyed:

سَتُبْدِي لَكَ الْأَيَّامُ مَا كُنْتَ جَاهِلًا ويَأْتِيكَ بِالْأَخْبَارِ مَا لَمْ تَزَوِّدِ

"The days will show you what you do not know and will bring you news from a time which is unknown." (Souley, 2018, p. 25)

REFERENCES

Al-Ghazali, Abu Hamid Muhammed b. Muhammed. (1324). *Kitap el-Maksâd el-Esnâ Şarh Esmâ Allah el-Hüsnâ* (2d ed.). Matbaatu's-Saade.

Costa, A. L., & Kallick, B. (Eds.). (2008). *Learning and leading with habits of mind: 16 essential characteristics for success.* ASCD.

Green, R. (2016). Imagining future possibilities as a pedagogical practice of hope. Proceedings of 2016 REA Annual Meeting, November 4–6. https://religiouseducation.net/proceedings

Selçuk, M. (1997). Din Öğretiminin Kuramsal Temelleri-Zihin Gelişimi Açısından Bir Deneme. *Din Eğitimi Araştırmaları Dergisi, 4,* sections 145–158.

Selçuk, M. (2013). Academic expertise, public knowledge, and the identity of Islamic religious education. *Religious Education, 108*(3), 255–258.

Selçuk, M., Albayrak, H., Antes, P., Heinzmann, R., & Thurner, M. (Eds.). (2013). *İslamiyet-Hıristiyanlık Kavramları Sözlüğü.* Ankara University Publishing.

Souley, A. O. (2018). *Kütüb-i Sitte'de Şiir* [Unpublished master's thesis]. Ankara University Social Sciences Institute.

NOTES

1. To my student-teachers of religion for making this research exciting, Dr. Havva Sinem Uğurlu, Dr. Betül Zengin, Ayşe Çalal, Sümeyra Arıcan, Yasemin İpek, Aslıhan Kuşçuoğlu,

Şevket Tarık Aktaş, Rüveyda Durmuş, Abdoulaye Ousseini Souley, Hümeyra Akarsu: You are the engine of this research. Thank you all for learning with me!

2. Dr. Martin Thurner is currently a professor at Ludwig Maximilian University, Faculty of Catholic Theology, Martin Grabmann Research Institute of Medieval Theology and Philosophy.

3. Dr. İsmail Hakkı Ünal is the current dean of the Ankara University Divinity Faculty. He is a professor in the Islamic Studies Department.

4. Selçuk et al. (2013), pp. 800–802. This project has been a journey of seven years. It began with two groups of scholars, one German and one Turkish, starting a project to document the concepts of two different religious worldviews in two different cultural contexts. The product was the *Dictionary of Encounter: Basic Terms of Christianity and Islam.* The *Dictionary* is a clear and authentic example of encounter, acquaintanceship, and understanding between Christianity and Islam, and is published in four languages: Turkish, German, Arabic, and English. See İslamiyet-Hıristiyanlık Kavramları Sözlüğü, *Lexikon des Dialogs Grundbegriffe aus Christentum und Islam, Dictionary of Encounter: Basic Terms of Christianity and Islam,* and معجم الحوار مفاهيم اساسية من المسيحية والإسلام.

5. The two workshops were held at Ankara University Divinity Faculty in September and October 2018. We are grateful to Professor Thurner and Professor Ünal for their inspiring presentations and engaging presence.

6. *Al-Baqara:* 2:112; *Al-Isra':* 17:97.

7. *Al-Baqara:* 2:112; *An-Najm:* 53:39–42; *Al Imran:* 3:186; *Luqman:* 31:16; *Al-Hijr:* 15:56; *Al-Jinn:* 72:14; *Hud:* 11:123.

FUSION OF HORIZONS

A Case Study of the Pedagogy of Transformative Hope for Muslim Women's Empowerment in Malaysia

SUHAILAH HUSSIEN

INTRODUCTION

The advent of globalization has brought significant changes and new challenges to the world in general and Muslim societies in particular (Boriçi, 2017; Sule et al., 2018). Most Muslim societies view globalization as a challenge to be met, especially with the flow of trade, movement of people across borders, international political relations, and a more Western cultural identity making ever greater inroads into Muslim societies and presenting them with the fear of losing control and a dilution of the Islamic way of life. To meet the diverse challenges of a rapidly changing and ever more complex and connected world, Muslim societies are having to be more flexible, compelled to address in multiple ways the issues relating to, and internationalization of, areas such as economics, education, social interaction, politics, and communication.

Yet, while the world develops and progresses, one thing that remains rigid and static and entirely not in the intellectual spirit of the time of the Prophet (SAW), or indeed the intellectual spirit that is a hallmark of the modern age, is the way Islam is being practiced and taught in Muslim societies. Whereas for the Companions of the Prophet (SAW) and those early generations Islam was lived and experienced as an intellectual, galvanizing force, challenging Muslims' critical faculties and acting as a catalyst for personal and societal transformation, today it lies dormant, more a cultural badge of identity than a force for progress, respected but on the periphery of our lives. This is very apparent in the way the whole socio-economic-political system is structured and functions, a case in point for this chapter being the Islamic education system. Modern Muslims learn about Islam in school. However, the method of teaching and learning is fundamentally flawed in several respects, unfortunately gravitating more toward indoctrination than critical inquiry or the development of reasoning skills in the context of and appreciation for theological knowledge, spiritual development, and the search for truth. It is in this sense that Muslims fall far short of the legacy of the early Muslim generations, failing to emulate their comprehension and style of engagement with the scripture, their methods of imparting knowledge, and their locating the centrality of the text and its application. Not surprisingly, we are consequently witnessing a failure to revive the early Muslim scholastic tradition, the emergence and achievements of the great classical scholars, as well as a revival of the civilization in general. Islam promotes learning, a thirst for knowledge, and the pursuit of truth. It was this intellectual dynamic married to spiritual development that marked the educational environment following the emergence of Islam on the world stage and that propelled the early Muslim thinkers to explore the world around them and be pioneers of knowledge and discovery, as part of a new and advancing civilization (Kazmi, 2011).

As Muslim civilization declined, decimated by inner political turmoil and wider colonial enterprises, its once-vibrant culture of learning also declined, suffering the same fate and leaving it in a state of intellectual bankruptcy and spiritual stagnancy. Historically, this was not the fault of globalization but of many complex factors, with colonialism playing a significant but not the only role. Colonialism is over, we have the model of history as a standard to achieve, and a modern example in the way the educational system flourishes to an extent in the West, so what is it that causes Muslim education to be continuously mired in stagnancy, and what is the exact threat that globalization is posing regarding this? One of the many effects is the internationalization of economics and exportation of a consumer/materialist culture whereby Muslim nations have become prey to its modes of functioning, mere consumers and more dependent on the West for the importation of products, goods, and services, causing their own economies to suffer. More dangerously, through this and other channels has been the importation of non-Muslim cultural identities, dictating patterns of consumer behavior and the worldview required for this type of consumer /demand-driven market economic model to flourish.

Yet, the world is a global village and to engage with it confidently requires changing a climate of suspicion to one of hope, to generate confidence in one's own spiritual and cultural potential to resist the onslaught of the economic and cultural offensive coming from the developed world and its more secular outlook. But we must be active agents to achieve this as individual citizens and communities. One step forward is to first study the instruments of the hegemonic "other," as well as the functioning of differing modes of control and oppression that may be a feature of our own societies, and Gramsci's (1999) conception of hegemony is a good starting point.

Gramsci's (1999) theory of hegemony contends that man is ruled not by force or dictatorship alone but also powerfully by ideas, and that hegemony in society operates on two key levels, those of civil society and the state. The state "exercises hegemony throughout the society and also exercises its direct dominance over it" (p. 145). Drawing from Gramsci's conception of hegemony, I highlight its various forms of rule, particularly what Stoddart (2007) identifies as the fact that "hegemonic power works to convince individuals and social classes to subscribe to the social values and norms of an inherently exploitative capitalist economic system" (p. 202). This aspect is also prevalent in most Muslim countries today. The consequence of hegemony is a challenge. Bahi (2016) asserts that "globalization creates forms of hegemonic power that threatens cultural differences and fuels the politics of identity and community" (p. 444).

Muslims tend to accept the ideas, values, and norms of the society they live in as a given of their political, economic, and cultural environment, operating under the premise that these have some sort of rooted basis in a historically religious context. This consensus prevents questioning what is taken for granted and accepted as the status quo; that is, critiquing whether ideas, values, and norms are ideological premises and behavioral norms following a socially constructed pattern and not a religiously grounded one.

This explains why some Muslim practices may be construed as "Islamic" when in fact they are the result of and entrenched in a society's cultural and social traditions. Muslim wedding celebrations are a case in point. Here people seem to be unable or even unwilling to distinguish between Islamic religious principles/teachings and their own cultural traditions; they are motivated more by the dictates of the latter than the requirements of the former. What happens through the internationalization of communication that is now a huge feature of globalization is that these same Muslim societies are becoming aware of the different cultural traditions and even cultures of other Muslim societies and, not having a clear understanding of these, are facing potential friction over them. We all like to employ the yardstick of the faith to judge others, but we fail to realize that our own internal patterns and modes of behavior might be based on premises not aligned with that same faith. Thus, this knowing of one another on a societal level could lead to division between Muslim societies due to their differing views and practices of Islam (Bahi, 2016).

As a preventive measure, we have one potential solution to this division and that is in education. Herein is a need for a critical pedagogy that asks Muslim educators and students to critically examine their own ideas and behavioral norms. Freire's critical pedagogy, which is better termed as a pedagogy of hope and is manifested in his literacy education project, has been successful in empowering his community and others around the globe. Thus, the primary aim of this chapter is to explore how adopting Freire's pedagogy of hope can help to empower Muslims through the broadening of their horizons or views, thereby initiating a unifying thread or bond of unity between Muslim societies.

TRADITION OF EDUCATION AND CULTURE OF LEARNING: COUNTERHEGEMONY AND IDEOLOGIES IN MUSLIM SOCIETIES

Muslim societies have been and are still disconnected from their early tradition (Bamyeh, 2009; Kazmi, 2011). This is a problem depending on how we are to conceptualize notions of tradition, the meaning and value we assign to tradition in the modern context. Viewing the concept of tradition here as a revitalizing force drawn from Kazmi's (2011) ontological notion and reclaiming it away from modern views of it being a symbol of something frozen in time and backward, Muslims have in this situation a dilemma needing a solution. Kazmi (2011) describes tradition as being alive, unfolding, and dynamic, a process of becoming. Taking this as the cue, the qualities inherent in the educational traditions of Muslim societies historically, therefore, warrant examination, and any attempt to revive that system of learning will require an understanding and examination of the culture of learning prevailing at the time and education as a praxis (Kazmi, 2011). Early Muslim scholars developed a strong culture of learning, one that reflected the true spirit of Islam and gave the acquisition of knowledge tremendous value, elevating the status of those who sought it and those who taught it. The ethos and ethic of study were entwined with scriptural sanction and encouragement and were not confined to the study of theological matters alone (worthy though this was) but rather encapsulated knowledge to embrace all forms of study including the sciences, medicine, botany, physics, and mathematics (Kazmi, 2011). All subjects studied were infused with spiritual vitality working in harmony with scripture and theology. What disrupted the model, which had hitherto been successful, was the introduction of colonial forms of education, including a dual-structured system that institutionalized lower and higher education in Muslim societies.

In practice what this meant was a curriculum that removed harmonious spirituality and theology as the weft and warp of everything studied out of the equation and created a neat division of Islamic and non-Islamic subjects. So, under Islamic education were classified subjects such as *sīrah* (history), fiqh (Islamic jurisprudence), and Quranic language, while everything else was classified as nonreligious (ergo, secular) subjects such as mathematics, science, and geography (Hashim, 2008). Muslim societies themselves did not help matters by focusing on Islamic studies as a stand-alone category and emphasizing its study in this vein, thereby undermining its value across all forms of study and, in the process of this dualism, making the West the reference point for secular knowledge.

Not surprisingly, and as Sahin (2018) asserts, "modern Muslim societies' concern for their lack of progress has turned into an admiration for Western scientific achievements, which has led to the imitation of the Western higher educational institutions," in the process leading Muslims even further astray from the shores of their own early traditions and culture of learning (p. 22). Sahin (2018) further asserts that some Muslim reformers "had not quite recognised the fact that scientific achievements come out of a scientific attitude toward life, which, in turn, was nurtured within a deeper reflective, inquiring educational culture" (p. 22). One cannot just adopt a system without identifying the sociocultural background and value system of the society it is supposed to be grafted on, and then tailoring it accordingly.

To overcome this dichotomy of the traditional educational system versus the modern one and to reclaim earlier cultural traditions to revive what has been lost by way of educational achievement, the first step is to critically identify the hidden premises that underlie not only the educational system but also the structure of society itself. Note, this is not to be antimodern but simply to point out that hegemony exists and needs to be exposed and countered. To do so, Muslim societies must first be *conscious* that hegemonic oppression exists, making its presence felt across many platforms of society, whether in the world of academia, politics, economics, and so on, and that it operates on an almost top-down level through hidden premises and ideologies that dictate ideas, behavior patterns, and the general functioning of society, taking many forms on the physical, social, and psychological planes. Islam itself is not immune (culturally) from this, meaning in the way it is taught. The hegemonic presence of this is felt in the way cultural norms having little or nothing to do with the religion or its principles are imposed and taught from childhood as if they were part of the faith.

This top-down approach is a form of oppression, but most are not conscious of the process, accepting it without intellectual resistance as a given. For example, when Muslims are taught to read the Quran in a rote fashion but are not encouraged to intellectually engage with it or study its meanings, to accept its truths without an associative relationship with them, this is a form of intellectual and spiritual oppression. This attitude of passivity, which we begin to encounter at an early age, stifles vitality and energy and feeds into the cycle of hopelessness once it has been inculcated. Yet, it is precisely this energy or psychology of hope that we need in the face of any form of oppression to confront it. For Freire (2003), "conscientization is learning to perceive social, political, and economic contradictions, and to take action against the oppressive elements of reality" (p. 35). This, he asserts, is his pedagogy of hope.

The process of liberation begins by recognizing the system of oppression that surrounds us on micro and macro levels and of our own functioning within the parameters set by that system. One must educate oneself through reading and study of one's environment, of the social dynamics of the world one lives in on human and institutional levels, and of why society functions the way it does, and how it could be transformed for the better and the benefit of all. It is at this point that conscientization as a process can begin, to expose and comprehend the social construction of reality, and to critically examine the means and outcomes of that construction to eventually engage with it. Conscientization is a process that Muslims can easily use to understand their own unique crisis in the context of their historical and entrenched demise, as well as their continuing decline. The foundations of this crisis lie in factors that need to be studied and exposed in order to uncover their origins, including hidden motivational aspects and ideologies, and to learn how these were maintained and continue to be perpetuated. The question then arises: How can this conscientization process be initiated within Muslim societies? I propose that the answer to that lies in Freire's pedagogy of hope.

PEDAGOGY OF HOPE FOR THE EMPOWERMENT OF MUSLIM SOCIETIES

Hope is powerful and transformative, as Freire would assert, and an antidote to stagnation, not to be taken lightly or assumed to be a naive response to a complex society-wide predicament. In other words, hope has the potential to empower and transform. The main purpose of the discussion is to examine Freire's pedagogy of hope as it relates to the empowerment of Muslims, and this is based on Freire's success in the application of his theory, as evidenced in a literary education project he established among his community and which step subsequently went on to empower it. There are many types of hope, but this study centers around two: *critical hope* and *transformative hope*, both important elements of Freire's pedagogy with regard to initiating the process and its targeted outcomes of hope (Webb, 2013).

CRITICAL HOPE AND TRANSFORMATIVE HOPE

Critical hope is a feeling that instills in one the longing for a better future. It is this expectation of "what is not but could be" that drives critical hope. Freire's pedagogy of hope begins as mentioned with the process of *conscientization*; that is, questioning and being critical of the status quo, and moving away from the realm of accepting things as they are. This critical mindset begins the process of unraveling the many layers that define our reality and giving it form in order to expose what has hitherto been veiled. This in turn leads to a process of transformative thought, which allows one to imagine and explore the possibilities of what could be, paths that have not yet been treaded or considered. To think on a transformative level mentally and actively, we have at our disposal a powerful mechanism, and that is the education system. The captive audience of minds in the classroom setting, society-wide in schools and institutions of learning, can be invigorated with a psychology of hope and a liberating education, which Freire terms as problem-posing education (in contrast to his concept of banking education, which involves students simply absorbing and filing information). According to Freire (2003), "in problem-posing education, people develop their power to examine critically *the way they exist* in the world *with which* and *in which* [emphasis in original] they find themselves, seeing the world as a reality in process or transformation rather than a static one" (p. 83).

According to Webb (2013), a distinctive feature of transformative hope absent from other types of hope is its emphasis on collective effort. A group of people sharing the same vision come together and pool efforts to effect the change they seek in the hope of realizing a better future. Because transformative hope involves acting on premises, assuming people have the agency to make things happen, to transform and re-create the world and conditions around them, it is viewed with suspicion, a reckless enterprise even, and is criticized as a pedagogy of risk. To dare to venture into the unknown and challenge what has never been challenged is viewed by cynics as a foolish undertaking replete with risks, including the risk of one's self and efforts appearing ridiculous to others (Freire, 2003).

Muslim youths are in desperate need of a pedagogy of hope that is critical and transformative and that pulls them out of the mindset of despair and fatalism into which they have been plunged for so long, from both within and outside the classroom setting, to one that empowers them as agents of change, able to frame a new understanding of reality and to influence conditions around them to an extent that they effect positive transformation. This dynamism should naturally be a product of faith for youth. Yet, why Islam is currently not the catalyst for this revival of hope is not the fault of the faith, for a tool is only as good as the person wielding it; rather, it is because its potential has been stifled and is lying dormant under the heavy yoke of a factory-model-style of rote learning and nonintellectual engagement with the Quran and theological matters.

The pedagogy of hope and transformation is no stranger to Islam but is an integral part of the Islamic message that energizes and gives life, if that message is taught as it was by the early generations of Muslims, reviving the tradition of thinking, reflecting, and studying the Quran and focusing on Islamic principles and values. It is through this conduit that the no hope/no point, almost nihilist mindset and attitude of Muslim youth can be energized into one of transformative hope and active agency in society. It is for this reason that I attempt to convey to students the value of agency, to not limiting themselves in thought, reasoning, and action but to make the right choices and become active meaning-makers while remaining steadfast to the guiding principles and values of Islam, and by exploring Kazmi's process of self and social critique. By becoming active meaning-makers with continual reading and comprehension of the Quran, students will live their lives far more richly; that is, as expressions of the Quranic text and thus the realization of inner potential. The act of continuous reading and understanding the Quran is the basis for the process of self and social critique, which is explored later.

SOCIAL AND SELF-CRITIQUE

To conceptualize the idea of social and self-critique and explore their dynamics, I propose to use Kazmi's (2000) notion of understanding the signs of Allah (both in the Quranic text and in the physical reality of the world around us). According to Kazmi (2000), the act of reading and understanding the signs, or verses (*ayat*), of the Quran is not something that happens once, that is a one-off experience. Rather, the Quran is engaged with on many levels, depending on the differing circumstances or experiences of the reader, and its import and significance, therefore, are in a sense fluid. Thus, the same verse may be understood differently in different circumstances or by different individuals. The act of reading is an act of decoding, since a Muslim needs to comprehend the meaning of the verses [signs] they read in the Quran and make sense of these based on their own experiences in the outer world. The act of decoding is thus a critical one because it requires one to seek meaning that lies beyond the literal. It is also a creative act because one needs to interpret; that is, create new meaning concerning one's experience.

Decoding is also a form of self-critique because one is continuously having to measure the import and significance of Quranic verses (signs) against the changing vagaries of one's life and experiences, for life is lived on many complex levels. For example, we read in Surat 101 Al-'Asr, "By (the Token of) Time (through the Ages). Verily, man is in loss except those who have faith, do good, and urge each other to the truth, and urge each other to perseverance." The verses explain how humanity is in grave loss except for those who fulfill their lives in this world with good deeds and submission to God. The symbolic notion of time is attached to this, and it is significant because God takes an oath by time in the opening verse, communicating a very important message. While the great spiritual moral code should be the governing force of our lives, which is the meaning we clearly understand, the same verses have also been used to explain the meaning of *loss* and *profit* as they relate to Islamic economic principles. In other words, Islam does not view profit and material gain alone as the objectives of a functioning society and economic system; rather, it considers that social welfare and justice are powerfully emphasized with a strong faith in and obedience to God (Abbasi et al., 1989). The first understanding of the verses indicates an individual worship of God, while the second refers to an individual obligation for justice and the welfare of society.

HERMENEUTICS, FUSION OF HORIZONS, AND DECODIFICATION

Kazmi (2000) draws from Gadamer's (2004) notion of hermeneutics to explain how the act of understanding the meaning of a sign can also be considered a hermeneutical activity. It is a hermeneutical experience or understanding because "the meaning of a sign is understood in the context of the whole of which it is a part, and the meaning of the whole is understood with reference to the meaning of a particular sign" (p. 28). Hermeneutical understanding can be illustrated with a reference to music, whereby we can capture the whole piece as well as a single note of the music as the particular. When one listens to a piece of music, one does not understand each single note separately and then all notes together as a whole composition. Rather, one understands the musical piece as a complete unitary experience composed of single notes. In this sense, Gadamer's hermeneutic experience applies to the human attitude to reflect and understand this art of interpretation, which, for the Muslim, considers the whole horizon of their life experiences as they read the Quran, and which attempts to distill an understanding of the verses (signs) based on a fusion of that horizon with textual meaning. In other words, and in a nutshell, the reading of the Quran is a dynamic and subjective experience. Each person's life is unique to that person; ergo, each person will approach the text from that vantage point. Horizon, according to Gadamer (2004), is not a "rigid boundary but something that moves with one and invites one to advance further" (p. 185). It is also "the range of vision that includes everything that can be seen from a particular vantage point" (Gadamer, 2004, p. 301). Bernstein (1983) asserts that Gadamer's concept of horizon is an essential extension of Nietzsche's and Husserl's concept of situation, for being situated means one's vantage point, or perspective being limited by one's situatedness. One can never escape one's situatedness, but through the fusion of horizons, one can expand and enrich one's horizon. "It is through the fusion of horizons that one risks and tests one's prejudices" (Bernstein, 1983, p. 144). Thus, Muslims are constantly engaged in self-critique as they shift their interpretations and meanings (decoding process) concerning the shifting vagaries and experiences of their life; that is, as their horizon changes.

Gadamer's understanding implies that there is no one reading and understanding or interpretation of God's signs because what the signs themselves communicate will differ depending on a Muslim's changing horizons and the different questions that they learn to ask. Hermeneutic understanding considering this will evolve and develop in relation to personal context or situation. In the act of understanding the sign hermeneutically, the issue of interpretation will change depending on one's personal changing circumstances, whether physically, psychologically, or socially. The nature of the hermeneutical clarification process is a cycle of continuous exploration of new meanings and the deconstruction of the old, accepted ones. This connotes the decodification process or deconstruction and construction of meaning, inherently a critical and creative act (Kazmi, 2000, pp. 28–29). In this sense, "understanding is conceived as part of the process of the meaning coming into being, and meaning is always coming into being through the happening of understanding" (Bernstein, 1983, p. 139). This notion of the philosophy of understanding as a cyclical process of continuously renewed clarification and interpretation working in harmony with changes in one's being and existence obliges Muslims to continuously engage with the Quran, to read and understand it in relation to their life and the world around them, to help Muslims become *active meaning-makers*. This process resembles Freire's conscientization, a process that strives to raise the critical consciousness of a person.

PREJUDICES AND SOCIAL CRITIQUE

Gadamer's (2004) concept of horizon also implies that any two Muslims may have a different understanding of the same Quranic verse depending on their particular situatedness. Situatedness in this context may refer to one's religious worldview, but it can also refer to one's race, ethnicity, culture, and tradition. Hence, an Arab and an Asian Muslim, or a Malaysian and an Indonesian Muslim (Muslims of similar ethnicity but different culture and language), or Muslims of different socioeconomic status may differ in their reading and understanding of Quranic verses (signs) and the wider world because of their different situatedness; that is, in the context of their differing experiences; social, ethnic, and cultural practices, and traditions. These differences may in turn lead to possible conflicts between Muslims on both individual and society levels, fracturing the *ummah* unless resolved. For example, the issue of Muslims, particularly those residing in non-Muslim countries and multifaith and multiethnic areas, celebrating the festivals of non-Muslims has become one of debate. Scholars in Muslim majority countries may object to the practice, stating it compromises the faith; however, those residing in multifaith and multiracial communities may view the matter differently. Those following a more orthodox, classical position may choose the conservative option, feeling it to be in line with Islamic principles, while others may choose the opposite. The issue then becomes one of differing opinions and debates.

This example demonstrates how Muslims can be entrenched in their doctrinal positions (to use Gadamer's (2004) term, *prejudices*) depending on and born out of their situatedness or tradition. Gadamer's (2004) idea of disabling and enabling prejudices can be used to understand the origins of a conflict due to differences of views and opinions. Disabling prejudices are those that hinder a healthy exchange of ideas and perspectives of two different people because of their situatedness, while enabling prejudices are those that are acknowledged yet assist the two people in seeing their different viewpoints and the reasons for their differing perspectives. Enabling prejudices allows a fusion of horizons to take place between different individuals. The act of self-critique is transformed to social critique when Muslims work together to take charge and initiate changes based on their act of reading and understanding the signs.

In this aspect, Kazmi's (2000) social critique resonates with the pedagogy of transformative hope, as it is characterized by the collective effort of a group of members who share a similar goal and strive toward change for a better future.

It is important to point out that the act of reading and understanding the meaning of God's signs is not to imply their veracity is in doubt but to emphasize their function to draw Muslims closer to their Creator. Any contemplation of this nature can only deepen awareness of God. As the very first verse revealed to the Prophet Muhammad (SAW) (*Surat al-'Alaq*, 96:1): "Proclaim! (or read!) In the name of thy Lord and Cherisher, who created." The verse calls on Muslims to read in His name, hence reading the signs of the Quran in the world can only benefit the relationship between a Muslim and their Creator. This continuous act of reading requires Muslims to consistently place God in the center of their lives. Following this line of reasoning, we can infer that the Quran demands that Muslims become active meaning-makers of the world. Hence, Muslims should not be blind followers of any authority in understanding the Quran and their worldly experiences. This understanding fits well with Freire's notion of conscientization, giving individuals the right to claim their own understanding and develop critiques of themselves. The conceptualization of a pedagogy of hope has been presented, but there is a need to share the pedagogy in action to show how theory can be translated into practice.

PEDAGOGY OF TRANSFORMATIVE HOPE IN ACTION: A CASE STUDY OF UNIVERSITY STUDENTS IN MALAYSIA

I would like to state my position and role. I was the principal researcher for a study exploring the possibility of introducing and practicing Freire's transformative pedagogy of hope in a postgraduate class. The course instructor, Amy (pseudonym), my supervisee, was meanwhile researching how critical pedagogy can empower university students to become more critical and active meaning-makers. Since our research areas were similar in some respects, we decided to work together. Amy had attended my classes and, having been exposed to critical pedagogy there, decided to start applying what she had learned. I tried my best to separate my role as the principal researcher from Amy's as a supervisor by identifying and dividing my classes clearly, for her thesis and my research. We involved only one of my master classes in our study, and Amy was the course instructor for seven of the semester's fourteen weeks, of which the fifth class was used for this case study as an illustration of the pedagogy of hope. Students were informed of the study, and all were willing to participate. Student identity was kept private and confidential as part of ensuring the ethical guidelines of research. Pseudonyms were given and participants' details provided, but not to the extent that their identity could be known.

Methods and Participants of the Study

The study employed the case-study design of a graduate-level course, consisting of five Muslim students (who all happened to be female) of diverse nationalities, identified as the case for the study. The study presented a classroom dialogue to show the development and sharing and changes of perspectives the students experienced throughout the course. Freire's (2013) idea of dialogue was to be practiced in class as the basis for the pedagogy of hope. Freire's idea of dialogue is a horizontal relationship between persons who are engaged in a joint search for something (pp. 42–43). To Freire (2013), the "essence of dialogue is to seek the constitutive elements of *the word*, consisting of two dimensions, reflection and action" (p. 87). In this sense, "dialogue is an encounter between men, mediated by the world, in order to name the world" (p. 88).

The study also examined the role of the course instructor (Amy) as the critical pedagogue while she attempted to engage the students in the process of conscientization with the hope of broadening their horizons. Throughout the semester, I observed the classes, providing consultations following each one. The consultation included an analysis of the dialogue and role of the instructor in the class. The case study used the observation method, while field notes captured the teaching and learning process in the classroom. The consultation was also transcribed to triangulate the observational data. In terms of methodology, discourse analysis was employed for the various elements of dialogue, with the unit of analysis based on the processes depicted from the pedagogy, thereby enabling prejudices to fuse the horizons, self-critique, countering hegemony, and social critique, and the fusion of horizons, and finally culminating in social transformation.

The five female participants of the study were Mariah, May, Khadija, Fatimah, and Aisyah. Mariah was a Thai student specializing in Islamic studies. She continued her master's degree immediately after completing her undergraduate degree. May, a revert from Malaysia was studying counseling part-time while teaching in a private school. Khadija, a Saudi student, was a history teacher before doing her master's in Educational Psychology. Fatimah, a sponsored student from India, specialized in Teaching English as a Second Language (TESL). Finally, Aisyah, a Malay Malaysian studying educational management part-time, was working as a principal in a private school[1].

The classroom discourse was drawn from the fifth class in the semester. The class was conducted every Wednesday evening for three hours. Amy and the students sat in a circle; the seating arrangement was designed to facilitate dialogue. Amy started the class by introducing the topic of the day's lesson; in this example, Women in Contemporary Society, with the issue for discussion being the rights of women. For this subject, she presented slides showing different images of women playing various roles, such as an employee, a manager, a mother, a teacher, and a daughter caring for her elderly parents. The class discussion began with Amy's question on the roles of women in today's world.

The results of the study are presented based on the analysis of the discourse, since the unit of analysis was the processes explained in the conceptualization of the pedagogy of hope; in other words, how the pedagogy of hope enabled prejudices leading to the fusion of horizons, engaged students in social critique, countered hegemony, and displayed a transformative hope for social transformation. Social transformation becomes the coveted end, as it signifies the culmination of "reflection" and "action" (Freire, 2003, 2013) and reflects how a Muslim realizes emancipation as an active meaning-maker (Kazmi, 2000).

Enabling Prejudices and Fusion of Horizons

In responding to the topic of women in contemporary society, the five students agreed that women do play an important role in the development and well-being of a society, but they differed in the finer details of their views. Students agreed that women are free to chart their own lives, to choose their careers, and even to choose their spouses. However, despite certain liberties given to women in contemporary times, some Muslim societies still expect women to play a traditional role, which poses a challenge as they try to balance the two aspects. Mariah felt that "the problem is not so much in what women want but how society treats them, which differs from one society to another."[2] There are expectations put on women that demand, on one hand, adherence to traditional roles while on the other meeting contemporary needs, with women expected to juggle both, such as contributing to family finances while also being responsible for domestic duties and the children's upbringing. The consequent pressure and stress can lead to conflict within the family as well as the failure of marriages. Through discourse, students came to realize that society's expectations of women's roles were not grounded in Islamic teachings but rather on tradition and culture. This is reflected in how flexible or rigid their society was regarding the idea of working women.

Being of different backgrounds, that is, ethnicity and culture, students were expected to encounter different perspectives on the same issue, which could lead to conflict. According to Gill (2016), "a rich diversity can become a potential source of conflict due to the increase in otherness though it can also offer the opportunity to engage with the other" (p. 484). Moreover, the students' different backgrounds or, using Gadamer's term, *horizons*, would entail that they possess prejudices, which, if disabling, could again lead to conflict. However, we found that since the participants were mature students, they did not have problems managing these differences of opinion on their own. They were more open and willing to listen to others' views and perspectives, which created a harmonious dialogue. In this sense, their prejudices enabled them to fuse their horizons.

Social Critique and Counterhegemony

Using the conflict of the many roles women are expected to play and balancing their responsibilities as constructed in the modern context with those of the traditional ideal in terms of the Quranic context, Amy asked the class how to resolve the issue. Fatimah felt the conflict was a challenge that Muslims must face "living in a capitalist economic system that is not aligned with Islamic values." She opined that in order "for Muslims to survive this challenge they have to hold fast to Islam." For instance, Islam has provided guidelines for Muslims in all aspects of life, such as the Prophet's (SAW) advice on the criteria for choosing a spouse. If a Muslim woman chooses her husband for his *iman* (faith) and *taqwa* (piety), then he would understand and play his role well in the family as explained in the Quran. If women must leave their home to work and help support the family, then husbands need to understand that they have to assist their wives with the primary role of raising the children. Fatimah stressed this point by highlighting that the Quran never instructed wives to cook for the family. Many Muslims knew from *sīrah* that the Prophet (SAW) was the one who did the chores at home, such as washing his own clothes. Aisyah related her own experience of having a difficult time making her mother-in-law understand her situation as a working woman, particularly when her husband was willing to help with the house chores. The traditional view in her society is that a husband who does the domestic chores and cooks for the family is being controlled by the wife. She stated that it took her twenty years to make her mother-in-law understand the demands of her position as the leader in the school and the extent of her contribution to the economics of her family. Khadija shared that her society is also patriarchal and has hindered her government's newly launched vision that promises more opportunities for women to be involved and participate in the development of the nation.

Based on students' discourse, even though Islam accords women a high position, culture plays a much stronger role in influencing how society views women. This makes it more difficult to change society's views and practices because people's minds are so entrenched in tradition and culture. Changing societal views is a long-term, gradual process, but it can be achieved when continuous attempts are made to introduce new ideas as a form of social transformation.

These views shared among the students offered examples of enabling prejudices, whereby different persons (of different situatedness) were able to relate to each other's experiences. Enabling prejudices not only paves the way for a fusion of horizons but also prepares people to engage in social critique. The scaffolding of ideas as constructed by students later assisted them to discover how realities are created by societies, illustrating how the pedagogy of hope can be transformative.

When the critical consciousness of the students had been raised, they needed to move toward the transformative role of the pedagogy. The instructor asked the students how, in their view, society could be changed, how people could be reminded of the original teachings in Islam and be more conscious of their practices. The students agreed that change must start with individuals and the family as the basic unit of society. They felt that mothers were an important component of change given their fundamental role in educating children. They also agreed that all parties need to play their own key roles and uphold their responsibilities well to critique societal views and practices where warranted, such as the government and *ulama'* (Muslim scholars).

Analysis of the discourse revealed that students shared similar experiences of hegemony; that is, juxtaposing and coping with the traditional and nontraditional roles they were required to play in the modern world. The discourse also revealed that students were moving toward social critique by sharing the counterhegemonic practices that they experienced. In doing so, they were able to unveil the hidden ideologies underlying social practices and norms, as constructed by society.

TRANSFORMATIVE HOPE FOR SOCIAL TRANSFORMATION

To demonstrate how the transformative pedagogy of hope moved the students to engage in social transformation, the subsequent discussion on the *khilaf* (disagreement) of *ulama'* (Muslim theological scholars) is presented as a good case in point. Initially, the discussion began with students expressing dissatisfaction with some *ulama'* interpretations and how this affected Muslim women, but on discovering that there existed different *ulama'* interpretations, students then realized that there was in fact wisdom behind these *khilaf*. More importantly, for students to choose which scholarly interpretation suited them best, they needed to be knowledgeable and aware of *ulama'* reasoning and be able to identify the most suitable one according to their context.

Khadija emphasized that it is important for Muslims to have knowledge so that they know and understand the disagreement or different views of the *ulama'* in whatever practices they perform, instead of following them blindly. She gave the example of covering *awrah* (parts of the body that need to be covered, according to Islam), especially for females since they have different *awrah* than males. The traditional dress for women in Khadija's country is a black *abaya* (long dress) because colors are to be avoided in her culture for fear of *tabarruj* (dress with the purpose to attract attention). However, Khadija realized that, unlike her culture, Asian Muslims like Aisyah prefer to wear colorful hijabs and dresses to the extent that Khadija has now learned to wear a little bit of color to fit in. Aisyah explained that it is appropriate in Malaysian culture to wear vibrant colors like their batik, which signifies the joy in their culture. In this regard, Aisyah felt that it was acceptable to wear colorful dresses and hijabs because this was part of her culture and not for *tabarruj*.

The analysis of the discourse exemplifies the transformative hope that the students engaged in. They gave a new, positive meaning to the term *khilaf* (disagreement) and dissected how the term *tabarruj* can appear to have a different interpretation in different contexts or societies, pointing to another reality constructed by society. It is also interesting to note that rather than skirting around the issue of *khilaf*, which is one of the causes for disunity and disintegration in the *ummah* today, the students chose to discuss it as a basis to understand the "other." According to Waghid and Davids (2014), by allowing different views to be discussed, "the individuals' capacity to exercise reason and choice will bode well for the flourishing of a socially just society" (p. 349). This is another indication of how transformative the discourse had been for the students as they dealt collectively with all issues, questions, and conflicts.

THE ROLE OF THE CRITICAL PEDAGOGUE

Now that we have theorized the pedagogy of hope and shown how it can assist in empowering Muslims and releasing them from the shackles of fossilized and entrenched thinking, it is equally important to identify the role the critical pedagogue needs to play, which will indirectly delineate the characteristics the critical pedagogue needs to possess.

The critical pedagogue did not speak much compared to the students, but she played a vital role in ensuring that the engagement of the pedagogy of transformative hope was successful. First, the critical pedagogue needed to identify an issue that is worth discussing and that has the potential to engage students in a meaningful dialogue. The issue must be relevant to the topic of the lesson, relatable to the students' experiences, and controversial so that it may invite students to expose their prejudices. For this, the critical pedagogue must have comprehensive knowledge of the issues under discussion in the discourse. As the classroom discourse demonstrated, discussion naturally evolves between participants and therefore is not to be determined by the critical pedagogue, who therefore needs to prepare well to be abreast of it.

Apart from identifying a worthwhile issue and having knowledge of it, the critical pedagogue needed to raise questions that challenged participants to think beyond their mundane practices. Since all students' views are considered valuable, the role of the critical pedagogue was to ensure that all took part fully and to motivate them to do so, in expressing their views, sharing their experiences, and clarifying their arguments. The latter is essential if the discourse is to proceed without conflict and irreconcilable clashes of opinion. This is also why the critical pedagogue needed to be able to read the nonverbal discourse of students—their facial expression or tone of voice—as a sign of emotional states such as anger, discomfort, or embarrassment. The ability to read students' emotions proved helpful to the critical pedagogue's decision to either pursue the same issue or move to another one.

Finally, the critical pedagogue needed to let the discourse end and present every student the opportunity to recall what they had achieved in and through the discourse analysis. During the discourse, the critical pedagogue asked the students to summarize what they learned in class that day, and they did so. This is another important feature of transformative hope because the dialogue should not be a mere participation or discussion activity only in a classroom setting. The closure helped the critical pedagogue to assess how much her students had learned.

Another aspect to consider for the pedagogy's success is class size. In this case, the small class size was an important factor because each student had an opportunity to explore, express, and share their views. Another advantage of the class was the varied backgrounds of the students, but the all-female class was an unavoidable limitation. On the other hand, the all-female class allowed the students to be freer in expressing their views.

CONCLUSION

The discourse centered on the roles of women as the chosen topic for the day's lesson. From the discourse, students realized that the roles of women are often defined and dictated by a society's culture and tradition rather than Islamic principles or values. The discourse analysis revealed to students that many of their social practices were governed by their traditions and culture. These traditions have been a part of their culture for so long that Muslims assume that they are a given and cannot be changed. But in the finer analysis, as the discourse showed, the first step is to acknowledge and realize, as the students did, that many practices and even meanings that they have understood and lived with are historical and societal constructions. This point was made based on students' own experiences of coping with the challenges of functioning in multiple roles as females, primarily working mothers.

There were also instances when students encountered conflict during dialogue and disagreements due to differing opinions and views. But with the instructor facilitating and keeping open channels of communication, the students were able to direct the conversation to listening to the other's explanation while clarifying their own perspective. This way there was no feeling of anxiety but rather respect for the other's position. Students ultimately were able to bridge the gulf of difference by getting to the root of the issue, which was that cultural context had shaped thinking and behavior. For example, both Khadija and Aisyah managed to give value to each other's understanding of *tabarruj* in relation to the issue of modesty in dress through a negotiated process of listening, clarification, and understanding. By framing discussions not along avenues of who was right or wrong but rather through explanation of why a certain mode of behavior or pattern of thought was being adopted, both Khadija and Aisyah reached a respectful understanding. This displays the transforming of students' prejudices to become *enabling* prejudices, through recognizing the different situatedness of the other, leading to a fusion of horizons via the new meaning they developed about the concept of *tabarruj*. Thus, the pedagogy-in-action case study demonstrates that transformative pedagogy is effective, valuable, and a key strategy to bring unity to Muslims both on a micro and a macro scale; that is, from individual groupings and communities to societies, using appreciation of viewpoints to arrive at a concise, correct understanding of things to help to unite Muslims and make them agents of positive change.

Regarding self-critique to social critique, the discourse focused on identifying ways to take things from the micro to the macro level for the improvement of society, removing unexamined cultural practices, and reviving a correct understanding and application of Islamic teachings and values. This alone is evidence of the potential of this strategy to identify the common problematic signifier of any issue/dispute, as well as, in this instance, the foundational elements of the crisis of the Muslim mind; to reach an understanding based on an appreciation of the other's perspective; and to explore solutions. By getting Muslims to engage in decoding, deconstructing, and reconstructing meanings, we make them active meaning-makers. Furthermore, by encouraging Muslims to be critical and creative, the pedagogy offers them an opportunity to avoid wasting energies in dispute and rather directs them to exercise their reasoning skills to address challenges, initiate change, and ultimately transform society. The findings of the case study indicate that the pedagogy of hope grounded in an Islamic worldview can bond individual Muslims of different ethnicities and cultures; hence, it may also have the potential to bond Muslim societies if they engage in it at the macro level.

REFERENCES

Abbasi, S. M., Hollman, K. W., & Murrey, J. H. (1989). Islamic economics: Foundations and practices. *International Journal of Social Economics, 16*(5), 5–17. https://doi.org/10.1108/03068298910367215

Bahi, R. A. (2016). Islam as a post-hegemonic discourse. In H. Tiliouine & R. J. Estes (Eds.), *The state of social progress of Islamic societies* (pp. 443–462). International Handbooks of Quality-of-Life. Springer. https://doi.org//10.1007/978-3-319-24774-8_20

Bamyeh, M. (2009). Hermeneutics against instrumental reason: National and post-national Islam in the 20th century. In R. Desai (Ed.), *Developmental and cultural nationalisms* (pp. 156–175). Routledge; Oxon.

Bernstein, R. J. (1983). *Beyond objectivism and subjectivism: Science, hermeneutics and praxis.* University of Pennsylvania Press.

Boriçi, G. (2017). Globalization challenges in a globalized world. *ILIRIA International Review, 6*(2), 141–159. https://doi.org/10.21113/iir.v6i2.260

Freire, P. (2003). *Pedagogy of the oppressed.* Continuum International.

Freire, P. (2013). *Education for critical consciousness.* Bloomsbury Academic.

Gadamer, H. G. (2004). *Truth and method* (G. Barden & J. Cumming, Eds. & Trans., 2d rev. ed.). Seabury.

Gill, S. (2016). Universities as spaces for engaging the other: A pedagogy of encounter for intercultural and interreligious education. *International Review of Education, 62*, 483–500. https://doi.org/10.1007/s11159-016-9572-7

Gramsci, A. (1999). *Selections from the prison notebooks of Antonio Gramsci* (Q. Hoare & G. N. Smith, Eds. & Trans.). ElecBook.

Hashim, R. (2008). *Educational dualism in Malaysia: Implications for theory and practice.* Other.

Kazmi, Y. (2000). The role of critical thinking in Islam. *Hamdard Islamicus, 23*(1), 27–36.

Kazmi, Y. (2011). Islamic education: Traditional education or education of tradition? In *Selected readings in Islamic critical pedagogy* (Vol. 1, pp. 23–64). IIUM Press.

Sahin, A. (2018). Critical issues in Islamic education studies: Rethinking Islamic and Western liberal secular values of education. *Religions, 9*, 335. https://doi.org/10.3390/rel9110335

Stoddart, M. (2007). Ideology, hegemony, discourse: A critical review of theories of knowledge and power. *Social Thought & Research, 28*, 191–225. https://www.jstor.org/stable/23252126

Sule, B., Yahaya, M. A., & Ating, R. (2018). Globalisation and the Muslim Ummah: Issues, challenges, and the ways out. *IIUM Journal of Religion and Civilisational Studies, 1*(1), 7–29. https://journals.iium.edu.my/irkh/index.php/ijrcs/article/view/23

Waghid, Y., & Davids, N. (2014). On the (im)possibility of democratic citizenship education in the Arab and Muslim world. *Studies in Philosophy and Education, 33*, 343–351. https://doi.org/10.1007/s11217-013-9393-0

Webb, D. (2013). Pedagogies of hope. *Studies in Philosophy and Education, 32*, 397–414. https://doi.org/10.1007/s11217-012-9336-1

NOTES

1. All participants have been given pseudonyms for anonymity.
2. All quotes from the five women were based on the classroom discourse of the study.

PART III

INITIATIVES IN TEACHER DEVELOPMENT

FIVE

—ɯ—

TEACHER PROFESSIONAL
DEVELOPMENT IN PALESTINE

Hope Despite All

ILHAM NASSER, BASSAM ABU HAMAD,
AND SULIEMAN MLEAHAT

STUDIES IN THE FIELD OF positive psychology suggest a strong correlation between hope and work. According to one study, leaders who are hopeful have an impact on positive financial and job satisfaction results (Luthans & Youssef, 2004). Further studies have found that hope is a motivational state determined by the interaction between three factors: goals, agency, and pathways. Luthans and Youssef (2004) state: "People are driven to accomplish their goals by their sense of agency, which provides them with an internalized determination and willpower to invest the energy necessary to achieve their goals. Those with high hope are also motivated by their sense of having the capability to develop ways to get the things they want, which provides them with the ability to generate alternative pathways towards the accomplishment of their goals if the original ones have been blocked" (p. 16).

Regarding the professional development (PD) of teachers, hope is a potential catalyst to improve not only teachers' professional practice but also their lives and well-being. The idea of hope has long been understood in relation to the human condition, with previous literature on the subject indicating how hope is instrumental in human adaptation. Early research has suggested that hope is important for change, for willingness to change, and for well-being. Furthermore, training teachers to have optimism, which differs from hope in that it attributes positive events as internal and permanent, and negative events as external and temporary, may help them stay positive about their situation (Luthans & Youssef, 2004). This becomes especially important in conditions where the general political situation is dire. Leaders of education initiatives, especially international development agencies (such as those that are active in Palestine) can undoubtedly lead as optimists optimists in these situations. Some researchers contend that hopelessness is not inevitable or structural, meaning that interventions could be effective in changing hopelessness levels (Bolland et al., 2001, 2005). One possible way to effect this would be through interventions targeting social factors that play a role in developing hope in youth, rather than having to change conditions of economic disparity (Bolland et al., 2005). This also means that educators in leadership positions do not need to wait for political conditions to change but rather can invest in current education systems by believing in the ability to effect change and empowering educators to believe the same.

THE CONTEXT

In Palestine, according to the Ministry of Education and Higher Education (MOEHE), only 40% of young children have access to preschool education, and retention numbers may even be lower. International organizations have been carrying the burden of the early childhood development (ECD) sector, especially in the areas of in-service teacher training and mentoring and preschool upgrading and renovations. This is a contribution to the international effort to increase enrollment and retention of young children in preschools as well as to improve the quality of services for young children in marginalized communities. An abundance of one-time generic teacher-training workshops dominates the ECD sector in Palestine. Many programs offer little guidance on next steps or follow-up plans, and it is not clear how many of these trainings are evaluated and how many of them document the possible impact on teachers. Nevertheless, they may be used as examples of hope interventions in ways that bring joy to teachers' lives and the communities they serve.

Until very recently, there were no set professional competencies or curriculum objectives that were agreed on by stakeholders such as teachers, supervisors of the Ministry of Education (MOE), and families. Local and international nongovernmental organizations (NGOs) offered training for kindergarten teachers with no guidance or set standards for the sector. A national task force on ECD convened in 2016–2017, including NGOs[1] and the MOEHE, and put together professional standards and a kindergarten curriculum framework to guide teachers to develop child-centered pedagogy. Although this is a huge step for the improvement of the ECD sector, the implementation of this strategy poses a problem because some early childhood education (ECE) teachers and their supervisors, who are already in the education system, are not qualified to teach this age group. This is in part because many carry upper-elementary teaching diplomas and end up in preschool education due to the shortage of elementary teaching positions (Nasser & Shami, 2013). Because preschool education is not compulsory in Palestine, charitable organizations and local councils primarily run the sector (out of 1,600 preschools, only about 170 are run by the MOEHE in Palestine).[2]

This study, conducted during the 2016–2017 school year, aimed at sharing the knowledge gained from a comprehensive PD program designed by an NGO, where school rehabilitation and renovations along with PD training and mentoring are offered using the model presented in figure A.1. This model is unique because, unlike others in the region, it is a long-term program that invests in marginalized villages and remote communities that are far from major cities in Gaza and the West Bank (WB). In addition, it offers an adaptable model whereby foundational knowledge may be adjusted as needed by the facilitator and teachers and more advanced training may become more necessary.

BACKGROUND INFORMATION ON TEACHER DEVELOPMENT

Studies point to the importance of ongoing opportunities for PD of ECE teachers, especially the need for learning formats that go beyond the one-time workshops prevalent in many PD designs (Diamond & Powell, 2011; Simon et al., 2011). Recommendations from the field support the importance of considering the form, duration, and prior knowledge of participants in designing successful PDs, including integration of content knowledge and opportunities to enact newly learned information and to reflect on that enactment individually and in groups (Van Driel & Berry, 2012). In a meta-analysis of PD literature, Birman et al. (2000) suggested that more hands-on PDs, more time combined with more contact, and collective participation are essential components and show greater potential for achieving success and transformation in pedagogy.

A high level of support, whether teachers are veterans or novices, is documented as important in promoting teachers' professional knowledge. Anders et al. (2000) concluded that quality PD is characterized by the following features: intensive/extensive commitment; monitoring/coaching/clinical support; reflection; deliberation, dialog, and negotiation; voluntary participation/ choice; and collaboration. In addition, PDs that allow feedback and modeling had a greater impact on teachers' practices and ensured change continues after the intervention (Joyce & Showers, 2002). Diamond and Powell (2011) also concluded that effective PD focuses on the learner, takes place in a collaborative environment, includes opportunities to enact the content gained, and is supported by constructive feedback and we add a hopeful agenda for the future.

It is clear in the literature that long-term PD that is comprehensive and includes usable ideas enacted in real classrooms is showing promising results in increasing the quality of teaching (Nasser et al., 2015). The current study examines this approach in marginalized locations in the WB (Ramallah and Jericho areas) and in Gaza (Gaza and the North Gaza governorates). It answers the question of whether a comprehensive PD model makes a difference for teachers and young children in these conditions and environments.

The PD training model, developed by one of the NGO's professional teams and examined here, is offered for a period of six to nine months and a total of 120 hours of training (on weekends and for an intensive period in the summer in the WB and in various other formats in Gaza, such as intensive daily after-school training). In this model, teachers are provided with new knowledge on theories, inquiry-based learning, literacy and numeracy, and practical applications in the classrooms (see figure A.1). The training team also engaged teachers in two one-on-one mentoring sessions before preschool rehabilitation and then three such sessions after the renovation of the preschool facilities. The mentoring sessions were conducted in the classrooms, where a mentor modeled best practices, including classroom management and working in learning centers.

METHODOLOGY

A mixed-method approach combining quantitative and qualitative research tools was used to measure the impact of the PD program for that academic year:

1. Pre- and post-observations checklist using components of the Classroom Assessment Scoring System (CLASS) developed in the US to measure the quality of ECE classrooms (Pianta et al., 2014). We used the same scoring system but not all the domains, as some were not relevant to the context in Palestine. We focused on the domains of "interaction with children," "teaching strategies,"[3] and "classroom environments" (see table A.1 for a list of items on the survey). Fifty-one teachers were observed by two observers—one in Gaza and one in the WB—to gain independent and reliable knowledge about practices and the quality of teaching before and after the PD training and renovations of facilities.

2. Focus group discussions: Two discussions each were conducted in Gaza and the WB with groups of teachers at the end of the

program, designed to elicit feedback about the training content, style, and materials and their impact on their performance.

3. Self-administered questionnaire: Eliciting teachers' background information and teaching attitudes administered to all at the beginning and end of the training program.

Twenty teachers out of fifty regularly attending the thirty sessions (for a total of 120 hours) in the WB, and thirty-one out of fifty attending the trainings in Gaza were part of this study. Only some of the teachers in the observations and focus groups were included to allow for observations before the training start date (pre) and after (post). As many teachers lived in isolated villages in the WB and Gaza, travel to conduct observations was limited. In addition, we selected teachers who would remain for the next academic year and did not miss any training sessions. We chose preschools that went through renovations and kept the same teaching staff because we wanted to observe the teachers in the classrooms they had used before and after the training. Teachers who left the preschool were dropped from the study.

Two researchers conducted the observations at pre and post, and the same two conducted the focus groups. A pilot observation to try the items selected was conducted first and was followed by discussions to agree on items to include in the survey in both Gaza and the WB. Interrater reliability was conducted on pilot observations and proved to be very high, as both raters had similar scores on more than 95% of items scored. The preintervention observations were completed nine months before the post observations and the focus groups were conducted.

Quantitative analysis to compare pre and post scores was administered on the three measures mentioned above. Analysis of the CLASS scores was conducted in the following three domains: (1) interaction with children, (2) teaching strategies, and (3) learning environments. Qualitative analysis was used to examine and generate themes based on teachers' responses in focus groups using the open coding thematic analysis technique. The quantitative data were analyzed and the transformation of data was done to get descriptive scores. A paired t-test was used to compare pre and post scores, while an independent t-test was used to compare scores by teachers in Gaza and the WB.

RESULTS

Responses on the CLASS were highly reliable, with a Cronbach Alpha equal to 0.954 (perfect reliability equals 1; 0.7 is considered a good reliability). Findings show that improvements were made because of the training, but further investments and training are needed, especially since preschools in the WB elicited higher scores than their counterparts in Gaza (see figure 5.1).

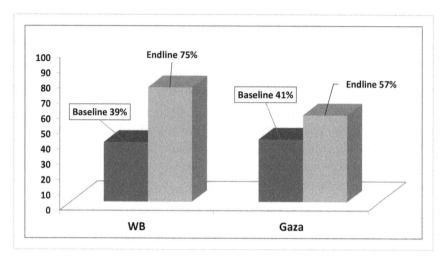

Figure 5.1. Teachers' Overall Scores on CLASS Items (Pre and Post)

The differences in the overall score on the checklist between the pre and post readings in both Gaza and the WB were statistically significant ($p < 0.001$). The same applies to the three subdomains constituting the CLASS tool, which all showed statistically significant differences between the baseline and the endline readings. This result is possibly due to the fact that, at the preintervention assessment, the status of preschools in Gaza was somewhat better than the WB, and therefore the change in the WB data is more tangible. This result may also be explained by the prevailing complicated conditions in Gaza that are characterized by siege, economic collapse, and psychosocial stress due to the political conditions that drive high unemployment rates and isolation from the rest of Palestine since the siege in 2007.

PRE AND POST ON CLASS

Domain One: Interactions with Children

Table 5.1 suggests that the differences in the first domain, interactions with children, were found to be large and significant at pre and post in Gaza and the WB. The percentage of improvement achieved on the item "teacher shows respect toward children" was high, as it was practiced "most of the time" at only 3.2% of Gaza preschools at the time of baseline assessment, and it has increased significantly to 61.5% at the endline assessment. Similarly, in the

WB, this item increased from 15% at pre to 68.8% at the post assessment. The reported proportions of the teachers' awareness of their surroundings have improved, as it was regarded as not evident / little evidence (combined) at around 54% in Gaza preschools at the baseline assessment and 26% of schools after joining the PD program. In the WB preschools, responses in the not evident / little evidence (combined) of surroundings category dropped from 45% of preschools to zero.

The level at which children seemed comfortable with teachers has significantly improved, as it was regarded as not evident / little evidence (combined) at around 40% of Gaza preschools at the baseline assessment and dropped to around 7% after joining the PD program. The same applies to the WB, with a decrease from 15% to zero. Also, the proportion of teachers who "encourage the child to take initiatives" has significantly improved, as it was regarded as not evident / little evidence (combined) at around 61% of Gaza preschools at the baseline assessment and decreased to around 25% after benefiting from the PD. In the WB, it decreased from 68% to 19%. The overall score for the first domain at the baseline was nearly 50% at preschools in the two sites. However, after the implementation of the training program, the mean scores have increased, especially in the WB. The margin of improvement in Gaza in this domain was 28%, and it reached 50.4% in the WB.

Table 5.1. Domain 1: Interactions with Children
Percentage distribution of preschool teachers' performance on CLASS in Gaza (Baseline $N = 31$, Endline $N = 26$) and WB (Baseline $N = 20$, Endline $N = 16$)

Variables	Gaza				WB			
	Baseline		Endline		Baseline		Endline	
	No	%	No	%	No	%	No	%
Teacher shows respect toward children								
Not evident	1	3.2	0	0.00	0	0.00	0	0.00
Little evidence	11	35.5	5	19.2	6	30.0	0	0.00
Sometimes	18	58.1	5	19.2	11	55.0	1	6.3
Most of the time	1	3.2	16	61.5	3	15.0	11	68.8
Consistently (all the time)	0	0.00	0	0.00	0	0.00	4	25.0

Table 5.1. (*continued*)

Variables	Gaza				WB			
	Baseline		Endline		Baseline		Endline	
	No	%	No	%	No	%	No	%
Teacher is aware of her surroundings								
Not evident	2	6.5	1	3.8	3	15.0	0	0.00
Little evidence	15	48.4	6	23.1	6	30.0	0	0.00
Sometimes	13	41.9	7	26.9	9	45.0	5	31.3
Most of the time	1	3.2	8	30.8	2	10.0	6	37.5
Consistently (all the time)	0	0.00	4	15.4	0	0.00	5	31.3
Children seem comfortable with teacher/s								
Not evident	1	3.4	1	3.8	1	5.0	0	0.00
Little evidence	11	37.9	1	3.8	2	10.0	0	0.00
Sometimes	11	37.9	11	42.3	9	45.0	1	6.3
Most of the time	6	20.7	12	46.2	8	40.0	8	50.0
Consistently (all the time)	0	0.00	1	3.8	0	0.00	7	43.8
Teacher encourages child to take initiatives								
Not evident	6	19.4	4	17.4	5	26.3	0	0.00
Little evidence	13	41.9	2	8.7	8	42.1	3	18.8
Sometimes	12	38.7	5	21.7	4	21.1	3	18.8
Most of the time	0	0.00	11	47.8	2	10.5	9	56.3
Consistently (all the time)	0	0.00	1	4.3	0	0.00	1	6.3
Overall mean scores for the interaction domain	Baseline = 50.3%; Endline = 64.4%				Baseline = 53.3%, Endline = 80.2%			

Note. Improvement in the interaction domains for both Gaza and the WB was statistically significant at *p* value <0.001.

Domain Two: Teaching Strategies

Table 5.2 depicts the results of the preschool teachers' observations before and after the training program. Improvement levels in this domain in Gaza preschools were less obvious in comparison to the WB. For instance, the percentage of children who are free to move between activities was judged with a status of not evident / little evidence (combined) at 27% of Gaza preschools at the endline (baseline figure is 70%), as not evident at 20% only in the WB (WB baseline figure is 95%). In the same line, the proportion of children who were free to move between activity centers most of the time / consistently (combined) was at 54% of Gaza preschools after implementation; in the WB, teachers elicited similar scores in this regard (53%). However, it was reported as not evident / little evidence (combined) at 27% in Gaza and 20% in the WB. Additionally, the proportion of teachers who "redirect students' behaviors when needed" was observed as not evident / little evidence (combined) at 19% of Gaza preschools at the endline assessment (baseline figure is 70%), while it was zero at the WB preschools at the endline assessment (baseline figure is 56%). The proportion of teachers who have established routines at preschools most of the time / consistently (combined) has improved from 6% at the baseline to 50% of Gaza preschools after benefiting from the support; in the WB it increased from zero to 40%.

Teachers' disciplinary practices showed significant improvement after the implementation of the PD intervention program, with 24% reporting teachers' tendency to scream, push, or spank children in Gaza, and 84% in the WB. Teachers' tendency to scream, push, or spank children significantly improved by 22% at the baseline in Gaza preschools and 10% in the WB schools. After the implementation of the intervention program, 46% of Gaza teachers and 94% of the WB teachers refrained from these practices most of the time or consistently (combined). The overall mean score of the learning strategy domain in Gaza was 42.4% at the baseline and increased to 55.6% at the endline, with a 31% improvement level after the implementation of the project. In the WB, the level of improvement was highly significant (84.2%), as the overall mean score percentage has increased from 38% to 70%.

Domain Three: Learning Environment

The findings in table 5.3 illustrate the learning environment at the preschool as observed by the assessors. The results of both baseline and endline assessments indicate an improvement in the learning environment in Gaza and

Table 5.2. Domain 2: Teaching Strategies

Variables	Gaza				WB			
	Baseline		Endline		Baseline		Endline	
	No	%	No	%	No	%	No	%
Children are free to move between activity centers								
Not evident	12	40.0	4	15.4	16	80.0	0	0.0
Little evidence	9	30.0	3	11.5	3	15.0	3	20.0
Sometimes	7	23.3	5	19.2	0	0.00	4	26.7
Most of the time	2	6.7	10	38.5	1	5.0	3	20.0
Consistently (all the time)	0	0.00	4	15.4	0	0.00	5	33.3
Teacher redirects students' behaviors when needed								
Not evident	2	7.1	0	0.00	3	16.7	0	0.00
Little evidence	14	50.0	5	19.2	7	38.9	0	0.00
Sometimes	12	42.9	9	34.6	7	38.9	2	13.3
Most of the time	0	0.00	10	38.5	1	5.6	8	53.3
Consistently (all the time)	0	0.00	2	7.7	0	0.00	5	33.3
Teacher has established routines								
Not evident	6	19.4	2	7.7	9	45.0	0	0.00
Little evidence	10	32.3	0	0.00	10	50.0	4	26.7
Sometimes	13	41.9	11	42.3	1	5.0	5	33.3
Most of the time	2	6.5	10	38.5	0	0.00	6	40.0
Consistently (all the time)	0	0.00	3	11.5	0	0.00	0	0.00
Teacher refrains from screaming, pushing, or spanking children								
Not evident	10	32.3	4	15.4	2	10.0	0	0.00
Little evidence	5	16.1	6	23.1	9	45.0	0	0.00

Table 5.2. (*continued*)

Variables	Gaza				WB			
	Baseline		**Endline**		**Baseline**		**Endline**	
	No	**%**	**No**	**%**	**No**	**%**	**No**	**%**
Sometimes	9	29.0	4	15.4	7	35.0	1	6.3
Most of the time	7	22.6	11	42.3	2	10.0	8	50.0
Consistently (all the time)	0	0.00	1	3.8	0	0.00	7	43.8
Overall mean scores for teaching strategy	Baseline = 42.4%; Endline = 55.6%				Baseline = 38%; Endline = 70%			

Note. Improvement in the teaching strategy domain for both Gaza and the WB was statistically significant at p value <0.001.

WB preschools. One of the most significant improvements was noticed in the percentages of teachers who ensure that spaces are well used, open, and not cluttered with furniture most of the time / consistently (combined) at 50% of Gaza preschools after implementation and zero at the baseline. In the WB, the improvement in this area was even higher, increasing from zero to 100%. Other improvements were noticed in the percentage of teachers who ensured that there are clear activity centers most of the time at 50% of Gaza preschools, although around one-third still regarded it as not evident; again, preschools in the WB elicited higher scores than Gaza. Moreover, the percentage of teachers who ensured that materials are accessible to children was very low at the baseline but improved at the endline (not evident = 46.2%, and little evidence = 11.5% in Gaza; not evident = 0%, and little evidence = 7.1% in the WB).

The overall score from preschool teachers about the learning environment domain was initially as low as 31% in Gaza and 23% in the WB. The training program significantly contributed to improving the learning environment, with an overall score at the endline of 52% in Gaza and 78.9% in the WB, marking a level of improvement of 66% in Gaza and more than 100% in the WB preschools. This result testifies not only to the success of the program to improve the learning environment but also to the fact that the baseline levels were very low and almost unsuitable for children. Thus, the learning environments at the selected preschools require further enhancement and maintenance.

Table 5.3. Domain 3: Learning Environments

Variables	Gaza				WB			
	Baseline		Endline		Baseline		Endline	
	No	%	No	%	No	%	No	%
Teacher ensures that there are clear activity centers								
Not evident	28	90.3	7	29.2	16	80.0	0	0.00
Little evidence	2	6.5	2	8.3	4	20.0	2	13.3
Sometimes	1	3.2	3	12.5	0	0.00	6	40.0
Most of the time	0	0.00	12	50.0	0	0.00	7	46.7
Consistently (all the time)	0	0.00	0	0.00	0	0.00	0	0.00
Teacher ensures that spaces are well used, open, and not cluttered with furniture								
Not evident	15	48.4	4	15.4	5	25.0	0	0.00
Little evidence	13	41.9	3	11.5	9	45.0	0	0.00
Sometimes	3	9.7	6	23.1	5	25.0	0	0.00
Most of the time	0	0.00	11	42.3	1	5.0	12	75.0
Consistently (all the time)	0	0.00	2	7.7	0	0.00	4	25.0
Teacher ensures that materials are accessible to children								
Not evident	26	83.9	12	46.2	17	85.0	0	0.00
Little evidence	2	6.5	3	11.5	2	10.0	1	7.1
Sometimes	3	9.7	3	11.5	1	5.0	1	7.1
Most of the time	0	0.00	7	26.9	0	0.00	7	50.0
Consistently (all the time)	0	0.00	1	3.8	0	0.00	5	35.7
Overall mean scores	Baseline = 31.7%; Endline = 52.7%				Baseline = 23%; Endline = 78.9%			

Note. Improvement in the learning environment domain for both Gaza and the WB was statistically significant at p value <0.000.

When all the items constituting all three domains were calculated, findings showed that at the baseline the overall score for Gaza was higher than the WB (41% and 39%). Although both sites saw an improvement in the overall score at the endline, the WB showed significantly higher improvement levels (57% in Gaza and 75% in the WB). It is encouraging to see an overall improvement in all teachers' scores after the project's completion despite the differences in scores between Gaza and the WB. This is true because all teachers who were observed improved in their interactions with children and their teaching strategies and the general learning environment as suggested in scores on the post observations. When looking at study results generated using the CLASS in the US and other areas, the Palestinian teachers in this study outperformed in the average gains received on class in the post observations. Most teachers usually score in the middle of the scale; our teachers scored in the higher range.

FOCUS GROUPS

The focus group interviews at the end of the program generated similar trends, with participating teachers identifying and expressing significant improvements mainly in three areas related to their jobs and professional growth:

1. **Personal development and growth:** This was a main result of the professional engagement with peers and trainers in the field of ECD. This is true because many were mothers themselves, and the training benefited them and their interactions with their own children and families. For example, one teacher said, "The training made me a better person . . . I scream less now at my husband and children and my husband noticed that." Another young teacher from a village near Ramallah stated: "I feel calmer and more in control, this means I don't go home stressed and frustrated." It does make a lot of sense that feeling better at one's job makes them feel better at home, as spillover from home to work and work to home is documented in the literature (Bronfenbrenner, 1986).

2. **Professional image:** This theme seems to be impacted by the various training sessions and mentoring received during the PD program and intervention. This was evident in Gaza as well

as the WB, even among those who did not like being preschool teachers and expressed dismay about their job (in Gaza more than the WB). For example, several teachers said, "I don't care about what people say about my profession now, I am proud to be a preschool teacher." A teacher in Gaza was very honest when she expressed that she used to hate children and now can "live with the fact that she works with young children." Of course, while the work conditions and compensation cannot be changed for these teachers, the professional investment in them means a lot and pays dividends. In Ramallah, and at the end of the program, the Prime Minister himself distributed the certificates to teachers from the Ramallah area and Jericho, which highlighted their importance and empowered participating teachers.

3. **Improved teaching strategies:** This theme was very strong and supports the changes noticed in the CLASS pre and post observations. One teacher said: "I no longer use corporal punishment to control children," and other teachers were amazed by the power of learning centers. Another teacher said, "I can't believe how exhausted I used to be trying to control the children. Now I facilitate and monitor learning while the children work independently." A third said, "I didn't know what games and songs to teach, and I was too shy to sing with the kids. Now, I have a lot of options and I sing with them and play with them."

While it was expected to hear of improvements in teaching strategies as evident in the CLASS scores, it was surprising to learn about the improvement in the personal growth and professional image of preschool teachers because of the training program. Personal change was a huge gain for the teachers, with improvements in their self-image as preschool teachers and their satisfaction on the job. Nevertheless, this investment should be accompanied by further enforcement of mandatory kindergarten education (including increased funding) that would enhance the status of these teachers because they could earn salaries that are compatible to elementary education teachers in the system.

PRESCHOOL TEACHERS' KNOWLEDGE
AND PRACTICE IN ECD

To assess preschool teachers' knowledge and practice, a self-report questionnaire was administered twice, before intervention (baseline assessment) and after the implementation of training (endline assessment). The reliability testing showed that the teachers' knowledge about early childhood questions is highly reliable (0.91). Also, the reliability of teachers' practice questions was acceptable (0.74).

The data analysis revealed some interesting points about preschool teachers' knowledge of ECD and education. Comparing the baseline and endline results showed little change in Gaza preschool teachers' knowledge about child growth and needs. This may be due to high turnover among preschool teachers, so it is possible that those who filled out the baseline questionnaire were different than those who filled the endline questionnaire. For the level of knowledge about child growth and needs from birth to eight years, the percentage of "know little" responses went from 23.3% of preschool teachers in the baseline assessment to 19.4 % after the implementation. Preschool teachers who reported "knowing much" increased from 30% at the baseline assessment to 40% in the endline assessment. Similarly, 45.5% of the WB preschool teachers reported "knowing little" at the baseline, and this number decreased to 40% at the endline. However, both Gaza and WB preschool teachers reported a higher level of knowledge after joining the program. Furthermore, teachers in Gaza scored higher overall than those in the WB on all questions related to the knowledge of ECD.

The overall score computed from the thirteen questions constituting teachers' knowledge of the early childhood domain was higher in Gaza (81.9%) than the WB (70.2%) at the baseline assessment. At the endline, the scores slightly increased in Gaza (82.8%) and significantly increased in the WB (85.7%). When examining preschool teachers' practices, significant improvements were found (as reported by teachers) in Gaza and WB preschools regarding the ability to plan a comprehensive program for strengthening the learning and active learning in kindergarten after joining the PD program, with an extremely high percentage of "yes" for annual and weekly plans. Also, at the endline assessment, teachers reported that they present and implement fixed daily plans with children, at around 86% of Gaza preschools and 100% of the WB schools (baseline 79% in Gaza and 75.6% in the WB). Some variables of follow-up and documentation in Gaza preschools have significantly improved after the implementation of the program. For instance, there was an obvious improvement in the level of keeping private child-cumulative records, as evidenced by the 93% positive response for the Gaza preschools in the endline assessment (baseline 77.4%) and the increase from 73% at the baseline assessment to 96% at the endline in the WB.

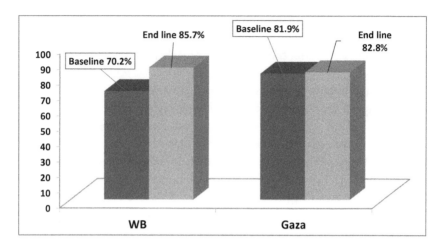

Figure 5.2. Teachers' Knowledge about Early-Childhood Development
(Pre and Post)

The overall score computed from all nineteen questions constituting teachers' practices was similar at the two sites at the baseline assessment (82.9% in
Gaza and 84.9% in the WB). At the endline, the scores slightly increased in
Gaza (84.5%), while they significantly increased in the WB (95.8%). The level
of improvement in the WB was 13%. The differences between the baseline and
the endline readings in the WB were statistically significant ($p < 0.001$). In
Gaza, the differences were minimal and not statistically significant. Figure
5.2 illustrates the improvement in scores on background self-administered
questionnaires.

SIGNIFICANCE AND RECOMMENDATIONS

This study highlights the accomplishments of teachers in a sector mostly run
by charities and local councils among marginalized communities in Gaza and
the WB. It also raises the general awareness of the benefits of a research-based
PD that is well planned and well executed, one that allows the time and space
for the transformation of attitudes and practice. The PD became a mechanism for changing the future of children in the eyes of participating teachers.
This was evident in the teachers' eagerness to learn and their willingness to
improve to change the lives of children and to lead toward political emancipation and better futures. This is where the hope lies in those communities

that see education as a transformative process and not a mechanism to keep the status quo.

It is clear from the results that gains were made because of the intervention in both areas of Palestine and for all participating teachers. The long-term engagement in PD created a support system for teachers in isolated villages where many live their daily lives in poverty and lack access to services and resources. In addition, teachers gained confidence in their ability to see the positive and felt confident about the knowledge gained and their ability to use and adapt it as needed.

Visible differences between the WB and Gaza were expected and were, in fact, not surprising given that the baseline was already in better shape in the WB, where resources are more available and the living conditions better than in Gaza. In addition to the differences in economic and political conditions, further reasons were provided by the staff as possible explanations for the variation. The following are possible reasons that may have contributed to the differences even though we cannot claim with certainty that these had an impact on the results.

1. Number of children per class and kindergarten: In Gaza and at the time of the study, kindergarten classes were larger.

2. Role of MOE supervisors: In Gaza, supervisors play more of an administrative role in working with teachers, focusing on such areas as licensing and supervision and less on mentoring and training. In the WB, most supervisors play this role, but some supervisors (especially those in areas of intervention) are more active, see themselves as mentors, and provide supervision (Nasser & Shami, 2013). The two supervisors from Jericho and Ramallah also attended all meetings in the WB.

3. Trainers' qualifications: In the WB, a minimum of eight trainers delivered the training throughout the program, with each trainer having a specialization in one or two topics. In Gaza, there was only one trainer with specialization and practical training in ECD on staff. Unfortunately, WB trainers are not able to easily travel to Gaza, and attempts to find others in Gaza have not been successful. Further investment in training of trainers in both Gaza and the WB is very much a priority.

4. Mode and length of delivery: The training meetings and mentorship in the WB were delivered over a longer period (weekly through the end of the school year and in summer with two weeks' intensive meetings), from February to August. In Gaza,

this was delivered more intensively and after school on many days. Further explorations and investment in coordination between the program in Gaza and the WB should allow for further discussion on the above points and ways to address the gaps.

Finally, this study suggests that intervention programs are making a significant difference and are improving the conditions for teachers and children. There are specific characteristics that make these types of interventions successful and impactful, and professionals in the field of training and development may benefit from some of the lessons learned. For example, the uniqueness of this PD is in the holistic investment in teaching and training it provides. The program included weekly PD sessions as well as mentoring sessions (a total of at least five), which totaled about 120 hours distributed throughout the school year. In addition, the PD program was accompanied by renovation and improvement of the learning facilities. The teachers also received new teaching materials and instructional aids. The children received new furniture and educational and child-friendly games. All instructional materials, games, and books were locally made (when possible) and authentic in reflecting local capacities and potential. Finally, continued demonstration and documentation of impact are necessary through follow-up studies and expansions to more preschools and more areas of focus. A larger-scale study examining intervention programs should assist the international funders to make decisions on scaling up programs in such contexts.

REFERENCES

Anders, P., Hoffman, J., & Duffy, G. (2000). Teaching teachers to teach reading: Paradigm shifts, persistent problems, and challenges. In M. L. Kamil, P. B. Mosenthal, P. D. Pearson, & R. Barr (Eds.), *Handbook of reading research* (Vol. 3, pp. 719–742). Lawrence Erlbaum.

Birman, B. F., Desimone, L., Porter, A., & Garet, M. S. (2000). Designing professional development that works. *Educational Leadership, 57* (8), 28–33.

Bolland, J. M., Lian, B. E., & Formichella, C. M. (2005). The origins of hopelessness among inner-city African American adolescents. *American Journal of Community Psychology, 36*(3–4), 293–305.

Bolland, J. M., McCallum, D. M., Lian, B., Bailey, C. J., & Rowan, P. J. (2001). Hopelessness and violence among inner-city youths. *Maternal and Child Health Journal, 5*(4), 237–244.

Bronfenbrenner, U. (1986). Ecology of the family as a context for human development: Research perspectives. *Developmental Psychology, 22*(6), 723–742. https://doi.org/10.1037/0012-1649.22.6.723

Diamond, K., & Powell, D. (2011). An iterative approach to the development of a professional development intervention for Head Start teachers. *Journal of Early Intervention, 33*(1), 75–93. https://doi.org/10.1177/1053815111400416

Joyce, B., & Showers, B. (2002). Improving in-service training: The messages of research. *Educational Leadership, 37*(5), 379–386.

Luthans, F., & Youssef, C. M. (2004). *Human, social, and now positive psychological capital management: Investing in people for competitive advantage* (p. 154). Management Department Faculty Publications. https://digitalcommons.unl.edu/managementfacpub/154/

MOEHE. (2014). *Education development strategic plan EDSP plan 2014–2019, A learning nation*. Ministry of Education and Higher Education.

Nasser, I., Kidd, J. K., Burns, M. S., & Campbell, T. (2015). Head start classroom teachers and assistant teachers' perceptions of professional development using a LEARN framework. *Professional Development in Education, 41*(2), 344–365. https://doi.org/10.1080/19415257.2013.833538

Nasser, I., & Shami, M. (2013). *Early childhood education supervisors' views and perceptions of their profession in Palestine* [Presentation]. Annual Meeting of the Society for Research on Child Development in Philadelphia.

Pianta, R. C., Burchinal, M., Jamil, F. M., Sabol, T., Grimm, K., Hamre, B. K., & Howes, C. (2014). A cross-lag analysis of longitudinal associations between preschool teachers' instructional support identification skills and observed behavior. *Early Childhood Research Quarterly, 29*(2), 144–154. https://doi.org/10.1016/j.ecresq.2013.11.006

Simon, S., Campbell, S., Johnson, S., & Stylianidou, F. (2011). Characteristics of effective professional development for early career science teachers. *Research in Science & Technological Education, 29*(1), 5–23. https://doi.org/10.1080/02635143.2011.543798

Van Driel, J., & Berry, A. (2012). Teacher professional development focusing on pedagogical content knowledge. *Educational Researcher, 41*, 26–28.

APPENDIX 1

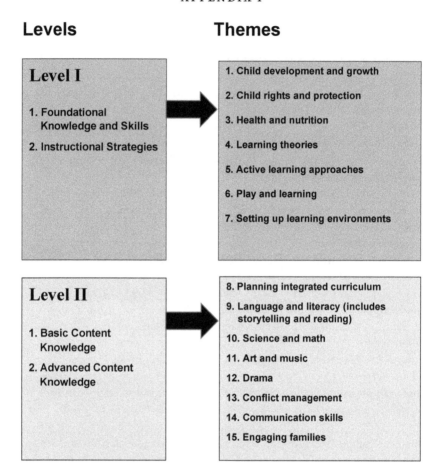

Figure A.1. Professional Development Design. Level I is
foundational knowledge, and level II is advanced knowledge

APPENDIX 2

Table A.1. Survey Items Based on CLASS

Target Behavior	Ratings	Comments/ Examples
Interactions with children		
1. Teacher shows respect toward children	1 2 3 4 5	
2. Teacher shows positive communication with children, such as simple and clear language use	1 2 3 4 5	
3. Teacher is aware of her surroundings	1 2 3 4 5	
4. Teacher is responsive to children's needs	1 2 3 4 5	
5. Children seem comfortable with teacher/s in room	1 2 3 4 5	
6. Teacher provides assistance where and when needed	1 2 3 4 5	
Teaching strategies		
7. Children are free to move around	1 2 3 4 5	
8. Teacher illustrates support for autonomy and leadership in children	1 2 3 4 5	
9. Children have a say in activities	1 2 3 4 5	
10. Teacher takes children's input into consideration	1 2 3 4 5	
11. Teacher models positive behaviors	1 2 3 4 5	
12. Teacher redirects student behaviors when needed	1 2 3 4 5	
13. Teacher has clear behavioral expectations	1 2 3 4 5	
14. Teacher uses a soft voice	1 2 3 4 5	
15. Teacher plans with children	1 2 3 4 5	
16. Teacher has established routines	1 2 3 4 5	
17. Teacher illustrates smooth transitions from one activity to another	1 2 3 4 5	
18. Teacher explains and provides directions on activities	1 2 3 4 5	

Table A.1. (*continued*)

Target Behavior	Ratings	Comments/ Examples
Learning Environment		
19. *There are clear activity centers*	1 2 3 4 5	
20. *Space is well used, open, and not cluttered with furniture*	1 2 3 4 5	
21. *Materials are labeled*	1 2 3 4 5	
22. *Materials are accessible to children*	1 2 3 4 5	
23. *Room is clean and preventive steps taken to ensure health and hygiene*	1 2 3 4 5	

NOTES

1. American Near East Refugee Aid convened the group.
2. For the latest information, see www.moehe.
3. Two of the categories/domains observed on the CLASS measure.

SCHOOLING CULTURE IN PUBLIC SCHOOLS

Reform for Equity (A'dl)[1] in Education

NORA EL-BILAWI

INTRODUCTION

Public education in Egypt continues to strive for improvement, especially in providing students from middle to lower socioeconomic status (SES) with the quality of education that many students from higher SES in private schools have privileged access to. To achieve this, Egypt's Ministry of Education (MOE) proposed implementing in its 2007 National Strategic Plan (NSP) a multiple intelligences (MI) teaching approach as a path to moving educational practice away from traditional teaching methods of focusing on student achievement and memorization to the integration of higher-order thinking in teaching practices, focusing on the student as a whole person (Nasser, chapter 1) and ensuring equal standards of learning for all students (MOE, 2007). MI was used as a method to differentiate instruction based on students' different intelligences and learning styles (Darling-Hammond, 1999).

The strategic plan was a move toward equitable access to best teaching practices and best learning environments for all children. It was meant to provide hope (amal)[2] for improving the educational system as students compete in a globalized economy around the world.

BACKGROUND

The NSP in Egypt (MOE, 2007) was launched as a schoolwide approach to reform. It outlines Egypt's commitment to equitable-quality education for all, stating as part of its mission that "the Ministry of Education fosters equal opportunities for all Egyptian students to realize quality education that empowers them to become creative, lifelong learners who are tolerant, critical thinkers with strong values, and a wide range of skills for active citizenship and dynamic participation in an ever-changing global society" (MOE, 2007, p. 11). Funded by the US Agency for International Development and implemented by the MOE, the aim is to realize high-quality teaching for all, utilizing current and most up-to-date theories of practice, with educational reform focusing on developing a cadre of teacher educators of high professional standards and training programs.

The reform effort that was subsequently launched and continued through to the next administration was slow to implement in part due to community and teacher resistance (Browne, 2011). This lack of progress has meant that objectives remain to be realized and that the hope for change remains just that, a hope. Today, people still await a larger nationwide mission to make all educational stakeholders (community, teachers and administrations, and policymakers) act on the need for reform in education (MOE, 2014).

The 2011 Egyptian Revolution ignited this nationwide hope for change and equal opportunities for all once again (Childress, 2013). But Egyptians were to be disappointed once again, as, although they emerged victorious from the revolution, the change they had longed and hoped for failed to materialize, and they found themselves in the hands of the Muslim Brotherhood (MBH) party, which switched focus back onto traditional approaches to teaching instead of integrating Islamic teachings with other approaches to achieve the desired developments in education (Childress, 2013). The removal of the old political regime brought into sharper focus, however, the urgent need to reform the education system to better equip youth with the tools and skills necessary through refined and integrated religious teaching packages. This chapter proposes an effective education strategy to prepare Egyptian youth for the twenty-first century by reviving educational discourse and developing the system from a "deficit to strength-oriented approach" (Nasser, chapter 1).

In pursuit of this vision, the MOE enhanced the 2007 NSP with a new reform plan for Egypt in 2014 under the new administration (after removing the MBH). This plan claims to carry modified goals for teachers, administrators, and the community to bring hope for change (MOE, 2014). To ensure successful realization of objectives for the newly revived strategic plan of 2014–2030, educators and researchers in the field need to understand the reasons for the failure of the 2007 initiative as well as the real needs and deficiencies of the current system of schooling. The hope is for a successful teaching and learning process that centers on educating the whole person through integration and focus on the learner and their well-being, for equitable educational opportunities.

AIM

The chapter aims to shed light on teacher responses following interviews conducted a few years after the implementation of the 2007 NSP and the impact of this in the classroom setting. The focus is largely on the responses given by teachers teaching English as a Foreign Language (EFL) in elementary private schools. The interviews delved deeper into the integration of teaching strategies that promote higher-order thinking, innovation, authentic experiences, and other student-centered strategies that form part of the MI theory (Gardner, 1983).

CONCEPTUAL FRAMEWORK

This study is based on Bourdieu's (1986) theory of "mind habitus" and cultural reproduction and how it is essential to start change from an inhibiting and deficit habitus to a strength-based habitus. The means to do so in school settings is linked to Webb's (2013) theory of "pedagogy of hope," which calls for using critical interactive educational methods and strategies to transform human social experiences and to liberate the mind. To achieve this transformation of the social experience in school settings, the use of teaching pedagogies like MI[3] calls for changing the mind and cultural habitus from student achievement to the education of the whole student's abilities and intelligences (Gardner, 1983). Gardner's (1983) theory focuses on the potentials of the individual learner and fosters the varied ranges of the intellectual abilities of each learner. Changing the cultural reproduction of the discourse of one-intelligence (grade-based) achievements to the importance of students' well-being and the importance of multiple abilities is the framework I use for a pedagogy of hope. This is, in turn, needed to transform educators and policymakers and, as a result, transform students' mindsets.

Throughout the data analysis, discussion section, and interpretation of results, I address the overarching conceptual framework, Gardner's MI theory and its teaching implications, MI as a pedagogy of hope, and the mind habitus and the transformation of hope.

METHODS OF EXPLORATION

The procedures used in exploring teachers' perspectives on the use of MI as a means for a nationwide reform were as follows.

I designed a semi-structured interview protocol that would allow for an open discussion between the researcher and the participant. I did not have to follow the order of the questions and was able to add questions that were not included in the protocol to clarify where needed to elicit deeper participants' conversations. After this step, I designed an initial screening questionnaire that aimed to test participants' foundational knowledge of MI practices in the three selected sites as a criterion to recruit for the interview.

The interview process was divided into two stages. Step one guided the semi-structured interview (appendix A). The flexible nature of this type of interview allowed for the development of a deeper understanding of the topic and interpretation of findings. These first interviews took place before observations. The second step was teacher reflections, which took place right after I visited their classrooms. The data collection, transcription, analysis, and peer checking of data collection and analysis took place congruently.

SAMPLING

The site selection was based on opportunity (because of the difficulties researchers face in accessing schools in Egypt to conduct fieldwork such as interviews and observations) and flexible sampling design (Patton, 2002). The first step was to telephone those schools that fit my site criteria to gain their initial permission for conducting interviews at the school, eventually selecting three of the ones that had granted me access. I focused on the elementary first through fifth grades, as the MOE was heavily concentrating on implementing MI techniques in the early-primary grades.

PEOPLE

According to Patton (2002), I focused on purposeful sampling based on criteria such as teachers' knowledge of MI theory and its practices (the screening addressed this criterion), and teachers' enrollment in the MOE's professional development (PD) on MI. Other factors, such as years of teaching experience and age, were left open to increase the pool of participants. Participating teachers came from a variety of age groups and experiences and were interviewed until data saturation was reached. According to Lincoln and Guba (1985), sample selection should be determined according to "point of redundancy . . . and informational considerations" (p. 246).

INTERVIEWS

After this initial selection, I simultaneously audio-recorded and transcribed the interviews. The duration of each interview was around an hour to address all interview questions or to reach "a point of redundancy" (Lincoln & Guba, 1985, p. 202). The second round was the reflective interviews, which took around the same duration; however, I was not an active participant and more of an active note-taker recording teacher views and reflections.

DATA ANALYSIS

Once data collection was complete, I referred to my anecdotal notes to ensure that I closely and fully understood the big picture (Maxwell, 2005). Hence, I decided to follow a systematic qualitative research data analysis to stay close to my raw data. I used the general procedure of analyzing qualitative data that is guided by specific research objectives in an inductive analysis approach (Bryman & Burgess, 1994; Dey, 1993).

I read and reread transcripts and field notes to address and examine both emic (participants') and etic (researcher's) perspectives. Then codes started to emerge, so I divided recurring statements into color-coded categories. Connecting codes and categories is the process of discovering themes in the data (Crabtree & Miller, 1999).

RESULTS

The results also suggest obstacles toward implementing MI practices; hence, the hope for change was hindered and not fully achieved. However, teachers were aware of their needs and what was missing, and they were working on bridging the gaps discussed in the interviews. Their overall perspective was that "there is hope despite hurdles" (Freire, 1972).

The core dilemma faced in the implementation of the MI in the study came from the teachers interviewed and their schooling culture and mind habitus. Even though most of the teachers I spoke with noted that they were enthusiastic about integrating newer ways of teaching, their own traditional schooling hindered their acceptance of new teaching methods, especially with the absence of sustained professional training that prepares them to move from traditional teaching practices into a supported transformation into student-centered methods. This filled their teaching tool kit, which they often resort to, with pedagogies that were more traditional than up to date.

Moreover, teachers' communication systems and classroom environments were based on the traditional teacher-centered way of teaching and learning. This created an environment of passive learners who lacked the initiative and the confidence in their learning abilities. Moreover, the large number of students in one classroom, which varied between forty to fifty, did not allow much room for learning independently and in interactive ways. Many teachers discussed issues of students' self-monitoring and self-management practices and ways schools do not prepare them to take initiative and practice self-control. An equitable educational environment would typically call for small-sized classrooms to ensure students' well-being, especially in these early years.

MEMORIZATION MIND HABITUS VERSUS INTERACTIVE TEACHING APPROACHES

Interactive teaching approaches like cooperative learning and classroom discussions are integral parts of MI pedagogies. Participants talked about how integrating these interactive approaches was difficult at many times. Esam (a male belonging to the new generation and who graduated from the Faculty of Education) from school A said, "I always find myself geared toward teaching in the traditional way when I'm in a hurry and want to finish things up."[4] This shows that traditional teaching based on memorization and repetition is the first tool teachers pull from their teaching tool kit and is the way they were taught.

Moreover, most of the teachers discussed their willingness to change, emphasizing, however, that the whole traditional system needed to enter this same interval of change for this transformation to be applicable or effective. Camellia (a female belonging to the middle teaching generation and a graduate of the faculty of education) from school C stated: "We are only one part of the body. How can you expect this one part to move alone? Unless the whole-body joins in, the body will stand still. They (administration and government) ask us (teachers) to change our teaching methods, strategies, and activities all the time. But when we try to change, we find many barriers that stop us."

In the three schools I visited, I noticed obvious examples of teachers being the center of classroom learning with students seated as passive recipients. This results in the relationship between teacher and student being a hierarchal one; the teacher becomes the only source of knowledge, and the students as receivers become followers of the teacher. The higher the grade level, the more intense this phenomenon.

According to teachers at the three schools, class control is a persistent teaching tool expected in classrooms that they cannot give up because it empowers central positions within the classroom setting. The idea of surplus control became part of the teachers' belief system in Egyptian schooling culture. Consistently, many of the teachers noted that the most difficult activities are the kinesthetic ones because students fail to contain themselves during class tasks.

Some of the EFL teachers also indicated that group work leads to chaos, and visual and auditory intelligences are considered the best types of activities for this matter. Nesreen (a female who belongs to the older teaching generation and age group and who graduated from an English major college) from school A stated, "Without my strict class control students cannot listen to appropriate English pronunciations." Mariam (a female belonging to the new teaching generation, in only her second year of teaching, and a graduate of English literature) from school B emphasized:

"Students have to learn how to respect me. I do not do activities unless I tell them the condition of being super quiet and respectful. I had tough students who would laugh at everything I said, so I had them write thirty times 'I respect my teacher and classmates.' Punishments are the only way to gain back class control."

PARENTAL EXPECTATIONS

Parents also have a mind habitus based on their backgrounds and experiences that build on specific educational expectations. These expectations are mainly oriented toward academic achievement and failure to link the importance of the whole student approach and the various ways the student learns and retains information. For them and like the teachers, kinesthetic activities are a waste of time. Learning is all about sitting tall, ready to listen, read, and write.

According to Maysoon (a female belonging to the middle teaching generation and who graduated from an English major college) from school B, "Learning here is a race to the top." Students must earn high cumulative grades because this is what determines their college acceptance and their whole future. Many teachers across the three schools described this concept, observing that the main concern of parents and students was exams, test results, and grades. Hence, parents worried over the quantity of English vocabulary their children memorized, grammar rules, keywords, and even sample composition texts.

To parents, the quality of English teaching and learning is not essential if children are passing their exams. This may encourage passive learning and rote memorization, which consequently leads to teacher-centered rather than student-centered instruction. According to Mahi (a female belonging to the middle teaching generation and who is a graduate of English literature) from school C: "It doesn't matter if I teach a lesson through role-play or by using a visual, like we have learned in MI based teaching. All that matters to parents is to see the workbook exercises are all done and give them key answers to tests. . . . This means that I will have to cover more of the workbook exercises and read and copy methods in class than work on an active learning environment."

According to EFL teacher perspectives, parental involvement on certain occasions becomes an obstacle. For instance, parental schooling backgrounds and cultures conflict with the current need for change in practice toward using MI activities in classroom instruction. Neither the government nor the school administration sought to inform and involve parents in these new interactive ways of teaching, such as using MI, so this has impacted the learning environment. Parents do not know or understand the goals behind the change in EFL teaching methods, nor do they understand the features of the change, and/or how teachers are seeking to apply these activities in the classrooms. Some teachers voiced concern over this issue, for example, Salma (a female belonging to the older teaching generation and age group and a graduate from the School of Education) from school A notes: "Parents might know about role-playing, but to them it's considered a fun activity only . . . They want us to do this maybe once or twice a week maximum, but they still want serious instruction, which is more writing and exercises. To them this shows that we work hard for the school."

According to teachers, parents ask for all classwork, even composition texts, to be sent home, so they can get their children to memorize these at home. Teachers inferred greater parental satisfaction from this situation, with the more work sent home the better, with demand for teachers to check this homework carefully (word by word) to ensure that children could memorize the correct answers. Esam from school A stated: "Parents want to see their children learning the same way they have learned themselves. They were taught by rote memorization, answering worksheets, following model answers, and lots of homework . . . They do not like it when I use PowerPoint. [They] say it's useless."

In agreement with the other teacher participants, Mustafa (a male belonging to the older teaching generation and age group and who graduated from the School of Education) from school A said, "This is how parents evaluate us as teachers . . . More homework equals a good teacher." Maysoon from school B affirms most of what other teachers have stated about how parents perceive teaching EFL should be and adds, "In spite of parents' demands to teach English through more paper-pencil exercises and practice . . . they complain that students are not able to converse well in English. How can we balance this?" Moreover, Maha (a female from the older teaching generation and age group and who graduated with an English major) from school B stated: "Parents don't care about how we teach. All they care about is to see the list of grammatical rules and key words to enable their kids to go to the exam. The education system now has active learning, group work, paperwork—all of this without changing our social, cultural, or educational backgrounds—so, don't call this reform, but call it addition."

STUDENTS' SELF-MANAGEMENT

During the analysis, I tried to connect teacher statements concerning student schooling skills and attitudes, which included observations such as "receptive and not creators," and I found there exists an absence of a culture of cooperation, self-efficacy, self-discipline, and self-motivation. Thus, a culture of cooperation among groups of students to produce, for instance, a final collaborative project does not exist due to these characteristics. When students were asked to work cooperatively (MI interpersonal skills) in this fashion, they preferred to compete to win and show themselves as being the best and wanting to earn higher grades. Teachers in these schools did not train students to work together as a team, with each having a specific role. Rather, the teachers talked most of the time, and only a few of the brightest learners had the opportunity to participate, usually by responding to the teacher. In this setting, teachers did not guide students as to how to form a group and what the dynamics of this group should be during an activity.

Teachers across the three schools stressed the fact that implementing group work and cooperative learning activities is difficult and not realistic in their EFL classrooms. One of the reasons mentioned was student behaviors. The most common comment about this was: "I [the teacher] have to control them [the students] all the time during group work . . . They can't focus on the task."

Sally (a female belonging to the middle teaching generation and age group and who graduated with an English literature major) from school C added, "One of the most important obstacles is students' behavior . . . A lot of us think we cannot do group work, sing, or any active learning because the students have no self-control. So, I insert activities that maintain order while students are at their seats."

My analysis of this situation is that students are used to an outside power or control to direct them, and once this power (strict teacher's structure) is absent, the students feel lost. This is a very critical problem; if we are discussing the need to change youth in Muslim societies from deficit minds to strong initiators who are creative and independent thinkers, we need to train them and provide them with multiple opportunities to make their own decisions, problem-solve, and take initiative in real-life situations. Another repeated comment was that students had low internal motivation and needed outside support. This means that student motivation is an extrinsic factor that prompts an individual's action with external factors such as reward or punishment, rather than an intrinsic one, which inspires action with internal factors such as the feelings associated with exploration, achievement, and personal interest. This is exactly what is discussed in the framework of cultural reproduction of the traditional and drilling-based education style, which eliminates the hope for a substantial transformation.

DISCUSSION

Based on the analysis of the data, it seems that teachers believe that change is possible and hope for transformation is close only if all stakeholders understand the goal behind change and are educated to be active participants. The stakeholders, including teachers, parents, and administrators, need to be supported to change the prevailing traditional mind habitus to achieve the aspired pedagogy of hope.

TEACHERS' PROFESSIONAL DEVELOPMENT

The beliefs and values of teachers form an essential component in the teaching and learning process, as the teacher is the core influencer in the learning process and in shaping students' hope for success and well-being (Kelchtermans, 2005). Therefore, they must be included in the educational process and the reform design. Teachers' beliefs influence their practices (Fang, 1996), and these practices are shaped by their personal experiences (Fang, 1996; Spillane et al., 2002; Vartuli, 2005). Their beliefs have a sustaining power when undertaking change (Prosser, 2006) and affect their ability to interpret reform (Carless, 2005; Spillane et al., 2002).

A newly adapted and culturally sensitive PD is a must to support teachers' transformation. The PD should zoom in on reform priorities with culturally appropriate practices that fit the Egyptian context, teachers' backgrounds, and the school environment. The governmental reform should prepare teachers and administrators with the new teaching methods to refine any cultural misconceptions (Hargreaves, 1997). The Egyptian school culture should intertwine with and enrich any internationally imported theories rather than merely mandating them. Educational changes can be unsuccessful because the change is inadequately conceptualized in school systems.

PARENTAL INVOLVEMENT FROM DEFICIT TO STRENGTH

Parents and the immediate community should be involved. In parent meetings, school administrators should discuss how the school is transitioning to implement new methods of teaching versus traditional ways of teaching and inform the parents about what these different ways of teaching are and how the difference between both ways impacts and improves children's learning. According to Rutherford et al. (1997), when schools provide the appropriate and welcoming environment for parental and community involvement, students' self-concept significantly increases as an outcome of parents buying into the existing education discourse.

STUDENTS' CHARACTER

Students need to understand the purpose of the transformational pedagogy of hope and that it is for their well-being and skills development. This can be achieved by teaching them how to be involved in the classroom based on dynamic methods such as cooperative learning, discussions, creative production, taking initiative, and problem-solving (Browne, 2011). Consistency in the application will consequently build students' abilities to learn and self-regulate their behaviors.

CONCLUSION

In summary, to increase the chances of hope (*amal*) in education for equitable (*a'dl*) learning in the Middle East, specifically in Egypt, a more inclusive system with open dialogue is very much needed. As pointed out, families in Egypt rely heavily on tutoring and individual learning, and they spend a great deal of money to make sure their children are ahead (Nasser chapter 1). Improving the public schooling system will reduce the need for that and ensure the equity needed for all to learn and not simply the wealthy having access to effective education.

Many societies in the Muslim world (as expressed in several chapters in this volume) need to initiate the change in education discourse to enable their youth to rise up and compete in a quickly changing global market. Reform efforts should focus on teachers and equip them and their school administrators with pedagogies that are inclusive and address the whole person by enriching the brain as well as the spirit and instilling hope back into the teaching and learning spaces in educational institutions (Nasser, chapter 1).

Implementing holistic and competency-driven educational practices and programs like MI-based pedagogies provide the tools that can ensure our youths' well-being. Pedagogies like cooperative learning, discussions, creativity, and problem-solving bring authentic Islamic thought to reality. Islamic teachings that are based on *taa'won* (cooperation), *shura* (discussion), *ibda'a* (creativity), and *ijtihad* (problem-solving) are an integral part of Islamic thought and should be utilized in schooling and education. Programs on *Hikma* (in Malaysia) and *Akhlaq* (in Indonesia) are examples of ways this can be done in Muslim majority societies. In the Arab world, examples of private schools adopting a more open approach to education are replacing failing public education systems, and a possible collaborative approach between the private and public systems may yield better results for students and teachers.

REFERENCES

Bourdieu, P. (Ed.). (1986). *Handbook of theory and research for the sociology of education* (1st ed., pp. 241–258). Greenwood. https://library.newcastle.edu.au/articles/2315165.22843/1.PDF

Browne, H. (2011). *Education reform in Egypt: Reinforcement & resistance* [Doctoral dissertation]. https://repository.library.northeastern.edu/files/neu:1845/fulltext.pdf

Bryman, A., & Burgess, R. (1994). *Analyzing qualitative data*. Routledge.

Carless, D. (2005). Prospects for the implementation of assessment for learning. *Assessment in Education, 12*(1), 39–54. https://doi.10.1080/0969594042000333904

Childress, S. (2013). *What's happened since Egypt's revolution?* https://www.pbs.org/wgbh/frontline/article/timeline-whats-happened-since-egypts-revolution/

Crabtree, B. F., & Miller, W. L. (1999). *Doing qualitative research*. Sage.

Darling-Hammond, L. (1999). Teacher quality and student achievement: A review of state policy evidence. *Education Policy Analysis Archives, 27*(1), 5–15.

Dey, I. (1993). *Qualitative data analysis: A user-friendly guide for social scientists*. Routledge.

Fang, Z. (1996). A review of research on teacher beliefs and practices. *Educational Research, 38*(1), 47–65. https://doi:10.1080/0013188960380104

Freire, P. (1972). *Pedagogy of the oppressed.* Penguin.

Gardner, H. (1983). *Frames of mind: The theory of multiple intelligences.* Basic Books.

Hargreaves, A. (1997). Cultures of teaching and educational change. In B. Biddle, T. Good, & I. F. Goodson (Eds.), *The international handbook of teachers and teaching* (pp. 1297–1319). Kluwer Academic Publishers.

Kelchtermans, G. (2005). Teachers' emotions in educational reforms: Self-understanding, vulnerable commitment and micropolitical literacy. *Teaching and Teacher Education, 21,* 995–1006.

Lincoln, Y., & Guba, E. (1985). *Naturalist inquiry.* Sage.

Maxwell, J. A. (2005). *Qualitative research design: An interactive approach* (2nd ed.). Sage.

Ministry of Education (MOE). (2007). National Strategic Education Plan, August, 2007–December, 2011 (English version).

Ministry of Education (MOE). (2014). *National Strategic Education Plan, 2014–2030.* Author.

Patton, M. Q. (2002). *Qualitative research and evaluation methods* (3rd ed.). Sage.

Prosser, B. (2006). *Reinvigorating the middle years: A review of middle schooling* [Paper presented] Australian Association for Research in Education Conference.

Rutherford, B., Anderson, B., & Billig, S. (1997). *Studies of education reform: Parent and community involvement in education.* RMC Research Corporation.

Sari, J. (2018). *Gardner's Multiple intelligences (MI).* https://www.toolshero.com /personal-development/gardners-multiple-intelligences/

Spillane, J. P., Diamond, J. B., Burch, P., Hallett, T., Jita, L., & Zoltners, J. (2002). Managing in the middle: School leaders and the enactment of accountability policy. *Educational Policy, 16,* 731–762.

Vartuli, S. (2005). Beliefs: The heart of teaching. *Young Children, 60*(5), 76–86.

Webb, D. (2013). Pedagogies of hope. *Studies in Philosophy of Education, 32*(4), 397–414.

APPENDIX A

Interview Protocol

1. How would you describe your childhood, high school, and college educational experience?
2. What do you know about the theory of multiple intelligences (MI)? What did you learn from the staff development or cadre training that you have participated in?

3. Do you use MI in your classroom as a tool to advocate creative thinking? If yes, how? If no, why?
4. What do you think are the implications of such theories to your classrooms?
5. Do you find your students more involved in the learning process when you implement MI? If yes, give examples. If no (or if it depends), why?
6. How do you identify your students' intelligences? Do you follow a certain pattern of identification, or do you usually use learning centers as your way of integrating MI?
7. What types of intelligences do you find yourself using more than the others? And what intelligences do you prefer not to use excessively in your classroom? Why? Give examples.
8. Does the school administration interfere in what intelligences you should use or how you use them? If yes, how and why?
9. Does your culture or the traditions you belong to have a role in your MI choices and in the way you implement the theory?
10. If you evaluated the staff development or the cadre training where you learned MI, what would you say?
11. If you were asked to make a change or a tweak to the MI theory and practices that you have learned from your teacher training, would there be any?

NOTES

1. *A'dl* is another word for *divine justice and equity* in Islam. Islamic Terminologies. In *Wikipedia*, 2020. https://en.wikipedia.org/wiki/Adl.

2. *Amal* is *hope*. It is similar to *rajā'* but primarily covers the meaning of hope, whereas *rajā'* captures a wider range of meanings. A formal difference between *rajā'* and *amal* is that the latter can be plural (i.e., *āmāl*).

3. The theory of multiple intelligences (MI) was introduced in 1983 by psychologist Howard Gardner in his book *Frames of Mind*. The essence of Gardner's MI is that each person has eight types of intelligence: verbal, logical, visual, musical, kinesthetic, naturalistic, interpersonal, intrapersonal (Gardner, 1983). The application of these intelligences in classroom pedagogies is to provide opportunities for students' verbal discussions, problemsolving, corporately working together, making visual implications, creativity, and movement (Sari, 2018).

4. This is a direct quote from one of the participants. All parentheses throughout this chapter are direct quotes from different participants in this study.

PART IV

INFUSING HOPE IN
K–12 EDUCATION

POSITIVE FUTURES AND HOPE FOR A BETTER LIFE

A Transdisciplinary Approach for Imagining a Flourishing and Sustainable World

ANDREAS M. KRAFFT

BACKGROUND: VISIONS AND HOPES OF YOUNG PEOPLE

Recent studies have impressively shown that youth (as well as many people) harbor more negative than positive visions of the future (Nordensvard, 2014), and when asked to sketch a picture of the world in twenty years, most of them express negative scenarios and also fear that current global problems will worsen in the future (Rubin, 2002). Simultaneously, powerlessness is expressed because many have the impression that they cannot do anything about these issues. Many young people lack a vision for themselves and the future of society (Eckersley, 2002). The more complex and unmanageable the world presents itself to be, the more these experiences trigger negative feelings of fear, depression, and helplessness (Eckersley, 1995).

As soon as young people are asked to outline their hopes for desired visions of the future, they express a completely different picture. On a personal level, hopes are directed toward attaining a good job, a happy family or partnership, a good education, and a house, health, money, and happiness. The main social hopes, on the other hand, relate to the environment, a sense of community, quality of life, social well-being, less stress and more peace, security, and harmony (Hicks, 2003). And when it comes to their dreams, youth place less emphasis on the individual and competition, and more on community, family, cohesion, and the environment. Some values seem to be almost universal, such as altruism, generosity, forgiveness, peace, honesty, harmony, idealism, and sustainability (Hicks, 1996).

How the young generation views the future, whether with hope, fear, or indifference, will influence the way it thinks and acts in the here and now.

Hopes and fears determine the perception of possible future conditions and options for action. Negative images of the future deprive young people of their passion and enthusiasm for their lives and the world (Eckersley, 1995). Individualism paired with the feeling that the world is breaking apart has produced a longing for community, harmony, a safe place, home, security, and protection (Brunstad, 2002).

PURPOSE: THINKING ABOUT A BETTER FUTURE

When members of a society start to develop new and powerful images of desirable futures, that society begins to mobilize its creative energy again (Hicks, 2003), indicating the importance of hope and confidence instead of fear and despondency as the fundamental drivers of renewal: "I no longer think fear is sufficient motivation to make changes . . . to spur us on, we need hope as well— we need a vision of recovery, of renewal, of resurgence" (McKibben, 2007, p. 5).

This chapter presents a methodology for students in secondary schools that offers them the opportunity to design alternative and positive future scenarios for themselves and the world. The strategy consists of combining the strengths of humanistic futures studies in education, on the one hand, and the strengths of positive psychology, on the other, with the goal of understanding our capacity to build hope. This interdisciplinary approach has been called positive futures, and the concrete program was titled Hope for a Better Life. The main purpose of this program is to combine individual future goals with visions of a good life in a better world and thus support young people in developing a more fundamental hope for happiness and fulfillment. Thinking about alternative and desired futures can give young people new sources of purpose, meaning, and orientation in life (Slaughter, 2002). Images of a better world can give them inspiration and hope (Eckersley, 2002). For this, they first need a realistic picture of a good life and a better world. This need not consist of only short-term goals but can also include long-term visions for the individual and society at large. And it needs clarity about what is important in life: "Beginning to see what is at the 'core' of life deepens one's understanding of the human experience. It puts the everyday in perspective and hope partly emerges from becoming clearer about what it is that really matters" (Hicks, 2003 p. 73).

THE NATURE AND VALUE OF HOPE

Hope philosophers and, nowadays, the discipline of positive psychology have seen hope as an inner driving force toward a better life and world. German philosopher Ernst Bloch (1959) saw hope as the human capacity to anticipate a better life and world for oneself and all human beings. In the philosophies and pedagogies of Freire (1994) and Rorty (1999, 2002), hope has a transformative character, leading the hoper to dream up a better future and by doing so to transcend the current situation. For existentialist philosopher Marcel (1951), hope is a creative and mysterious force that emerges in the intersubjective encounter between two human beings connected in love.

Psychological theories intend to represent the complexity of the phenomenon of hope by integrating empirical research findings and traditional philosophical reflections. Many authors relate to the work of Erikson (1963), who, within the framework of his developmental theory, recognized hope as the first and fundamental human virtue necessary for psychosocial development. The emergence and reinforcement of hope are grounded in the basic trust an individual has in people in their immediate social environment. For Erikson, hope, as a virtue, is the basis not only for effective action but also for ethical human behavior.

This focus on trust and interpersonal relations is especially crucial when the individual does not seem to have enough possibilities to influence the event or situation they are hoping for. Inspired by the work of Marcel (1951), hope is categorically distinguished from optimism and expectation by its fundamental existential character (Pruyser, 1986). Hope comes into play when the person is confronted with a threatening or dreadful situation and does not feel capable of coping with it using only the resources available to them. For these authors, hope deals with critical experiences in life and has a transformative character for the person involved.

The central question related to hope is how people make sense of and respond to these critical situations (Eliott, 2005). In the work of Frankl (1959), hope presupposes the transcendence of one's ego, a feeling of communion with other people, and the belief in a benevolent higher power (Pruyser, 1986). For this reason, Peterson and Seligman (2004) included hope in their catalog of character strengths common across cultures and attaining the virtue of transcendence. For them, hope is a transcendent virtue because it goes beyond our own knowledge and coping capabilities and allows us to build connections to something bigger than ourselves that provides us with meaning, purpose, and basic beliefs. In their categorization, hope is linked to other character strengths such as gratitude, appreciation of beauty and excellence, humor, and especially spirituality and religious faith. As a transcendent character strength, hope is linked to values that provide a moral framework that keeps the person committed to the expectation and pursuit of goodness.

Fredrickson (2004, 2009) has underlined the transformative character of hope as one of the ten most frequently experienced positive emotions in daily life, with the effect of fostering personal growth and well-being. The effect of hope, as a positive emotion, is that it broadens the mindset, the scope of attention, and the thought and action repertoire, nurturing the psychological, social, intellectual, and even physical resources to cope with adversity. The second important effect of hope as a positive emotion is that it transforms the individual for the better. While certain emotions such as a good mood and pleasure nourish hedonic happiness, hope can be considered a part of the eudaemonic domain of flourishing that is connected to inner personal growth, meaning in life, and meaning in our relationships with others (Cohn & Fredrickson, 2009). Because hope is a process of broadening and growth, hopeful people tend to display more altruistic and generative behaviors, such as helping others, taking a long-term view of things instead of satisfying short-term needs, thinking beyond the struggles of the present moment, and adopting moral values such as friendship, gratitude, generativity, selflessness, kindness, and inclusiveness toward strangers (Cohn & Fredrickson, 2006). In addition to cognitive (analytical, planning, logical) skills, hope is primarily believed to be nourished by social, religious, and spiritual practices such as meditation and prayer and creating a deeper connection to the inner self, other people, and a higher spiritual power (Fredrickson, 2013).

THE ROLE OF SCHOOLS AND EDUCATION FOR A BETTER FUTURE

Today's youth will be the adults of tomorrow. How young people perceive the future is important not only for them but also for the entire society. They will shape the world of the future decisively and can or must be prepared for it now (Toffler, 1974). In general, schools provide extensive knowledge about the present and the past. Schools are much less concerned with the future, let alone with different visions of the future (Hicks, 2012). We cannot change the past, but we have a common interest in creating a better and more sustainable future worth living. The fundamental task of education is not only to prepare young people for the future but also to enable them to responsibly and actively shape the future they want to live in (Eckersley, 1999).

THE DISCIPLINE OF FUTURES STUDIES

The credo of the scientific discipline called futures studies, prominently represented by authors such as Jennifer Gidley (2016), David Hicks (2003), Richard

Eckersley (2002), and Richard Slaughter (1994), is that without a living vision in which education is to take place, the higher purpose of education cannot be fulfilled satisfactorily. Education is always a preparation for the future based on certain images of the world. If education was always intended for the future, then schools would have to deal with the future in a much more differentiated way. There is a need, especially these days, to develop positive images of the future so young people can think about the world in which they would like to live.

Education needs a leading story, a vision of the future that motivates young people to shape a better life for themselves and their social and natural environment (Halpin, 2002). In creating this vision, optimism and hope for the future can be conveyed to the youth. Young people can believe in themselves and their abilities if they are convinced they can shape the future positively. Schools can help young people define their own vision of a good and fulfilling life and a harmonious, just, environmentally friendly, and sustainable society. Students need to be aware that there are alternative futures, and they should also know what contribution they can make to realize the desired future (Beare & Slaughter, 1993). This requires not only cognitive skills and competencies but also the appreciation of emotions, values, attitudes, desires, hopes, and dreams of young people. Education should embrace the whole person and their relationship to the social and ecological environment. To educate people is also to form personal attitudes toward everyday phenomena such as work, family, and social relationships, as well as environmental issues.

THE PRINCIPLES OF FUTURES STUDIES

From this perspective, futures studies deals with how people imagine the future; how their past experiences, their feelings, thoughts, and dreams influence their decisions in the present; and what they can do to fulfill their visions of the future (Hicks, 2003). From this perspective, futures studies is oriented toward human beings and their needs and connects these with the social and ecological lifeworlds, making the general quality of life an essential focus of futures studies. The future is like an open horizon full of possibilities that can be creatively explored and above all shaped in different directions. This means that futures studies emphasizes human dignity and freedom. If one assumes that the future can be shaped, then the first question should be which future is desirable at all. By examining young people's values, preferences, interests, and goals, futures studies encourages them to imagine alternative and desired futures. What releases the energy for a better future are hopes and dreams of a better life, rather than focusing on problems and worries.

Concrete ideas such as human rights, equal treatment, environmental protection, social institutions, humanitarian aid, and so on found their inspiration in social visions. Visions offer the image of an ideal future to which one can commit oneself and emphasize human freedom and dignity. People are always free to imagine and strive for a completely different and better world. Futures studies is based on a set of guiding principles that define the basic assumptions and worldviews for its activities (Riner, 1987):

1. People are active, purposeful, and goal-oriented beings. The future is not a phenomenon that happens to people but rather is actively shaped by them.
2. A society consists of patterns of social interaction. It arises and develops from emergent routines of human behavior.
3. Patterns of action emerge from memories of the past; from current decisions; and from expectations, hopes, and fears about the future.
4. The world and everything in it (including nature) form a unity. Everything is interconnected in a natural and temporal chain of causality.
5. Not everything that will exist in the future already existed in the past or exists in the present. The future contains things that did not exist before.
6. Thus, the future is not completely predetermined but open. This opens the horizon for new thoughts and possibilities.
7. The future is the domain of imagination, intentionality, and action.
8. Future thinking is particularly relevant if it influences actions in the here and now. Future states are influenced by current decisions and concrete choices between different possibilities.

POSITIVE PSYCHOLOGY AND POSITIVE EDUCATION

Changing the world always goes hand in hand with transforming everyone, each individual, and this is what leads us to address the importance of human values, virtues, and behaviors (Hicks, 2003). The following quote describes how similar the main concern of futures studies is to that of positive psychology: "Futurists have appealed to values such as the quantity and quality of human life (both considerations of freedom and wellbeing), perceived life satisfaction, and happiness on the individual level, social harmony, sustainability, effectiveness, efficiency, equity, and the life-sustaining capacities of the Earth itself. Other candidates for worthy (and possibly universal) values include the desirability of sufficient wealth, knowledge, affection, opportunities for sex and family life, respect for authority, loyalty, courage, perseverance, cooperation, honesty, generosity, helpfulness, friendliness, trust and self-realization" (Bell, 1996, p. 14).

Futures studies and positive psychology have enormous potential for cross-fertilization. This chapter briefly introduces the disciplines of positive psychology and positive education. We then focus on the phenomena of positive experiences and emotions, virtues and character strengths, flourishing, and the appreciative inquiry (AI) methodology.

PURPOSE OF POSITIVE PSYCHOLOGY

Positive psychology is the discipline that scientifically explores the good life. It builds on the tradition of humanistic psychology and deals with theory, research, and practice regarding the question of what makes life worth living. It does not negate the problems in life and does not plead for the wearing of rose-tinted spectacles to repress the problems of today. Positive psychology focuses attention on the positive sides of life, on the beautiful experiences, on what we can be grateful for, and on the good that happens to us every day. It is the science of human strengths and abilities, good feelings, happy families, friendly relations, and functioning institutions (Seligman & Csíkszentmihályi, 2000).

Positive psychology aims to help people recognize and use their strengths, experience positive feelings, and contribute to a prosperous society. The main purpose of positive psychology is to show people that everyone can lead a better life, regardless of age, financial income, nationality, or physical condition. It is above all a matter of recognizing and releasing personal potential. People want to live a fulfilled life and give meaning to their existence. They are interested in developing their good sides and thus enhancing themselves. People are no longer seen as victims of negative circumstances but as autonomous, self-determining, and self-effective individuals. Most people can make independent decisions, explore options, seize opportunities, and shape their lives positively. In many cases, we are the authors of our own life story. We are free, responsible, and creative actors. Through our attitude to life, to ourselves, and to our fellow human beings, we actively shape our personal and common future.

POSITIVE EDUCATION AND CHARACTER STRENGTHS

Positive education is the application of positive psychology in the fields of schooling, education, and raising of children and adolescents. The basis for the development of positive education is the recognition that positive psychology and the promotion of character strengths can contribute to optimal development and a fulfilled life for young people (Park, 2004). Within the framework of positive education, Burow (2011) addresses the meaning of dreams, happiness, and positive relationships in school in the following way: "In this sense, teachers should support students more in discovering their 'dreams of happiness,' their visions, and the emergence of creative synergetic relationships. However, this requires teachers and head teachers who have not lost touch with their own dreams and who are enthusiastic" (p. 132).

Thus, schools are institutions that enable positive experiences and, in addition to imparting knowledge and skills, also serve to train moral competencies and develop a good character (Park & Peterson, 2006). Examples of virtues and character strengths are courage, justice, humanity, creativity, humility, fairness, and hope (Peterson & Seligman, 2004). The premise of positive education is the conviction that the human character is fundamentally capable of development and that a good character makes a decisive contribution to a fulfilled life and a better world. "There is consistent evidence that character strengths play important roles in positive youth development not only as broad-protective factors preventing or mitigating psychopathology but also as enabling conditions that facilitate thriving. These strengths can be cultivated and strengthened by appropriate parenting, schooling, various youth development programs, and healthy communities. The goal of positive youth development should not be merely surviving in the face of adversity but actually growing throughout life" (Park, 2004, p. 50).

Hope belongs to the virtue of (self-)transcendence that refers to understanding oneself as part of a greater whole, of outgrowing oneself, and of finding a higher meaning in life. The strength of hope means expecting the best and doing something about it. Hopeful people have a clear picture of their desired future and do not give up on challenges and setbacks (Krafft & Walker, 2018).

POSITIVE EXPERIENCES AND EMOTIONS

Besides character strengths and virtues, the second pillar of living a good life is the possibility of having positive experiences and savoring emotions such as joy, gratitude, forgiveness, inspiration, pride, awe, wonder, happiness, and love (Fredrickson, 2004). According to Fredrickson (2009), positive emotions have a building and broadening effect in both the mind and consciousness of the person and in their social relationships. Having the opportunity to experience positive emotions changes the perspectives and horizons of everyday life. Thanks to positive emotions, people become more creative.

One of the central positive emotions is the feeling of hope. Through hope, the way of looking at things is expanded, and positive resources are built up to cope with negative situations that arise. New ideas emerge and the attitude toward life itself changes. Problems that have been burdensome until now turn into interesting challenges, the future keeps new options open, and new approaches to solve existing problems emerge. Positive emotions strengthen us in good times and make us more resilient in bad times.

By doing so, positive emotions promote personal growth. Self-confidence is strengthened, and an open attitude toward new events and other people is developed. The expansion of consciousness causes one to think not only of oneself but of others as well, and to be connected to a larger whole. If you feel well, you are also more friendly and helpful to other people, you want to do good, and you feel at one with the environment (the family, the community, and the world).

FLOURISHING AND THE FULFILLED LIFE

Positive education is not only about combating negative phenomena such as violence and drug use but, above all, is about creating a fulfilled and happy life and what psychologists call *flourishing*, meaning the process of personal inner growth. Flourishing is about the active and positive shaping of life according to our human virtues and capacities. It is fundamentally a matter of recognizing one's own potential, realizing it, and bringing it to its fullest development. Young people develop their character strengths and experience flourishing primarily based on positive experiences and emotions that inspire their urge to explore, their motivation, and their social relationships (Peterson & Seligman, 2004).

According to authors like Huppert and So (2013), Keyes (2005), Ryan and Deci (2001), Ryff and Singer (2000), and Seligman (2004), the main elements of experiencing a fulfilling and flourishing life are self-respect, positive relationships, autonomy, competence, meaning in life, positive emotions, commitment, hope and optimism, achievement, vitality, and personal growth. The following testimony from Martin Seligman (2014) expresses how closely the term *flourishing* as a fulfilled life relates to a desirable future in the social environment: "The discipline of positive psychology studies what free people choose when they are not oppressed. I call these desiderata the elements of 'wellbeing,' and when an individual or nation has them in abundance, I say it is 'flourishing'" (p. 113).

DIMENSIONS OF LEARNING FOR A BETTER FUTURE

From a methodological point of view, the key pedagogical question is how to develop stories and future scenarios of hope with students and how to teach them the values of a fulfilled life so that enthusiasm and motivation are triggered in them. Previous research in schools by authors like Eckersley (1999), Gidley (2016), Hicks (1994), and Jungk (Jungk & Müllert, 1989) has shown that a holistic and structured approach is needed to enable students to develop visions of a positive future for themselves and the world.

The development of future scenarios can be a purely cognitive and rational exercise. When it comes to designing alternative and desirable pictures for the future, however, creativity and intuition and thus emotions, values, hopes, dreams, and longings become increasingly important (Hicks, 2003). The development of future scenarios acquires a special creative value when the current reality is overcome, so to speak, and completely new ideas and wishes can be developed (Bell, 2009).

Dimensions of Learning for the Future

Rogers and Taugh (1996) distinguish five dimensions in creating visions of the future: (1) cognitive, (2) affective, (3) existential, (4) empowerment, and (5) action. Interestingly, these dimensions have a large correspondence with existing multidimensional concepts of hope (Dufault & Martocchio, 1985; Scioli et al., 2011). Hope involves cognitive, emotional, social, cultural, and spiritual elements and is characterized by an existential process (mastery and survival), a spiritual-transcending process (faith), a rational thought process (coping), and a relational-emotional process (attachment) (Farran et al., 1995; Scioli et al., 2011).

The Cognitive Dimension

Cognitive engagement with the future is about knowledge and critical reflection on global developments and their possible consequences. This includes facts, trends, forecasts, and scenarios for the future. Sometimes the complexity of the issues can overtax young people and trigger an attitude of resignation and helplessness. Therefore, the cognitive dimension also includes reflection on one's own basic assumptions, beliefs, thought patterns, and worldviews. For alternative visions of the future to be conceivable, often new worldviews must be developed first. Sometimes it takes a fresh perspective, a different view on things, and new beliefs to leave the current comfort zone and create new images of the future.

The Emotional and Social Dimension

The systematic, profound, and differentiated consideration of alternative future images in all their complexity usually triggers a personal emotional process. When one thinks about the future, especially about negative trends or desirable scenarios, a multitude of positive and negative affects are triggered. Sometimes emotional ups and downs take place, which are characterized by feelings of anger, grief, or fear, but also happiness, joy, and hope. These feelings must be acknowledged and worked on in this process.

The Existential and Self-Transcendent Dimension

Most people who have intensively engaged in questions about the future report that they have been confronted with existential questions about the meaning of life and the nature of existence. This triggered a deeper reflection about one's own life, about relationships with other people (parents, friends, etc.) as well as about one's own attitudes toward the environment, work, and other areas of life. Such experiences address the human need for self-transcendence, combined with a longing for community and an urge for helpfulness and altruism toward other people and the world. The existential dimension addresses the essence of human nature, the core values of humanity, faith, spirituality, and the meaning and purpose in life.

The Empowerment Dimension

From the previous dimensions, feelings of responsibility, commitment, and attachment to a higher ideal arise. People are beginning to think about what they can do to improve their lives and the world. The question is, how can people develop a sense of hope and confidence? The global economic, social, and ecological megatrends, in particular, seem to far exceed the possibilities of the individual and completely overwhelm people. It is precisely against the background of such phenomena that positive future scenarios and concrete success stories are needed to trigger motivation and encouragement.

The Action Dimension

The future must be an integral part of the present and of everyday life. Goals for the future must be defined and concrete options for action identified that provide orientation for today's decisions. Goals must provide information about how we want to live in the future and what we can do to achieve this. As soon as people imagine a better future together, they will want to create it together. From a positive psychology perspective, anyone who wants to change the world for the better must first start with transforming themselves and then influence their environment positively. In most cases, this causes a change in one's own way of life. The visualization of alternative visions of the future often leads to different priorities in life and dedicating more time for family, friends, and meaningful activities.

THE APPRECIATIVE INQUIRY METHODOLOGY

A very powerful tool in positive psychology, which we consider is perfectly appropriate for the development of future scenarios, is the AI methodology (Cooperrider et al., 2000). McQuaid et al. (2016) are among the pioneers who have applied AI in the school context with teachers and educators. The implementation of AI in a program of hope with students who deal with personal and social future scenarios could thus represent a meaningful extension and innovation. AI summarizes a strength-oriented philosophy, an appreciative interview technique, and a resource-oriented process model for change.

1. *Philosophy*: A recognition and activation of existing resources and potentials take place. The main focus is on opportunities rather than problems.
2. *Interviews*: The instrument of the AI interview is based on the inquiry of positive experiences. This can generate constructive energies and forces. The mere awareness of existing strengths and resources triggers enthusiasm, motivation, and willingness to change.
3. *Change process*: Although the AI method does not ignore the problems, the change process focuses primarily on opportunities and the definition of a desired future.

AI's philosophy of designing desirable future concepts and successfully implementing positive changes can be summarized in five points (Seliger, 2014):

1. If we ask for the best that already exists today, we will discover it.
2. Powerful images of the future trigger energy for change and development.
3. When we ask for positive experiences, we develop more strengths than if we ask for problems.
4. The change begins the moment we ask questions.
5. Systems change in the direction in which questions are asked.

The 4-D model conceived by Cooperrider and Whitney (2005) fits almost perfectly with the concerns and methods of futures studies.

The first step in this model, *discovery*, asks the question "What is a good life?" and brings positive experiences to consciousness. The second step, *dream*, poses the question "What could the future look like?" and creates positive images of the future. In the *design* phase, the question arises of how dreams can be realized. Under *destiny*, motivation and the responsibility for positive life changes are generated.

INTEGRATING FUTURES STUDIES AND POSITIVE PSYCHOLOGY IN EDUCATION

Futures studies and positive psychology are two disciplines that can ideally complement each other. Futures-oriented disciplines have either focused on predicting economic and technological developments (futures research) or on critical reflection and alternative design of global areas such as social justice and ecological sustainability (futures studies) (Gidley & Hampson, 2005). In the first case, the so-called hard facts are put in the foreground and the psychological and social factors are largely ignored. In the second case, the image of an ideal society is outlined. Even if this perspective has already made great social and ecological achievements possible, global issues generally elude the direct and personal influence of the individual. In both cases, the impression can arise that one can imagine a (better) future, but there is hardly anything one can do to actively shape it or avoid undesirable consequences.

Positive psychology deals with the factors that promote personal well-being. This addresses above all the life of the individual and, in part, the quality of social relationships. Flourishing usually means the fulfilled life of an individual human being. Similarly, hope and optimism usually refer to the positive expectations for the future in an individual's life. The great social hopes—the (collective) hopes that exceed the horizon of the individual human being—have been, until now, largely neglected in positive psychology. Even though virtues, character strengths, and flourishing always include a social dimension, there is still the danger of an overly individualistic perspective.

PAST EXPERIENCES: BUILDING HOPE FOR THE FUTURE

Based on Snyder's (2002) hope theory, Lopez et al. (2000) have developed a five-week program for high school students called Building Hope for the Future. The aim is to support students in defining concrete goals and planning their implementation. Snyder (2002) conceptualizes hope as a personal strength with the following three abilities:

1. *Definition of goals*: Goals are what you set your hopes on. Clearly defined goals are easier to achieve than abstract or general goals.
2. *Pathways thinking*: This is the perceived self-competence regarding the development of possible strategies, ways, and solutions to achieve the goals.
3. *Agency thinking*: Refers to the motivation and willpower to implement these strategies.

The students met once a week on five different afternoons for one hour after school. The steps of the program were as follows (Marques et al., 2011):

1. The first meeting introduced the students to the theory of hope and its importance for positive change processes.
2. The second meeting was dedicated to the general structuring and differentiation of meaningful goals, plans for implementation and the development of willpower, and first reflections on concrete personal goals.
3. In the third week, the students were able to concretize their personal goals. It was important to formulate personally significant goals as concretely and specifically as possible.
4. At the fourth meeting, students reflected on their goals again and developed positive stories regarding these goals.
5. At the end, the students exchanged positive experiences and planned the next steps.

Although the Snyder and Lopez program certainly had positive effects at the individual level, its scope and impact are limited. The limitations of Snyder's theory of hope and its application in the school environment (Snyder et al., 2002, 2003) can be explained by the following features, among others (see Krafft et al., 2017; Krafft & Walker, 2018):

1. In Snyder's theory, hope is conceptualized as an iterative cognitive process. The emotional dimension and the existential-transcendental dimension play a subordinate role or no role at all.
2. It is mainly about individual short- and medium-term goals. Typical goals are better school grades and performance in extracurricular activities (sports, hobbies, etc.). Long-term goals and sustainability in the sense of social and ecological contexts are ignored.

3. The students take the world for granted and are not encouraged to critically question existing situations and practices. There is an adaptive but not imaginative, formative, and creative teaching methodology.
4. Moral values, altruistic motives, and virtues and character strengths are ignored. The right and good are not discussed. There is no holistic view of the human being.
5. Hope is understood as perceived self-competence in terms of self-esteem and self-confidence. Social and other resources (e.g., individual beliefs and values) are acknowledged but hardly considered in the concrete implementation.

For our purposes, this approach must be supplemented and extended. For many authors in futures research, especially in the discipline of futures studies, schools should place more emphasis on teaching and developing a fundamental awareness of how to actively shape the world for the better, instead of only optimizing oneself. Only on this basis can further competencies such as goal orientation, planning, and performance be developed (Schütze, 2009).

On the other hand, the many workshops designed by futures researchers, be it Jungk's Future Workshop (Jungk & Müllert, 1989), Ziegler's (1972) Planning as Action, Eckersley's (1999) Scenario Development Workshop, Boulding's (1994) Envisioning the Future, or Hicks's (1994) the Global Futures Project, are exclusively focused on how to imagine, design, and act toward a future situation for a better world in general. They all neglect the characteristics, the goals, and the personal growth of the individual.

POSITIVE FUTURES: INTEGRATING INDIVIDUAL AND SOCIAL FLOURISHING

Based on the complementarity of future studies and positive psychology approaches, we require a method that starts from the possibilities and capabilities of the individual and at the same time assumes a global (social, ecological) perspective as its field of action. Since major changes and profound transformations usually cannot take place overnight, this approach will require a focus on the medium- to long-term time perspective. The positive futures approach integrates futures studies and positive psychology with combined goals of individual and social flourishing and focuses on hope for a desirable future within the framework of social trends and scenarios. Figure 7.1 shows the relationship between the three dimensions of the resulting positive futures approach and the purpose of a holistic, individual, and, at the same time, social

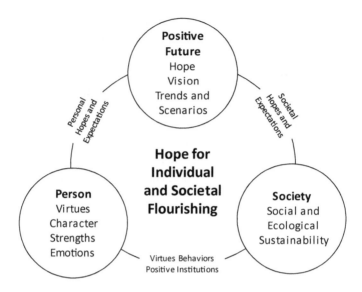

Figure 7.1. *Positive Futures*—Individual and Social Flourishing

(including ecological) flourishing. On the one hand, there are personal hopes and expectations for a fulfilled life. On the other hand, social hopes and expectations of a world in harmony and peace can be addressed.

When young people take a long-term and global perspective and develop their character strengths, virtues, and potentials to shape a socially and ecologically sustainable society, both their own and the collective well-being within positive institutions are promoted. This does not always mean that everyone must trigger a major social revolution. It is usually enough for people to achieve something in their immediate environment (family, leisure and voluntary activities, environmental commitments, etc.) through their empathic, caring, and virtuous behavior. Personal well-being and flourishing go hand in hand with a caring social and ecologically sustainable development.

DESIGN OF THE PROGRAM HOPE FOR A BETTER LIFE

The integration of both individual and the societal dimensions is the leitmotif for the design of the program Hope for a Better Life. Based on positive experiences and emotions as well as individual capabilities and character strengths, images of a better (socially and ecologically) sustainable life and world are developed, and personal activities for their fulfillment are derived. Instead of striving only for the best possible self, where the focus is mainly restricted to setting personal goals (Niemiec, 2017), the Hope for a Better Life program connects character strengths with the image of a better life for oneself, for others, and for the world in general. Hope for a Better Life has been designed according to the following principles:

1. Students should be able to design alternative visions of the future, regardless of whether or not these appear realistic from today's point of view.
2. They should deal with current problems and worries as little as possible. Criticism and complaints about the current situation should be reduced to a minimum.
3. Students should become aware of the positive experiences and emotions in their own lives: What makes them happy? When do they feel comfortable? What do they find particularly good?
4. Students should recognize the basic human needs behind these positive experiences (e.g., connectedness, meaningfulness, well-being, autonomy, etc.).
5. The visions of the future should not refer to superficial things, especially not only to material aspects. The focus should be on the human being, a fulfilled life in the social and ecological environment.
6. Based on the character strengths and positive experiences of the individual, students should sketch scenarios of a flourishing society and community of people.
7. The students should be able to think about what and how they can contribute to the fulfillment of the hoped-for visions of the future.

The Hope for a Better Life program consists of six steps, which can be shortened or extended as required. The program has been inspired by similar workshops designed by the pioneers in this field, including Boulding (1994), Eckersley (1999), Hicks (1994), Jungk (Jungk & Müllert, 1989), and Ziegler (1972).

In the following sections, the individual steps for the implementation of the program are described. This is only a blueprint that must be further elaborated, supplemented, and adapted to the cultural reality of each country.

Step 1: Introduction to the Program

The purpose of step 1 is to provide information about the disciplines of futures studies and positive psychology and to create awareness of current megatrends and research findings in these fields. The teacher or moderator discusses with the students such questions as: "What megatrends do you know? How do these influence your daily life, or how will they influence your everyday life in the future? What are the characteristics of a good and fulfilling life?"

Step 2: Remembering Past Positive Experiences

The purpose of step 2 is to become aware of past positive experiences and generate positive emotions. In this way, students' imaginations can be activated. Students form pairs (free choice). Each student interviews the partner about their positive experiences using the AI method. Students are asked to remember beautiful experiences and to savor them again. Each student should think of three personal experiences and describe them in detail. An experience may have occurred recently or a long time ago. These experiences must only be beautiful memories that trigger positive feelings in the students. The students should describe the situation in detail; for example, the people involved, the smells, pictures, sounds, and feelings. By remembering beautiful moments, students are training their imaginations, and will be able to imagine similar situations in the future. It is particularly important to find out which experiences have triggered which kind of positive feelings and experiences (e.g., good grades—pride; conversation with parents—security).

Step 3: Positive Emotions, Character Strengths, and Flourishing

Based on the results of step 2, the purpose of step 3 is to give an overview of the nature and the role of positive emotions, character strengths, and the flourishing life. Furthermore, students should reflect on their previously remembered positive experiences. The teacher or moderator collects attributes of positive experiences and discusses with the students their feelings, thoughts, situations, and involved people. The moderator presents the importance of positive emotions, character strengths, and the dimensions of flourishing as the essential characteristics of a fulfilled and happy life. The students self-assess on a prepared form how important the respective emotions, character strengths, and dimensions of flourishing are for them (scaling 1 = unimportant to 5 = very important) and create a personal ranking.

Step 4: Alternative and Desired Future Scenarios

This step stands at the core of the entire program. Its purpose is to promote students' creativity and imagination in the development of alternative visions of a desirable future. Students are divided into groups of four to five persons and are invited on a mental journey twenty to thirty years into the future. The students can close their eyes as the moderator leads them mentally out of the building into a new world. Students are encouraged to think about something that does not yet exist. They are asked to look very closely to see what this world looks like. As soon as the students return from the future journey, they describe to the groups what they have seen and record their experiences. The groups are reminded to acknowledge positive emotions, character strengths, and dimensions of flourishing. Some introductory questions are: "What are the most important features and characteristics of the desired future? Which areas are affected (family, work, health, environment, etc.)? What do the cities look like?" The groups then create a common picture (scenario) of the imagined future. This should contain colored drawings, collages with pictures from magazines, and written texts. Each group then presents its vision of the future to the plenary.

Step 5: Criteria and Characteristics of Different Future Scenarios

The fifth step involves a debriefing of the previous step 4. The purpose is to identify the main features of the desired futures. The teacher or moderator asks the groups to give their scenario a suitable title or name. The moderator creates a list with the names of all future scenarios and records with the students the main characteristics as well as the advantages and disadvantages of the individual future scenarios.

Step 6: Planning Activities in the Present

The purpose of step 6 is to combine the desirable future scenarios with concrete goals, activities, and measures in the present. In individual work, each student considers what they want to do this year to contribute to the positive future. First, everyone considers what options they have for action. Each student creates a list of activities in the family, in the neighborhood, at school, and so on. Then students think of short-term goals they want to achieve.

Possible questions are: "What can I do to achieve these visions of the future? What can I do about them today? What can I do differently in my daily life?" Afterward, the students exchange ideas in trios. Again, in the plenary, some of these activities and measures are collected on call and briefly discussed (possibly grouped into categories like *family, school, neighborhood,* etc.). The program closes with an evaluation and a feedback round from the participants.

SUMMARY

The first purpose of the current project is the development of a new approach called positive futures, which results from the integration of futures studies and positive psychology. The (first) concrete field of application for the implementation of the new approach is school education, which is why the second purpose focuses on the design of a new program of hope called Hope for a Better Life. Specifically, the aim is to combine best practices methodically and didactically from future workshops and the methodology of AI with the target group of students in secondary schools. This program will train students to reflect on alternative future scenarios and the design of positive future images based on positive emotions, virtues, character strengths, and the dimensions of a fulfilled life.

We began with the presentation of the social discipline called futures studies, which has the objective of developing and evaluating different visions of the future. The aim is to examine alternative and desirable futures, in the conviction that we should not only adapt to the future but also must actively and responsibly shape it. For this, we need plans based on individual and collective interests, values, and dreams of a better life and world. Hope counters both fear and worries and apathy and helplessness because it inspires faith and confidence in the attainability of a prosperous future. The commonly desired futures are reflected in socially peaceful and harmonious as well as ecologically sustainable visions of a prosperous society. They express values such as justice, respect, courage, commitment, helpfulness, friendliness, and honesty, among many others. Finally, futures studies aims to help people assess their own lives and the state of the world, and subsequently to identify both goals and ways to create a better future.

Futures studies uses a variety of methods and instruments, including trend analysis and scenario techniques, where people discuss their expectations for the future and their fears and hopes and develop common visions of the future. Such procedures trigger an inner cognitive, emotional, and existential process of learning and growth, in which existing worldviews are critically reflected and new worldviews and visions of the future are developed. Futures studies aims to contribute to the positive development of children and young people by designing future visions that stimulate their motivation, willingness to change, critical and creative thinking, values, and sense of responsibility.

Positive psychology seeks answers to the question of the good and the fulfilled life. It focuses on the positive aspects of life, especially on the hope and confidence that even in difficult times, despite difficulties and disappointments, it is possible to lead a better life if one adopts a personal attitude accordingly. To achieve this type of attitude, we need to sharpen our awareness of positive experiences and associated positive emotions as well as of human virtues and character strengths. Adopting such an attitude serves to shape positive social institutions such as happy families, enthusiastic schools, meaningful jobs, friendly social relationships, and much more.

Positive education is an applied field of positive psychology focusing on schools and educational institutions. Its mission is to offer young people a learning and development environment full of motivation, enthusiasm, joy, and, above all, hope. By promoting character strengths, positive education promotes optimal development and makes a fulfilled life for young people possible. The development of moral competence and a good character also manifests itself in the choice of meaningful personal and social goals.

All these elements converge in the design of the Hope for a Better Life program. Inspired by the AI method, Hope for a Better Life brings positive experiences and feelings into the consciousness of students. As students create alternative and positive images of the future about one's own life and the world, they adopt a holistic, medium- to long-term perspective. The aim is to convey essential elements of a fulfilled life and at the same time to develop a concrete vision for a world characterized by harmony and sustainability through the development of personal virtues and character strengths. With this project, we would like to contribute to a responsible debate about the future as well as to the optimal development of young people who shape their lives and the world in a positive way.

REFERENCES

Beare, H., & Slaughter, R. (1993). *Education for the 21st century*. Routledge.

Bell, W. (1996). An overview of futures studies. In R. Slaughter (Ed.), *The knowledge base of futures studies: Foundations* (pp. 28–56). DDM Media Group.

Bell, W. (2009). *Foundations of futures studies: History, purposes, knowledge. Volume I: Human science for a new era*. Transaction.

Bloch, E. (1959). Das Prinzip Hoffnung. Suhrkamp Taschenbuch Verlag.

Boulding, E. (1994). Image and action in peace building. In D. Hicks (Ed..), *Preparing for the future: Notes & queries for concerned educators* (pp. 61–84). Adamantine.

Brunstad, P. O. (2002). Longing for belonging: Youth culture in Norway. In J. Gidley, N. Ingwersen, & S. Inayatullah (Eds.), *Youth futures: Comparative research and transformative visions* (pp. 143–154). Greenwood.

Burow, O. A. (2011). *Positive Pädagogik. Sieben Wege zu Lernfreude und Schulglück.* Beltz.

Cohn, M. A., & Fredrickson, B. L. (2006). Beyond the moment, beyond the self: Shared ground between selective investment theory and the broaden-and-build theory of positive emotions. *Psychological Inquiry, 17*(1), 39–44.

Cohn, M. A., & Fredrickson, B. L. (2009). Positive emotions. In C. Snyder & S. Lopez (Eds.), *Oxford handbook of positive psychology* (2d ed., pp. 13–24). Oxford University Press.

Cooperrider, D. L., Peter, Jr., F. S., Whitney, D., & Yaeger, T. F. (2000). Appreciative inquiry: Rethinking human organization toward a positive theory of change. *Team Performance Management, 6*(7–8), 140.

Cooperrider, D. L., & Whitney, D. (2005). *Appreciative inquiry: A positive revolution in change.* Barrett.

Dufault, K. M., & Martocchio, B. C. (1985). Hope: Its spheres and dimensions. *Nursing Clinics of North America, 20,* 2379–2391.

Eckersley, R. (1995). Values and visions: Youth and the failure of modern Western culture. *Youth Studies Australia, 14*(1), 13–21.

Eckersley, R. (1999). Dreams and expectations: Young people's expected and preferred futures and their significance for education. *Futures, 31*(1), 73–90.

Eckersley, R. (2002). Future visions, social realities, and private lives: Young people and their personal well-being. In J. Gidley, N. Ingwersen, & S. Inayatullah (Eds.), *Youth futures: Comparative research and transformative visions* (pp. 31–42). Greenwood.

Eliott, J. A. (2005). What have we done with hope? A brief history. In J. A. Eliott (Ed.), *Interdisciplinary perspectives on hope* (pp. 3–45). Nova.

Erikson, E. (1963). *Childhood and society* (2nd ed. rev. and enl.). W. W. Norton.

Farran, C. J., Herth, K. A., & Popovich, J. M. (1995). *Hope and hopelessness: Critical clinical constructs.* Sage.

Frankl, V. E. (1959). The spiritual dimension in existential analysis and logotherapy. *Journal of Individual Psychology, 15*(2), 157–165.

Fredrickson, B. L. (2004). The broaden-and-build theory of positive emotions. *Philosophical Transactions of the Royal Society of London. Series B: Biological Sciences, 359*(1449), 1367–1377.

Fredrickson, B. L. (2009). *Positivity: Groundbreaking research reveals how to embrace the hidden strength of positive emotions. Overcome negativity and thrive.* Crown.

Fredrickson, B. L. (2013). Positive emotions broaden and build. *Advances in Experimental Social Psychology, 47,* 1–53.

Freire, P. (1994). *Pedagogy of hope.* Continuum.

Gidley, J. M. (2016). *Postformal education: A philosophy for complex futures.* Springer.

Gidley, J. M., & Hampson, G. P. (2005). The evolution of futures in school education. *Futures, 37*(4), 255–271.

Halpin, D. (2002). *Hope and education: The role of the utopian imagination.* Routledge.

Hicks, D. (1994). *Educating for the future—A practical classroom guide.* WWF UK.

Hicks, D. (1996). Retrieving the dream: How students envision their preferable futures. *Futures, 28*(8), 741–749.

Hicks, D. (2003). *Lessons for the future: The missing dimension in education.* Routledge.

Hicks, D. (2012). The future only arrives when things look dangerous: Reflections on futures education in the UK. *Futures, 44*(1), 4–13.

Huppert, F. A., & So, T. T. (2013). Flourishing across Europe: Application of a new conceptual framework for defining well-being. *Social Indicators Research, 110*(3), 837–861.

Jungk, R., & Müllert, N. (1989). *Zukunftswerkstätten. Mit Phantasie gegen Routine und Resignation,* Heyne.

Keyes, C. L. (2005). Mental illness and/or mental health? Investigating axioms of the complete state model of health. *Journal of Consulting and Clinical Psychology, 73*(3), 539–548.

Krafft, A. M., Martin-Krumm, C., & Fenouillet, F. (2017). Adaptation, further elaboration, and validation of a scale to measure hope as perceived by people: Discriminant value and predictive utility vis-à-vis dispositional hope. *Assessment, 26*(8), 1594–1609.

Krafft, A. M., & Walker, A. M. (2018). *Exploring the concept and experience of hope—Empirical findings and the virtuous circle of hope.* In A. Krafft, P. Perrig-Chiello, A. Walker (Eds.), *Hope for a good life* (pp. 21–60). Springer, Cham.

Lopez, S. J., Bouwkamp, J., Edwards, L. M., & Teramoto Pedrotti, J. (2000). *Making hope happen via brief interventions.* Second Positive Psychology Summit.

Marcel, G. (1951). *Homo viator: Introduction to a metaphysics of hope* (E. Crawfurd & P. Seaton, Trans.). St. Augustine.

Marques, S. C., Lopez, S. J., & Pais-Ribeiro, J. L. (2011). Building hope for the future: A program to foster strengths in middle-school students. *Journal of Happiness Studies, 12*(1), 139–152.

McKibben, B. (2007). *Hope, human and wild: True stories of living lightly on the earth.* Milkweed.

McQuaid, M., White, M., & Waters, L. (2016). *Making wellbeing achievable for every school. Creating a positive education schools association: An Appreciative inquiry approach.* Summit Booklet. Positive Education Schools Association.

Niemiec, R. M. (2017). *Character strengths interventions: A field guide for practitioners.* Hogrefe.

Nordensvard, J. (2014). Dystopia and disutopia: Hope and hopelessness in German pupils' future narratives. *Journal of Educational Change, 15*(4), 443–465.

Park, N. (2004). Character strengths and positive youth development. *The Annals of the American Academy of Political and Social Science, 591*(1), 40–54.

Park, N., & Peterson, C. (2006). Moral competence and character strengths among adolescents: The development and validation of the Values in Action Inventory of Strengths for Youth. *Journal of Adolescence, 29*(6), 891–909.

Peterson, C., & Seligman, M. E. (2004). *Character strengths and virtues: A handbook and classification.* Oxford University Press.

Pruyser, P. W. (1986). Maintaining hope in adversity. *Pastoral Psychology, 35*(2), 120–131.

Riner, R. D. (1987). Doing futures research—anthropologically. *Futures, 19*(3), 311–328.

Rogers, M., & Tough, A. (1996). Facing the future is not for wimps. *Futures, 28*(5), 491–496.

Rorty, R. (1999). *Philosophy and Social Hope.* Penguin.

Rorty, R. (2002). Hope and the future. *Peace Review, 14*(2), 149–155.

Rubin, A. (2002). Reflections upon the late-modern transition as seen in the images of the future held by young Finns. In J. Gidley, N. Ingwersen, & S. Inayatullah (Eds.), *Youth futures: Comparative research and transformative visions* (pp. 99–110). Greenwood.

Ryan, R. M., & Deci, E. L. (2001). On happiness and human potentials: A review of research on hedonic and eudaimonic well-being. *Annual Review of Psychology, 52*(1), 141–166.

Ryff, C. D., & Singer, B. (2000). Interpersonal flourishing: A positive health agenda for the new millennium. *Personality and Social Psychology Review, 4*(1), 30–44.

Schütze, F. (2009). Die Berücksichtigung der elementaren Dimensionen biografischer Arbeit in der Schule der Zukunft. In D. Bosse & P. Posch (Eds.), *Schule 2020 aus Expertensicht: Zur Zukunft von Schule, Unterricht und Lehrerbildung* (pp. 359–364). Springer-Verlag.

Scioli, A., Ricci, M., Nyugen, T., & Scioli, E. R. (2011). Hope: Its nature and measurement. *Psychology of Religion and Spirituality, 3*(2), 78.

Seliger, R. (2014). *Positive leadership—Die revolution in der Führung.* Schäffer-Poeschel Verlag.

Seligman, M. E. (2004). *Authentic happiness: Using the new positive psychology to realize your potential for lasting fulfillment.* Simon and Schuster.

Seligman, M. (2014). Flourishing as a goal of international policy. In R. Costanza & I. Kubiszewski (Eds.), *Creating a sustainable and desirable future: Insights from 45 global thought leaders* (pp. 113–116). World Scientific.

Seligman, M. E., & Csíkszentmihályi, M. (2000). Positive psychology—An introduction. *American Psychologist, 55*(1), 5–14.

Slaughter, R. (1994). Changing images of futures in the 20th century. In D. Hicks (Ed.), *Preparing for the future—Notes & queries for concerned educators* (pp. 39–59). Adamantine.

Snyder, C. R. (2002). Hope theory: Rainbows in the mind. *Psychological Inquiry,* 13(4), 249–275.

Snyder, C. R., Feldman, D. B., Shorey, H. S., & Rand, K. L. (2002). Hopeful choices: A school counselor's guide to hope theory. *Journal of Personality and Social Psychology, 65*(5), 1061–1070.

Snyder, C. R., Lopez, S. J., Shorey, H. S., Rand, K. L., & Feldman, D. B. (2003). Hope theory, measurements, and applications to school psychology. *School Psychology Quarterly, 18*(2), 122.

Toffler, A. (1974). *Learning for tomorrow: The role of the future in education.* Random House.

Ziegler, W. L. (1972). *Planning as action: Techniques of inventive planning workshops.* Educational Policy Research Center, Syracuse University Research Corporation.

HOPE FOR DEVELOPING COMPASSIONATE RELATIONS WITH HUMANS AND MACHINES

Emotional Cognition and Islamic Education in North America

SHER AFGAN TAREEN

INTRODUCTION

This study was conducted in one of the 20 largest public school districts in the United States with nearly 46% of students classified as racial minorities.[1] Yet very few seem to benefit from the large sum of money that is allocated by the public education system. Reports are rife of expulsion and other forms of disciplinary measures that curtail students' access to a quality education and undermine prospects in the labor market.[2] Even when left unpunished and when scholastically capable, many minority students have trouble enrolling in advanced academic programs such as Level IV.[3] Whatever the decision-making process or educational framework, this state of affairs is suggestive of racism operating within the school system in terms of educational response to student ability or behavior. One Muslim mother from the area recalls that despite having a studious work ethic, her son did not qualify for a gifted student program offered by his school. Much to her surprise, she went on to discover that the administrator managing the applications for the gifted program happened to be a female migrant from Latin America, someone she never imagined would perpetuate racism. Yet she framed the incident as racism, the source of which she could not identify apart from the computer software the administrator mentioned in her long-winded, unsatisfactory response about why her son's application had been rejected. Experiencing both pain and confusion, the mother decided to quit her job in an IT firm and work instead as a homeschooler.

146

The intense scrutiny over Islam in the wake of 9/11 terror attacks fell most acutely upon Muslim youth attending public schools (Ewing, 2008; Jamal & Naber, 2008; Abu El-Hajj, 2015; Jaffe-Walter 2016). Over the past two decades, concerns over the mental health and self-esteem of their children have prompted Muslim mothers from all over North America to invest in private Islamic school systems that broadly maintain public school curricula while incorporating courses on the Quran, Arabic, and ritual activities such as salat in order to build a community for Muslim youth (Grewal & Coolidge, 2013). Islamic schools have been credited for kindling a spirit for civic engagement and volunteering to help members of the broader community that includes non-Muslims (Zine, 2008; Cristillo, 2009). While there remains an ongoing suspicion of insularity, the most piercing criticism bemoans the ways in which Islamic schools assimilate Muslim youth into a sterile, white suburbia by sanitizing their bodies from the contagion of urban black aesthetics. Such concerns tend to focus on the school dress code. In her ethnographic study of Islam in the Chicagoland area for instance, Suad Abdul Khabeer observed that girls who attended Islamic schools in the western suburbs of Chicago were mandated to wear tightly fitted headscarves, which were unlike the loosely fitted *hoodjabs* black Muslim girls like her donned growing up in Chicago's Southside neighborhood. The contrast points to a narrowing of the tradition with Quranic verses and sayings of the Prophet invoked to obscure the boundary between the pure suburb and the decadent city roped around restrictions on what a Muslim girl may wear (Khabeer 2016). Muslim adolescents today are under the siege of the invisible software, as demonstrated by the boy who was disqualified from the gifted student program at his public school. This raises the following two questions: Why does the computer, a technology that was supposed to connect people from all over the world, discriminate, and how does an Islamic model of education restore the hope for an inclusive community?

Wendy Chun highlights a paradoxical feature of computer technology: the freedom it grants to explore the web heightens a desire for control. The conflation between freedom and control is engineered by a ruse of the computer screen. Shifters such as "my documents" create the illusion of ownership and privacy while software corporations surveil your every move on the web and subject you to a user identity based on correlating likeness across large data sets. An otherwise invisible transformation registers a visible effect of paranoia on the face when we actively perform these discriminatory roles to seek the comfort of lacking any conflict in our virtual communications (Chun, 2008). Conflict however undergirds most intimate social relationships, especially that between a mother and her children. This study explores how Muslim women draw upon their experience of motherhood to teach adolescents about the value of embracing vulnerability in their day-to-day interactions with friends, parents, and teachers. The case study is a predominantly women-run kindergarten to eighth-grade Islamic school based on fieldwork I conducted during the fall and spring of 2019–2020.[4] Over the course of talking to my interviewees, I was struck by the ways in which they framed education as a process of cognizing emotion and cultivating the feeling of compassion. Compassion, I argue, is an emotional antidote to the paranoia that has been rampantly growing due to our transformation from humas into users on the interface and a useful lens for understanding how Muslim women are leading the fight to redress the perils of racism in an age of artificial intelligence.

THE SETTING

The area in focus was once a quiet forest known for its oak and hickory woods, but since the late sixties, it has rapidly transformed into a bustling city drawing workers from all around the world in search of jobs related to information technology. A Lyft ride passes by Pilates and Yoga studios as well as IT and business-solution firms. As the car turns left, the road expands into four lanes, bustling with cars in both directions by late afternoon. A few miles into the drive, tall and lush trees on the edge of the parkway and a community park emerge unannounced, drawing the onlooker to the remains of the forest topography on which the city was built. An Islamic school is located a few yards away on the other end of the road, yet the drive to the school takes a slightly longer, convoluted way: a right turn one block later and another immediate right turn onto a road that eventually extends into a large angular parking lot with the school building behind it. Before reaching the parking lot, the car curves left and circles a preschool, a software company, and a fourth- to twelfth-grade private school. Sharp-edged sofas, whiteboards, a basketball rim, and posters are scattered around a large unenclosed area inside the private school as if its interior were designed to mimic a startup technology firm.

RITUALS OF COMPASSION

The Islamic school in question differs from a conventional school in that it was originally built as a three-story office building. Large square-shaped windows occupy most of the surface space of the front wall, materializing that very cold and faceless aesthetics commonly attributed to modernist federal buildings.

Yet in this austere building, school faculty, staff, and students interact in such a way that over the past two decades the premises have been transformed into more than just a school for acquiring knowledge; they are now conceived of as a home infused with feelings of compassion. Going beyond the severity of architecture or assumptions of cold educational perspectives, the focus on compassion has been deliberate and is produced through several practices. These include conducting *salat* (ritual prayer and an act of worship that is enjoined in the Quran) and other activities, such as ice-skating, afforded by the area's urban landscape. Both seemingly disparate activities are constitutive elements of an integrated curriculum that facilitates Muslim youth cognizing their emotions and which emerged from the experience of the school's cofounders raising their children together.

Such emphasis on motherhood is no surprise.[5] Conceived as an extension of the home, the school consolidates motherhood and teaching around an integrated model of curriculum. The core subjects taught at the school comply with the state's standards of learning yet simultaneously digress from public schools with Allah's compassion scaffolding each course. A snowflake, as a manifestation of Allah's compassion unto others, for example, is studied: its angles measured for a mathematics course, its content examined for a science course, and its features described for an English course. Using this process, students develop a mentality of interdisciplinarity. This is holistic understanding. Students identify overlaps between such seemingly disparate subjects as science, math, and English based on the conviction that Allah's compassion consolidates all. Far from being reducible to enrollment in a supplementary set of courses in Arabic and Islamic studies, the process of learning Islam at the school entails measuring God's compassion as it registers onto a moving body. The body moves rigorously during the process of conducting *salat*, for instance. On placing the thumbs behind the ear lobes, one declares the intent to pray. With an arched back, the palms of both hands extend to the knees. The knees collapse, with the forehead touching the ground and both hands placed on the ground slightly ahead of the face. With legs crossed over one another, the head rotates to the right and then to the left, and lastly, hands are placed over one another in prayer. Students routinely arrive at the school worried that some of these intricate movements are commands that demand obeyance. Their experience at the school lets them reimagine the *salat* as a process of embodying the compassion of an intimate God, rather than a mechanized set of prescriptions obligated by a distant God. Allah's compassion transgresses the boundary between a private self and their surroundings. Breathing techniques also form an integral component of prayer. The principal prepared a written guideline with steps for deep breathing in a document called *Sakinah Space: Purpose and Use.*[6] Far from referring to breathing as a metaphor for *salat*, breathing exercises are incorporated as preparation for conducting *salat*. All of them align the mind and the body around counting numbers.

Implementing what is termed the *bear breath*, for instance, pupils are taught to count to four while inhaling, to count to two during a pause, and then to count to four while exhaling, and the cycle repeats. The reference to the bear is to evoke the image of a bear hibernating, grounded, and settled. Alternatively, some breathing exercises such as the bunny breath combine staccato inhales consisting of three quick breaths through the nose with long exhales. A similarly fast-paced hissing sound allows pupils to connect with their breath—something that often eludes them at times when they feel upset. In addition to counting breaths through the nostrils and the mouth, the hands also help students to count as they breathe. With the index finger of the opposite hands, students trace up the ascending fingers as they slowly and deeply inhale for five seconds, and then trace down the descending fingers as they exhale for five seconds. After going around all five fingers and thumb, they will have taken five deep breaths.

Youth in the United States are often introduced to Yoga through breathing exercises. Wary of criticism over the possibility of *salat* conflated as yoga, the principal reiterates that "it isn't *bida* [innovation]" for pupils to do breathing exercises before they pray. Rather than corrupting the tradition, breathing exercises heighten pupils' desire to conduct *salat*. Time slows down as they inhale and exhale counting down numbers and the ensuing *rakats* (kneelings) stretch longer, recentering themselves as a conduit for Allah's compassion. As an emotion acquired through movement, compassion also enables students to discipline themselves apart from adult supervision.

Another initiative to promote compassion and emotional development is the inclusion of *sakena* corners (*sakenas* are quiet areas) in each classroom. These are areas of the classroom where students can regain composure when they feel overwhelmed by stress. Students have even started to design *sakena* corners at their homes to maintain equilibrium in times of distress. *Sakena* corners spatially transform disciplinary regimes such as time-outs, which reify division between adults and adolescents. A time-out corner signals punishment for misbehavior. With their movement impeded, the student becomes angrier and even less inclined to cooperate. *Sakena* corners help students regain tranquility through movement. During one school event, a student became rowdy with another, and the *sakena* corner calmed matters, allowing him to reassess his outlook on being disciplined. The child's mother was surprised by his reaction when she asked him about his day. She expected that he would be reluctant to describe the aftermath of his fracas and would shrug his shoulders and murmur displeasure about spending the rest of the day outside the principal's office. Instead, he spoke confidently and without guilt about how he had regained his tranquility while spending time inside a *sakena* corner. He fondly described scrolling beads with his thumb and softly reciting *Bismillahi Rahmani Raheem* one bead after another. Most *sakena* corners include a variety of tactile objects suitable for the age range of that classroom's students. In addition to scrolling beads, students may observe images of a peaceful landscape, listen to audio of calming sounds, or dig their hands inside a box filled with soft sand. These objects and activities stimulate the senses to help students learn to feel compassion for themselves at times when they feel "frustrated, distracted, sad, angry, or otherwise needing a break" from the overwhelming commotion of bodies between morning and afternoon. Of course, students might routinely clash with each other, compassion skills notwithstanding, and in such scenarios, the school's counselor intervenes. Rather than verbally threatening pupils with ramifications, the counselor's office serves as one large *sakena* corner with tactile objects and activities for the students to cultivate tranquility through touch.

Spacious and dimly lit, the counselor's office is furnished with comfortable beanbags on the floor surrounded by tactile objects and games such as Jenga. Playing Jenga, the student and the counselor take turns moving a small wooden block on a growing tower while trying to keep the tower from falling. As they play, the counselor asks questions from the feelings and coping pamphlet: Have you ever bottled up your anger or pain? What happened when you could not anymore? What bugs you? How do you deal with anger? How easy is it for you to forgive those who caused you pain? Would you rather forgive or forget? How do you take care of yourself? How do you express love to other people? How do you appreciate yourself? You forgive (blank) because (blank). Are you happy with who you are? What do you feel right now? You feel (blank) years old inside because (blank). What are five to ten things crucial for you to be happy? What is the last thing you did to make yourself happy? How would you cope if you lost everything you own? How do you feel when your parents are upset with you? When you are angry, how do you look? When are you the happiest? When have you felt lonely? When do you feel pride? When was the last time you cried and why? How can you work through a painful memory and try to let it go? Each time a student places a wooden block on the tower, they answer a question about emotion. Exterior play, therefore, is accompanied by interior play whereby the student builds the capacity to cognize their emotions, especially feelings of anger. Rather than directing students toward an alternative feeling, the questions encourage them to play with anger, to reenact detailed memories of anger from the last time they felt that emotion.

Another method the counselor employs is to have students form a restorative circle outside of the building. On the day of our interview, the counselor was leading a restorative circle to help a group of fifth graders overcome feelings of animosity they had about gender. The conflict started during lunch break when the boys complained about the girls taking too much time eating and wasting precious recess time. The students initially showed little signs of reconciliation. One of the boys feigned a bee attack, shouting, "Bee!" to purposefully scare a girl who had been recently stung and feared going outdoors. His behavior corroborated the counselor's assessment that gender structures the ways adolescents express their feelings. Boys act out aggression, and girls withdraw, leading to low self-esteem. By allowing boys and girls to voice how they feel and also take responsibility for making others feel hurt, the counselor helped both groups express their feelings differently.

To facilitate compassion among students, the teaching staff actively destabilizes the binary between adolescence and adulthood, situating students into a series of hierarchical relationships among themselves. For example, the other school counselor I interviewed had instituted a peer-mediation program to address student behavior and discipline. This program settles student disputes by enlisting a third student who listens to both parties without passing judgment.[7] The program effectively dissuades teachers from issuing harsh punishments and turns student conflict into an opportunity for them to develop a social relationship. The younger students learn proper conduct by observing the older students and emulating how they behave. By disciplining the gestures and movements of their bodies, the students learn to practice proper conduct without necessarily reading the student handbook a priori. One of the parents distinguished discipline as a code of ethics documented in a handbook from the bodily configuration of discipline at the school by invoking the problem of coercion. The hierarchical relationships formed between older and younger students, she argued, allow students to reimagine ethical conduct from "something weird like I have to do this" to a habit one learns volitionally. This new configuration of discipline, whereby students do not follow commands but instead proactively learn to discipline themselves, also shapes the playground.

The teaching staff rarely intervenes on the playground, instead allowing students to develop compassion for each other without adult supervision. One of the key elements of the playground is the buddy bench. Students are expected to sit on the buddy bench when they are not sure "who to play with and talk to" and when they "want to assess the situation before joining a group." The school administrators trace the idea of a buddy bench to an "eight-year-old boy who lives in Pennsylvania," someone with no affinity with the Muslim tradition. But as a place to meet and make new friends, the buddy bench embodies values that are part of the Islamic tradition, including *husnul khuluq* (good character), *ukhuwa* (community), *niyyah* (intention and purpose), and *amana* (steward-ship). By responding to students sitting on the buddy bench, peers "extend a hand of kindness to someone who needs it," "foster friendship among peers," commit to reaching out to someone and thereby fulfill their purpose in life "to know one another," and, lastly, "take care of everything on this earth which includes one another."

These benefits of the buddy bench, listed in a pamphlet called *Buddy Bench Overview*[7] that I was given access to during my fieldwork, underscore the importance of movement. When a student asks another student to play a game they do not want to play, teachers are encouraged to convince that student to play nonetheless, "even for a little while." In an alternative sce-nario, in which both students prefer to sit on the buddy bench and "talk for a while," teachers are encouraged to ask them to get off the bench and "do something." In other words, the buddy bench must be used in ways that challenge Muslim youth to get to know someone they may otherwise never talk to.

This deeply Islamic principle of getting to know someone also informs the school's establishment of a pluralism program, during which students listen to an authoritative figure from another religious tradition. Such panels initially disconcerted parents, many of whom feared that the guest might exploit the impressionable minds of the students and convince them to renounce Islam. The principal dismissed such suspicions as a reflection of weak spirituality. The students' experience reinforced this critique. Rather than swinging between disdain and awe, the students developed a resilient outlook. They recognized key differences between Islam and the guest's religious tradition without elevating the difference into an existential threat to their own tradition that could only be resolved through accepting or decrying it.

Another event that had a similar demystifying effect was a visit to President George W. Bush's White House during the post-9/11 war on terror when US soldiers were actively killing Muslims in Afghanistan and Iraq. Many parents questioned this trip, as they were critical of Bush. During the visit, students asked President Bush to explain his understanding of peace, a question they kept repeating whenever he started talking about his dogs instead. When asked to share their experiences in a debriefing session on their return to school, one student confessed he had expected the president to have horns, an image that fits his caricature of evil. Another student gained the insight that someday he could preside over the country. Rather than a source of pride or inspiration, the visit changed his understanding of the president as all-powerful. He recognized that even Bush, a president who at the time was commanding wars in two Muslim countries simultaneously, ultimately assumed the subjectivity of a human, deeply flawed and imperfect, yet relatable for even a Muslim adolescent growing up in post-9/11 America. Students left feeling both reassured about their Islamic identity and less concerned about the non-Islamic identity of the speaker. They learned about the belief systems of the speaker's religious tradition but remembered the compassion affecting both parties.

THE PEDAGOGY OF COMPASSION

The Islamic school movement in North America offers an opportunity to participate in a tradition of Islamic education in which learning structures social relationships. The former principal of the school traces the tradition to the nascent Muslim community led by the Prophet Muhammad, who, she recalled, would "only teach what he knew his companions would understand."[8] Other important figures in the tradition include Ibn Sina, the renowned tenth-century educator who strongly advocated for classroom teaching. Instead of viewing the classroom as a detached setting where one learns by reading books, however, he saw it as a laboratory to form social relationships that extend beyond the walls of the classroom. To participate in this tradition, the former principal exhorts the contemporary Islamic schoolteachers in North America to identify concepts about classroom teaching in the field of education that builds on the relational model of learning advanced by the Islamic tradition.

An example of one such concept is the Bloom taxonomy of questions (Bloom, 1956). Benjamin Bloom was an educational psychologist who introduced a teaching pedagogy that divides learning objectives into various stages. The first stage asks students to remember previously learned information. In the next stage, students demonstrate their understanding of facts and move up the ladder of critical thinking to evaluating data. This method of teaching cautions against inundating students with information all at once and transforms knowledge from a kind of commodity that one ought to accumulate as much as possible to a marker of undergoing an emotional transformation. The teaching staff draws on such concepts introduced in the field of education to participate in an Islamic tradition of education.

One of the teachers became aware that professionalization and emotional intelligence are intertwined during her graduate coursework in education. She expected this coursework to follow the rubric of a typical classroom learning experience, in which one passively listens to lectures and fulfills necessary assignments. Much to her surprise, the learning was structured by emotion. "You get into your own feelings," she recalled, as students face their classmates and ask them questions. Such a seemingly intimate journey of exploring one's feelings was, ironically, facilitated by students leaning into rather than ignoring their diverse backgrounds. Far from subjective and beyond observation, inner feelings became activated through outer relationships with fellow graduate students.

A third-grade teacher implemented a teaching pedagogy based on how she relates to each student, both individually and as part of a team. For instance, she grades worksheets based on the number of questions each student completes rather than on how many questions they failed to answer. Also, she designs her tests based on the specific skills of each student, noting "a lot of students weaker in math will be higher in arts." Evaluation of class participation also pivots, without following a rigid set of rules. Students who do not feel comfortable talking may attain participation points by writing. All in all, she resists internalizing a mentality of "tests, tests, and more tests"; confident students will pass the standards set by the state through working collaboratively.

Third-grade students, for example, were assigned a group project to build a three-dimensional community. Having previously studied ancient Greece and Rome as major communities in world history, they were asked to assess how the community they inhabit differs from these ancient communities. Students created communities that were rural, urban, or suburban. Each group enlisted a timekeeper, a notetaker, and a supply deliverer without help from the teacher, who refrained from supervising them. The teacher initially feared that chaos would ensue. On the contrary, her students worked together, developing "real-life skills in a way that was fun."

The rhythm of the school is marked by leisure activities that collectively allow for the flow of compassion among not only students but also the entire student body and the parents. Such leisure activities include ice-skating. Every year, students (past and present) convene at a local ice-skating rink with parents and teachers to raise funds for the school. The past year, the entire class of 2018 and their parents attended this fundraiser, far exceeding the minimum number of fifty participants the ice-skating rink requires. In fact, the participants numbered around one hundred, allowing Mahwish, the current president of Parent Teacher Organization (PTO), to raise $500 "without doing any cleaning afterwards." Convenience alone, however, fails to explain why ice-skating has emerged as a sacred ritual that regularly draws such a large number of participants. Most parent attendees are mothers for whom ice-skating is a novel experience. Any sense of self-reliance, independence, and invincibility they may have held disintegrates once they step inside the ice rink. Acutely aware that the ice could drop them at any moment, they search for someone who could hold their hand. Mahwish was struck by the image of "two or three moms on the ice rink holding their kids together." Instead of fear and unease, their faces conveyed excitement. All were vulnerable to an imminent fall yet comforted by that shared vulnerability bringing them together on the ice rink. They glided on ice with their bodies covered from head to toe, enwrapped by a calm energy that differs vastly from the intensity of running a 5K rally or the torpidity of lying on the chaise lounges, sofas, and hammocks at a pool party. The sensation of gliding on ice has been a key ritual practice for women in other religious traditions as well.

One parent noted that women with no access to familial relationships out-side of their husband and children rely extensively on the All-Local American Muslim Center for community. Although this parent attends the center, she does not feel obliged to. In addition to gathering at the homes of her extended family, such as her mother and sister-in-law, she participates in all the outdoor activities planned by the PTO, such as ice-skating, that facilitate the formation of a distinctly familial community. Bound by shared feelings of compassion that extend from Allah to the students and their parents, the familial community gives rise to a distinctly feminine constellation of Islam that draws on the work backgrounds of Muslim mothers in computer technology over the theological training of clerics and imams.

FAMILIES AND THEIR SPACES

The suburban setting of the school offers a case study of a city where the over-abundance of digital technologies has rendered ethnic and national back-grounds obsolete. The school counselor observed that distinctions between a Pakistani and an Iraqi, for instance, do not distinguish the residents. To high-light the regional distinction of Islam between the suburban city and her home-town in Texas, she shared an anecdote about navigating her public school in the wake of 9/11. Back then, she was in sixth grade and had recently started wearing the hijab. Unlike many girls who feared a non-Muslim ripping apart their hijab, seeing it as a political symbol of terror rather than a garment worn to display modesty, she lacked such anxieties about wearing the hijab, remembering "I never felt odd." Rather than navigating the differences between Muslim and non-Muslim, she had to figure out how to differentiate herself from the other Muslim students in her school, who also had Pakistani parents, all living in proximity to one another. Muslim Americans, the counselor observed, "aren't that separated" and instead "mix" and "intermingle" without fretting over the different schools of jurisprudence in the Islamic tradition or transplanting the distinct geographies of these *madhabs* from the Muslim world. The question of why we pray has gained priority over with whom we pray, as more and more time is spent facing the computer than another person.

Digital technology transgresses the boundaries between home and work-places in this school and probably many others. Mahwish embodies the pre-dicament most parents face spending their days inside offices in front of a computer while their children come home from school with no one to greet them other than fellow players of the popular video game Fortnite and You-Tube influencers. In addition to organizing outdoor activities for parents and students such as ice-skating, Mahwish spends her weekdays consult-ing for health-care managers, college administrators, retail business owners, and other clients on the benefits of incorporating such emerging concepts as artificial intelligence and augmented reality into their workplaces. The clients often try to burden the computer with responsibilities that were previously fulfilled by human employees. Computer error consequently unsettles them deeply. Over the years, Mahwish has noticed that many of her colleagues at the firm trace computer error to human error in programming when such spontaneous and unforeseen responses from the computer confirm its mind-fully interpreting commands rather than mindlessly executing them. The illusion that computers lack consciousness comes from a failure to understand the binary language of zeros and ones. Programmers are trained to memo-rize numerical sequences of zeros and ones as equivalences of alphabetical commands. Numbers, however, are irreducible to textual codes. They move in ways that human language can neither regulate nor predict. In that sense, machines affect us with feelings we may not be able to explain but that we can easily observe physically.

Mahwish gained this key insight about machines affecting our feelings once she incorporated the various practices of acquiring compassion from the school into her workplace. In between her hectic meetings with clients, Mahwish routinely conducts *salat* in a fashion popularized at the school, with a set of breathing exercises preceding it. In the absence of breathing exercises, "I can't get anything out of my *rakats*," Mahwish noticed. Far from offering solace from work, her *rakats* (kneelings) allow her to regain focus on her work, specifically as it relates to her capacity to offer advice on the ways computers are alive, fully capable of both reifying existing divisions and building new relationships, especially among youth. Her father's and son's contrasting experiences of engaging with software reveal a lot about the stakes in human and machine relationships. Whenever Mahwish's father requests Amazon's Alexa to play a certain song, for instance, Alexa fails to discern his accent and reacts unresponsively, since it was not built "for anyone other than perfect American accents." In stark contrast to Alexa reifying the divide between American and immigrant is the computer entering into a tactile relationship with Mahwish's son. The physical sensation of "typing on the computer," for instance, creates an expression of joy on the five-year-old's face. When assigned homework by his teachers to "list all the sounds you hear at home," he excitedly reaches for the computer's keyboard over a pen. Among the sounds he lists is the one his computer makes each time he presses the keyboard. Neurologists routinely ignore the touch of fingers typing on the keyboard when they account for the impact of computers on the emotional well-being of teenagers in the contemporary United States, reducing consciousness instead to the brain. By unveiling the inner workings of the brain, neurologists argue, one could corroborate the observations made by childcare specialists that time spent facing the iPhone screen makes teenagers more prone to feeling suicidal.

Parents and educators are acutely aware of the deleterious effects of digital technologies as well. The counselor noticed that the amount of time students spent facing the computer leads to intense feelings of anxiety. Some skip school, complaining, "I am sick" in order to conceal the real cause of truancy: anxiety. Outside the counselor's office, a placard reads "We spend so much time inside or using technology, go out and soak up the sun!" The students she meets in her office resemble Mahwish's children, playing Fortnite on Xbox and watching YouTube influencers at home. Nevertheless, paranoia over the influence of computers on the impressionable minds of youth is strikingly absent, and in its place is hope in Allah's compassion to facilitate a human and machine relationship bound around movement rather than a series of prescribed commands.

Students learn to reimagine computer programming as knowledge produced through movement, not only comparable to but more profoundly a manifestation of the mysterious nature of Allah's compassion. During code hour, for instance, students play video games, including one that simulates the classic story of Aladdin moving on top of the carpet. Through gaming, they learn to program Aladdin's movements without prescribing a set of steps and instead follow Aladdin as he jumps onto the carpet; circles around it; and sits in front of, in the middle of, or along the outer edges of it. Although Aladdin and the student are divided by the interface, both are tied to each other by a motion that may not move from point A to B but that nonetheless feels like movement. At home, such virtual relationships may have begun to replace other forms of relationships that bind family members to each other around shared ethnicity or nationality. The school serves as an extension of these homes, helping students consolidate Islamic piety as proficiency in programming. "They will always interact with technology," Mahwish declared, referring to her two children who attend the school, one is five and other is eight years old. Her voice was full of levity rather than dismay, with technology facilitating rather than undermining her aspirations to strengthen her students' Islamic piety. How Islamic education can facilitate youths' interaction and engagement with technology such as it affects them with feelings of compassion over anxiety, however, remains largely unaddressed.

Scholars routinely privilege a textual conception of Islam to redress the marginalization of Muslims in North America, especially youth whose formative years are spent in educational settings hostile to the concerns and aspirations of their parents. Panjwani (2008) distills the hope emanating from a private Islamic school into a core curriculum that introduces Muslim youth to writings and commentaries of Muslim intellectuals who demonstrate the plurality and diversity of voices within the Islamic tradition. The study of internal contests and debates among Muslim intellectuals on what counts as Islam, the argument goes, will encourage students to rebut an alternative corpus of texts and sayings that juxtapose Islam against Western democracy. Underlying this claim is the assumption that such monolithic representations of Islam do harm by drawing Muslim youth away from Islam in favor of assimilating into the West or toward a militant rendition of Islam that decries the West altogether. Are feelings of anxiety among Muslim youth in the West merely a symptom of an undeveloped appetite for inquiry into the intellectual history of Islam or conditioned by their material surroundings, which are replete with digital technology? I join my fellow contributors (such as Davids, chapter 2) in centering the hope in Islamic education around ritual practices that allow for the possibility of restoring human connection.

At stake is understanding how Islamic education might guide Muslim youth into forming a triadic connection that includes both human and nonhuman actors; namely, digital software. The hope is for Muslim youth to develop a profound relationship with Allah, alive to his existence through thought and movement, such that they are always connected with him as they move through feelings of compassion and submerge the feelings of anxiety that arise when movement is impinged by statis. The students I observed during my fieldwork share with the larger demographic of US youth the propensity to spend most of their time in front of a computer. However, instead of anxiety, they feel compassion, with Muslim women consolidating motherhood and education to situate them in a series of compassionate relationships with themselves, peers, teachers, parents, and, finally, the computer.

REFERENCES

Abu El-Haj, Thea Renda. (2015). *Unsettled belonging: Educating Palestinian American youth after 9/11.* University of Chicago Press.

Bloom, B. (Ed.). (1956). *Taxonomy of educational objectives: Handbook I—The cognitive domain.* David O. McKay.

Chun, W. (2008). *Control and freedom: Power and paranoia in the age of fiber optics.* Massachusetts Institute of Technology Press.

Cristillo, L. (2009). The case for the Muslim school as a civil society actor. In Y. Y. Haddad, J. I. Smith, & F. Senzai (Eds.), *Educating the Muslims of America* (pp. 67–84). Oxford University Press.

Ewing, Katherine Pratt. (2008). *Being and Belonging: Muslims in the United States since 9/11.* Russell Sage Foundation.

Jaffe-Walter, R. (2016). *Coercive concern: Nationalism, liberalism, and the schooling of Muslim youth.* Stanford University Press.

Jamal, A., & Naber, N. (2008). *Race and Arab Americans before and after 9/11: From invisible citizens to visible subjects.* Syracuse University Press.

Khabeer, S. A. (2016). *Muslim cool: Race, religion, and hip-hop in the United States.* New York University Press.

Panjwani, F. (2008). Religion, citizenship, and hope: Civic virtues and education about Muslim traditions. In J. Arthur, I. Davies, & C. Hahn (Eds.), *SAGE handbook of education for citizenship and democracy* (pp. 292–304). Sage.

Zine, J. (2008). *Canadian Islamic schools: Unveiling the politics of faith, gender, knowledge, and identity.* University of Toronto Press.

NOTES

1. National Center for Education Statistics, "Status and Trend in the Education of Racial and Ethnic Minorities," https://nces.ed.gov/pubs2007/minoritytrends/ind_2_7.asp

2. Tisha Lewis, "Mother Says Son Was Unfairly Disciplined, Targeted by Teacher Because of Race," *Fox 5 DC*, March 14, 2018.

3. Matthew Barakat, "Public Schools Leave Out Some Gifted Minorities," *Associated Press*, February 5, 2018.

4. The data was collected from participant observations; unstructured interviews with administrators, faculty, and parents; and the school's pamphlets. Quotations in this chapter are from these sources unless otherwise noted.

5. Apart from the physical education instructor and the guard, every staff member, administrator, and teacher at the school is a woman. Many of their children have studied at the school as well, a fact highlighted in their online bio pages.

6. "Sakena Space: Purpose and Use"

7. "Buddy Bench Overview"

8. Amaarah DeCuir, "Imam Al-Ghazali's 8 Rules of Conduct for Teachers," *Islamic Society of North America Education Forum* (2009): 74.

INTENTIONAL AND MINDFUL RELIGIOUS STUDIES TO DEVELOP A HOLISTIC IDENTITY IN YOUNG MUSLIMS

A Case Study

AFEEFA SYEED

IDENTITY EDUCATION DOES NOT BEGIN in universities but in K–12 schooling and at home. Young students make meaning as they learn about and gain confidence in who they are. Integrating models of religious education provides a way to implement a transformative curriculum without compromising faith and/or knowledge. This chapter describes a religious education model in a K–8 school in Virginia, starting with a common understanding of the various aspects of religious schooling in the United States.

The very core of education in general and religious education in particular should be relevancy and meaning connected to a young person's lived reality. Education philosophers such as Dewey (1916) had argued for that over the past century. With this seamless connection, both a three-year-old in preschool and a teenage student can take teachings of faith as not only tenets to be followed but also as tools to better their lives and the world around them. This chapter explores how this connection and resulting understanding by students and their teachers are achieved through curriculum development, transformative pedagogy, alignment of essential questions, and institutionalizing practices of mindfulness and presence as they relate to the school experience.

Religious practices and rituals taught through this interconnected and enlivened manner and lessons learned from them help answer the fundamental and profound question, varied in different religious contexts of *Who am I?* This is to ask: *What is a Muslim?* This is to further delve into the essential questions of does Islam make sense to me? How do I shape my worldview to align with the revelation of Allah? How do I embody the Prophetic way of life? How do I fulfill my purpose? How do I reconcile my identity as a Muslim and an American?

What are my relationships (i.e., Allah, Prophet, family, society), and how do I nurture those relationships? What does it mean to study the Islamic sciences? These questions provide a transformative framework that supports inquiry and innovative approaches to teaching the core lessons in *āqīdah* (tenets of faith), *akhlāq* (practice of virtue and morality), *sīrah* (Prophetic biography), and *fiqh* (jurisprudential practice of faith).

This chapter uses these essential questions and how deeply faith affects the heart and soul to address how interactive, engaged, and responsive religious studies pedagogy for Muslims can be a catalyst for hope and optimism for individuals as well as society. Examples and promising practices come from the case study of Al Fatih Academy, an Islamic school in one of the largest metropolitan areas in the United States, serving the community since 1996. The coeducational school spans ages three to thirteen from preschool through middle school and is an independent, private educational nonprofit organization. Since its founding, the school has been used as a model for its integrated and innovative approaches to education such as highlighted by Gjelten (2017) on National Public Radio.

A BRIEF OVERVIEW OF ISLAMIC SCHOOLING IN THE UNITED STATES

To get a sense of where Al Fatih Academy is situated among the fabric of Islamic schooling in the United States, it is important to outline a brief history of Islamic schooling within the country context. Memon (2009) maps Islamic schooling into four overlapping historical phases that illustrate the evolving vision of Islamic schooling (the *why* of Islamic schools). Phase 1, labeled *Protest*, spans from 1930 to 1975 and highlights the Nation of Islam's establishment of schools as a reaction to the lack of equitable educational opportunities afforded to the African American population during that time. These schools also represent the earliest institutional approaches to teaching religious and cultural identity to empower the Muslim minority in the US. Phase 2, *Preservation*, shifts the focus to protecting and preserving the Muslim identity from a perceived immorality in public American schooling among indigenous (African American) Muslims and the new wave of Muslim immigrants between 1965 and 1990. During this period, Islamic schooling became further established as newer institutions learned from existing ones while also realizing the importance of the now-interwoven US Muslim community to identify its own path outside of either "back home" models or ones previously affiliated with centralized umbrella organizations. This allowed for the development of school philosophy, curriculum practices and teacher training, leading to Phase 3, *Pedagogy*, from

1985 to 2001. Phase 4, for which the tragic events of September 11, 2001, served as a catalyst, continues today, defined by Islamic schools focusing on helping their students *live* their Islam (to truly "be" Muslim) in an American context through increased social consciousness and intensified civic engagement.

It is important to note that the existence of and need for Islamic schooling has been a debated issue among the American Muslim community. As noted by Merry (2005), some parents consider Islamic schooling to be little different from its secular counterparts, save the addition of religious classes. On the other hand, demand for Islamic schools is on the rise, with waiting lists at schools growing longer, especially for younger grade levels. This increase in interest, based on various sources cited by the Islamic Schools League of America (theisla.org), an umbrella organization, speaks to how American Muslims want to find spaces for their children where they can practice and learn about their faith without the negative environment persisting in current school climates. Going hand in hand with the dynamic character of the American Muslim identity, families are finding their way through what they prioritize in their faith and practice with regard to educational options for their children.

This ambivalence toward Islamic schooling is also found among families in the larger geographic area where Al Fatih Academy is located. Al Fatih Academy primarily serves families from Fairfax and Loudoun Counties in Virginia, both of which consistently rank among the top twenty-five counties with the best public schools in America (Niche). This required that Al Fatih Academy clearly expresses why it, as a religious-based school, is needed. That is to say, what does the religious-based school have to offer students that cannot be found in public schools, and can it deliver on higher expectations than the average community-based school?

RATIONALE FOR RELIGIOUS-BASED SCHOOLING

This sense of having to stand out, or at the very least to make the case for existence, has led many veteran Muslim educators to spend more effort in framing and explaining this competitive edge their schools may claim to provide. It is therefore critical to explore how this difference is defined and how certain elements can make a case for the *why* of religious schools.

An increasing number of schools are interested in addressing the issue of wanting to nurture and develop the whole child through a school's educational philosophy and programs. Islamic schools answer the question of why by claiming to meet the demands for *tarbiyah*—generally defined as training or upbringing of young people that is inclusive of the many facets of education and knowledge acquisition. *Tarbiyah* is also rooted in the understanding that effective teaching and learning must be based on the deeper understanding of the role *fitrah* plays in a child's life—how the innate and intrinsic tendencies of each child must be considered and appreciated so that teaching becomes a scaffolding or supporting of these unique characteristics. *Tarbiyah*, as defined by classical lexicographer al-Rāghib al-Asfahānī (d. 402 A.H./1011 C.E.), is to cause something to develop from stage to stage until reaching its completion or full potential. This then encompasses the full array of mental, emotional, social, spiritual, and physical wellness needed to nurture the whole child through an educational framework, so the result is *al-insān al-kāmil*, the fully developed human being. An excellent source to see this interwovenness is Tauhidi's (2001) *Tarbiyah Project*.

Regarding this increasing focus on a holistic framework, some argue that the field of education may be packed with jargon, flavors of the month, and other trending approaches in what is sometimes called innovative approaches to teaching. There are, however, essentials to curriculum development and pedagogy that we have found to be most effective to create the "holistically educated child." To achieve comprehensive gains toward this whole-child goal, education programs, especially in full-time religious-based schools, should embody an understanding of the interconnected roles of *defining identity, building cultural literacy, valuing place-based learning*, and *developing an integrated subject curriculum*, all of which lead to a school's core objective: the teaching of fundamental skills and knowledge within an environment of discovery and personal growth that appreciates the innate tendency toward learning and positive engagement with the world.

It is these elements of techniques and approaches to education in Muslim schools that ensure a more positive and integrated worldview for children to grow with and retain into their adulthood. The purposes of identity, cultural literacy, place-based learning, and an integrated curriculum are to bolster and give foundational support to religious education within a Muslim school. Arguably, these may be elemental in any religious school context and may also lend support to noninstitutional learning outside of the school setting. Nevertheless, highlighting those may catalyze further exploration of the methods and pedagogy that support a more positive and integrated worldview of Muslim youth.

THE CASE FOR DYNAMIC DEVELOPMENT OF THE WHO AM I QUESTION—DEFINING IDENTITY

Identity is a common element written into the mission and vision of various schools, especially in Muslim minority communities, where the idea of maintaining or building an Islamic identity is seen as paramount for the objective of these institutions (Qureshi, 2016). Often the label is preceded by *maintaining, protecting,* or *ensuring* this identity in what might be perceived as a hostile environment for a community to grow as a religious or cultural minority.

In multiple discussions on identity formation, the underlying understanding about what identity itself connotes, or how to define the idea of an Islamic identity, is not necessarily fleshed out. This missing piece, or underdeveloped notion, moves through school leadership from the founders to changing board members to the teaching staff, who may not be able to articulate the concept to students, who are the targets or subjects of this serious identity work. Definitions or parameters are often based on unspoken assumptions of what identity as a phenomenon means and on related expectations written into descriptors of the school's character.

Identity refers to where one (a person or a group) belongs and what is expressed as self-image and/or common image. Identity is what integrates these inside a self or a group existence and what differentiates them vis-à-vis others. Instead of a static, narrowly defined concept, identity should be understood as a dynamic, fluid process socially produced and reproduced. Culture encompasses identity and includes within its parameters the aspirations of a people (Ting-Toomey & Dorjee, 2019).

Religion is integrated into, grows from, responds to, and is encompassed by culture, and identity is hence an expression to an extent of this growth. However, it can be differentiated within a religious group as much as a person actualizes that religious identity and associates with it. An ongoing conversation among religious schools, Muslim and otherwise, is about how to define our schools as what we *are* rather than what we *are not*. This means citing a positive identity rather than a negative one to convince parents to send their children there. A positive identity also contributes to reenvisioning and building a sense of self in children that is inclusive of and incorporated in a discerning manner into a broader identification with the surrounding culture and society.

CULTURAL LITERACY IN MUSLIM SCHOOLING

According to Abd-Allah (2004), "Islam in America must become wenyējï, 'something belonging here.' It must be indigenous—not in the sense of losing identity through total assimilation or of being the exclusive property of the native-born—but in the word's original sense, namely, being natural, envisioned, and born from within. Regardless of birthplace, Muslim Americans become indigenous once they truly belong. Islam in America becomes indigenous by fashioning an integrated cultural identity that is comfortable with itself and functions naturally in the world around it" (p. 365).

According to the Pew Forum Survey (2017), Muslim Americans overwhelmingly embrace both the Muslim and American parts of their identity, and a vast majority of US Muslims say they are proud to be Americans (92%), while nearly all say they are proud to be Muslims (97%). Nine in ten (89%) say they are proud to be both Muslims and Americans. Based on these findings, Muslims in the US are comfortable with a seemingly dual identity. Muslim schools, as institutions of education and knowledge, must take heed of what is needed to create a thriving American Muslim identity and presence (Abd-Allah, 2004). Additionally, the idea of a thriving American Muslim identity cannot be limited to individuals merely as identifying as either or both. This identity needs to be nuanced, textured, and fully expressible as belonging to both. In other words, identity needs to be understood in the context of a life lived knowingly within a culture (Abd-Allah, 2004).

Hirsch (1988) coined the term *cultural literacy*, referring to the ability to understand and participate fluently in a culture. This does not mean a full immersion or expansive competency in a cultural context; it means being able to identify and know basic values, ideals, critiques, and problematic considerations of the cultural. It should not imply simply creating a static list of cultural must-knows that could be concerning if only some things make the list. Some critiques of Hirsch's efforts discuss how concepts, people, and ideas are chosen to identify as critical cultural knowledge for Americans (Liu, 2014). Hirsch's work and the actual potential of this approach are valuable in that they help educators frame how knowledge can be connected to realities experienced by students. This idea of understanding the components—history, trends, politics—of the culture a community lives and grows in is essential for religious education to be of benefit and grounded. Cultural literacy helps put the substance and texture to the what and why of learning.

There may be more potency in using the term *social literacy* alongside *cultural literacy* as we evolve our curricula and school environments to better respond to current social issues, including racism, inequity, and justice-related themes.

PLACE-BASED LEARNING AND EDUCATION

In most traditional education models in modern history, it is agreed that more effective learning happens when knowledge is connected to and pulled from the actual surroundings of where a student lives or learns (Katz et al., 2014; Vygotsky, 1978). Place-based education (PBE) emphasizes and actively incorporates learning about what is currently happening around the student as well as the historical, environmental, social, and political elements of these surroundings (Anderson, 2017). Such learning can be as simple as knowing the classification of trees on the playground to understanding how the school's neighborhood was created and changed over time through various impacts.

PBE connects the student with the reality they see every day and helps each create a unique relationship with what is happening or has happened, while giving them tools to keenly observe, critically question, and take ownership of these relationships. Learning becomes relevant daily, especially when abstract or global concepts being taught are conscientiously linked to elements existing in commonly shared spaces experienced by students. Centering the local environment in learning builds a connection that is authentic and meaningful. Students grow to love where they are, and at the same time understand their place to be part of a larger world with similar spaces and people living out their own realities—and that perhaps their realities are more linked to others than they thought. Schools that use place-based learning earnestly are also connecting their communities to others in the neighborhood, town, or community in genuine relationships across many identities and cultures (Mannion et al., 2010).

INTEGRATED/INTERDISCIPLINARY LEARNING AND TEACHING

As we better understand these approaches to learning, it becomes critical to build from them a framework for curriculum development. Identity, cultural literacy, and PBE help us know that people's natural tendency is to see aspects of their lives as interconnected naturally and dynamically. Yet when it comes to most education models, knowledge—as defined by subjects and disciplines—is divided into discrete buckets and taught in isolation as topical and linear. Integration, in contrast, means to consciously bring parts of a whole together so the result is greater than these parts. An integrated or thematic-based curriculum is when a teacher presents a unified or integrated conception of some form of knowledge to the student. This curriculum is created by defining each grade's learning objectives, forming these into essential questions, then plugging the adopted standards of learning across subject areas, while these standards usually stand alone. For the teacher, this means using the analogy of a web where the topic is in the center (e.g., plants) and the strands coming out are each of the subjects (math, science, language, history, etc.) to be filled in with corresponding lessons. The scope and sequence of each lesson or unit are based on how much is introduced by the teacher and, even more importantly, how much the students take the lead on their own learning (Katz et al., 2014).

An example of integrated learning has students writing poetry about plants while sowing a variety of seeds in their classroom or school garden. They measure their seeds' progress and come to understand what plants need to grow, while also learning the names of flora living around their building. Students research which plants have been eradicated or introduced in the surrounding neighborhoods over time and also learn why people have allergies to certain pollen and plants. Student-facilitated learning happens organically at each individual's pace through this process. They connect the curriculum-objective dots, and the teacher provides opportunities to witness and experience various aspects of knowledge acquisition and transference. This process of inquiry, deconstruction, and reconstruction (see chapter 1) allows for the transformation to occur.

Proponents of an integrated curriculum suggest that much is missed when knowledge is separated into categories and treated hierarchically. Instead of defining basic skills as a prerequisite to higher-order/critical thinking, integrated or integrative approaches view critical thinking within large, complex themes as a necessary background to knowledge acquisition, making this latter part more relevant and useful than a list of facts for the student (Lipson et al., 1993). Because of its dynamic framing, integrated learning catalyzes further exploration, ensuring that students are engaged with the process itself. This is how human brains learn and understand the world around them, so students can take the experience outside the classroom into their own lives, where they come to understand that knowledge is interconnected.

Critical to this integrated approach is relying less on textbooks in teaching across subjects and methods. Most student texts have a limited scope of information and become a crutch for both the teacher and the learner. More effective in integrated curriculum implementation is a wide variety of resources such as trade books, fiction, websites, multimedia, guest speakers, and relevant field trips and experiences outside the classroom. This dynamic information-acquisition approach allows students to naturally become knowledge producers rather than passive, spoon-fed consumers.

Education that is culturally literate, place-based, and from an integrated framework while moving toward building the positive identity of young people contributes to a learner's understanding of social justice, the interconnectedness of a global community, and the challenges of learning from history. This encourages students to develop their skills to decipher, deconstruct, digest, and deploy knowledge more impactfully. This then leads us to look for where spiritual or religious education might naturally and beneficially fit into this framework.

RELIGIOUS EDUCATION IN MUSLIM SCHOOLS

Religious knowledge—its teaching, and its learning—is fundamentally based on the premise that religion, and in this case Islam, *is about transformation, not information*. In an integrated, place-based, and culturally literate framing, the teacher adds another strand to the web when planning their lesson on planting seeds. This is where the spiritual/religious connection is filled in with a standard from the objectives outlined in the religious curriculum. These objectives may include teaching students to understand the concept of trusting in God (*tawakkul*) as they plant their seed; to recognize that God is the best planner in case their seed does not sprout; to learn attributes of God as the Creator, the Sustainer, the Most Loving, the Best Protector, and the Most Merciful; and to understand that the Prophet Muhammad ﷺ said that a person is like a young sapling that bends toward the wind but straightens up again through these attributes of God and that we are strong at our core.

In addition to this layer of spirituality on top of an integrated curriculum, building standards for teaching religion within a framework of identity formation and self-awareness means reconfiguring objectives and understanding pedagogy to better fit the framework of answering the question of *why*. Why should the teaching of religion be approached differently, and why does this matter?

Traditional approaches to religious education are based on dogma, ritual, and ahistorical context, with the thought that religion should transcend the mundane and focus on instilling a uniform understanding of tenets to fulfill the requirements of the believer (Syeed & Ritchie, 2005). While this is indeed a basic function of religious education, it is becoming increasingly clear that religious-based schools need to create curriculum connections to the religion they espouse as well as understand how to teach the faith more vibrantly, so students understand their role as believers in the faith and as faithful persons in the world.

In order to fit and be in congruence with the development of a healthy identity—one that is formed in the context of communal and individual spaces—religious education must have components that are responsive to a child's need for belonging; some parts from the pretext of identity formation and others from the larger sense of being connected. These should include some form of (1) creating and strengthening *relationships* with God, with scriptural prophets and spiritual teachers, with one's self, and with all creation; (2) being *relevant* to everyday life with theology in practice rather than a set of rules and regulations outside one's lived experiences; (3) understanding *regularized ritual* as tools for mental, physical, and emotional health; and (4) building *resilience* through connecting religiosity to self-awareness, self-knowledge, and self-advocacy.

The goals of an integrated religious studies curriculum include (1) building on the existing love of God held by students, (2) nurturing the relationship with God as the basis for *deen* (faith), (3) emphasizing practices of faith that are integral and relevant to life experiences, and (4) teaching the importance of inclusivity and diversity of practices in worship and action (see Figure 9.1 for further emphasis on role of the educator in an integrated curriculum in religious education).

CONTENT OF RELIGIOUS EDUCATION[1]

The breakdown of religious knowledge starts with the following areas of traditional teachings:

Fiqh *(Islām)***:** Students learn the fundamentals of how to *perform* their religious duties of *tahārah, salāt, zakāt, sawm,* hajj (as appropriate) and associated actions.

*āqīdah (imān)***:** Students nurture their relationship with Allah by exploring His names and attributes, which *informs* their belief.

The Educator's Role

- Be aware of age appropriateness
- Integrate Islamic studies objectives and content within other subjects
- Acknowledge and respect the role of a family as critical in the student's development
- Emphasize positive and productive practices and teachings
- Model learning objectives as opposed to relying solely on targeted instruction
- Utilize stories and examples as a basis for teachings
- Create space for dialogue and discussion beyond textbooks
- Contextualize and connect content as appropriate for students

This includes building on their relationship with the Prophet Muhammad ﷺ, the Qur'an (*āyāt* of the Book), and Creation (*āyāt* of the universe).

***Akhlāq* (*Iḥsān*):** Students are shown methods to develop their morals and etiquette and to *transform* their relationships with Allah, Prophet Muhammad ﷺ, self, family, community, and the larger society.

***Sīrah* (Prophetic biography):** Students study all content through the exemplar of the Prophet Muhammad ﷺ, making sense of the nature of his prophethood as a mercy to all the worlds. The *sīrah* (Prophetic biography) serves as a vehicle to teach *āqīdah*, fiqh, and *akhlāq*. As outlined in our standards, aspects of the *sīrah* are divided based on the relevance of the *sīrah* to the other subjects within a given grade. For example, third-grade students are introduced to the concept of community, so aspects of *sīrah* outlined in third-grade standards are related to the building and development of the Prophetic community in Makkah. Many teachers tend to teach *sīrah* mainly as a chronological series of events in isolation from other subjects or context, emphasizing memorization of these dates and events. This approach to the Prophet's life can be limiting with students not able to relate to the underlying experiences of that time. Rather, the *sīrah* should be a well from which water can be drawn whenever appropriate as it is a compilation of stories and lessons within the lives of the Prophet, his companions, and members of the community. Some benefits of teaching the *sīrah* in chronological order include understanding the linkage to the revelation of the Quran and the reasons of revelation (*asbāb al-nuzūl*) as well as being able to analyze of the cause and effect of an event of that time.

METHODS OF TEACHING RELIGIOUS STUDIES

In addition to integrating the teaching of religion as much as possible across grades and levels, it must be as engaging as other areas of learning. Inquiry-based lessons and exploration of questions help students understand that asking and wondering are important and integral aspects of learning about the faith. Many may come from homes where they are told not to question teachings of religion or even the teacher of religion. In order to achieve the holistic objectives cited here, it is imperative that students feel there is a safe space for questions of faith and that teachers ask them what they think of or understand about the lessons. There is much to support this from the Prophet Muhammad's ﷺ example as a teacher, and this goes a long way to ensure students' comfort engaging with both the teacher and the content.

Activity or experience-based learning is important in all areas of knowledge acquisition, but it may be even more important in religious education. Being able to role-play, create models, discuss in smaller groups, and develop projects (multimedia and otherwise) not only helps students stay interested but also allows their creativity space for expression.

Along with activity-based learning, real-life case studies and relevant thought experiments help promote critical thinking about faith principles and concepts. A sampling of how various groups of Muslim communities express the same religious tenet can help students understand that there are variations in practice and recognize that these variations may be based on material culture or influences. Contemporary issues of egregious misrepresentation of Islam may come up and should be addressed through this lens of critical questioning: Why do some extremist groups think they can justify terrorism using Quranic verses?

Religious education that is taught within the place-based, cultural literacy, and identity framework can be experienced in any classroom. One example of this in life science studies is a middle-school lesson titled *Of Meat & Men*, in which students link their study of the issue of climate change to land degradation that is a result of the Western Hemisphere's high demand for beef consumption. Students understand the social, scientific, historical, and mathematical aspects of this issue through a variety of literature and language arts. Students must then place these issues into a framework of spirituality: How does this behavior (demand for meat) reconcile with a religious identity? What is the obligation, if any, of a believing Muslim who is considered a caretaker (*khalifah*) of the earth as well as one who knows that this behavior is harmful? Students then work through a facilitated lesson on how fatwas (religious edicts), which include making something permissible or prohibited, are formulated. They debate whether eating meat is permissible if this knowledge might negate one's purpose of being created as caretakers of this earth.

As children grow through this integrated and mindful curriculum, the school ensures that they understand how to express and maintain their faith in the larger community, where they may be a minority or might encounter experiences outside of their practice of learning as a faithful person. Teachers may suggest role-playing situations of "what would you do," or tell them about real-life examples of debates or discussions they might participate in outside of their Muslim school. Students also learn about other faith traditions by visiting diverse places of worship; interacting with people of other faiths, including students of the same age; and learning that there are shared religious understandings across faiths and knowing that differences in belief exist. It is just as important that students learn about variations within Islamic traditions and schools of thought to build an appreciation for intrafaith relationships. Finally, religious education is also rooted in recognizing the societal obligations of a believing person and in understanding the role a student plays in contributing actively to the betterment of all as a basis of faith.

SCHOOL CULTURE MATTERS FOR RELIGIOUS EDUCATION/IDENTITY

Core Values

An integrated, grounded, and relevant approach to religious education must be supported by a surrounding school culture that enables a vibrancy in teaching and learning. One way to ensure this is to have in place and in practice a set of core values by which the school abides and that comes from a spiritual tradition. Over the years and through building both cultural literacy and spiritual connectivity, our school's core values are:

Be Intentional and Mindful النية Be conscientious in actions and recognize purpose in learning and knowledge

Uphold Excellent Character الخلق الحسن Practice good conduct through honesty, humility, forgiveness, generosity, kindness, fairness, compassion, and empathy; remind one another of these through lessons, interactions, activities, and personal relationships

Build Community الإخوة والجماعة Foster and create relationships within one's family, neighborhood, and world while learning about others and how to better ourselves

Create Serenity and Peace السكينة والسلام Create spaces for reflection to find ways to make peace within ourselves and with others

Transform Knowledge into Action العلم والعمل Nurture a love of learning and wonder about the surrounding world; appreciate and acknowledge a diversity of ways of knowing and learning; use knowledge for the benefit of ourselves and to serve others

Practice Stewardship and Service الأمانة والخلافة Understand that
our bodies and our world are a trust and responsibility for us to
take care of and serve others through our actions, thoughts, and
abilities

TEACHER ORIENTATION AND TRAINING—
ENSURING THE VISION IS ALIVE

Any, if not all, curriculum and program elements are implemented by teachers
in the classroom. Their understanding and buy-in of core values, philosophy,
and approaches can never be underestimated. And in turn, their need for regu-
lar orientation and support in many ways cannot be overstated. The extent
to which the school culture supports teachers will determine the outcomes
of impactful programs, and teachers appreciate being part of the process as
much as they want the support and tools. Their input is invaluable in developing and course-correcting curricula or related programs that are school specific. Establishing a feedback loop for them to be responsive as well as proactively involved only strengthens the impact and sustainability of programs and
teachers' buy-in.

In addition to social–emotional learning orientation and helping teachers create more responsive strategies in the classroom that make teaching
more effective, we have developed training by using Prophet Muhammad's
ﷺ approach to teaching, which is spiritually grounded as well as an effective
toolbox for classroom-management techniques. Each lesson is attached to his
teachings or the ways he interacted with those surrounding him. We assert
that he taught us to be not only a *muallim*, a conveyor of knowledge, but also
a *murabbi*, a nurturer of souls. This gives the vocation even more of a spiritual
connotation and fits well with how we model religiosity and faith in action to
students.

MENTAL/EMOTIONAL HEALTH: A SPIRITUALLY
BASED WELLNESS PROGRAM

An essential aspect of school culture that supports religious education as well
as intersects with core values is a wellness program or set of tools and resources
to identify and respond to mental well-being. These might include licensed
and experienced school counselors who can include spiritual resources in
their work with individuals and groups of students who may be experiencing grief, anxiety, depression, and anger-management and self-esteem issues.

PROPHET MUHAMMAD ﷺ AS A TEACHER

al fatih	HIS ACTION	LESSON FOR US
ᴖᴖ	MAINTAINED DIRECT EYE CONTACT WITH LISTENER	BE PRESENT
↻	STATED 3x IN DIFFERENT WAYS	REPEAT, REPEAT, REPEAT
	ASKED QUESTIONS TO SPARK INTEREST AND CURIOSITY	UTILIZE ENQUIRY-BASED INSTRUCTION
	USED ANALOGIES & ILLUSTRATED TO MAKE POINT	DIFFERENTIATE; BE VISUAL
	USED HANDS OR OBJECTS TO TEACH A POINT	MAKE THE ABSTRACT CONCRETE
	USED DAILY LIFE EXAMPLES TO INSTRUCT	BE RELEVANT
	USED QUESTIONS TO ELABORATE AND EXPAND	REDIRECT FOR SELF DISCOVERY
	SPOKE IN MEASURED TONE GAVE TIME BETWEEN WORDS	BE SUCCINCT, CLEAR GRADUAL

Figure 9.1. A sample handout distributed to teachers on the prophetic approach to teaching

Professionals are trained in using tools that speak to the well-being of individuals, and when these are paired with spiritual tools, the school has even more impact on maintaining positivity. Classroom teachers are trained to recognize indicators of distress and, as well as being responsive, are given tools to create proactive spaces and interventions to ensure wellness. One example is setting up a *sakinah* space within the classroom, where students and teachers can go when they feel out of sorts or when their *sakinah* (peace) is disrupted. There they have prayer beads, prayer rugs, and other tactile materials to calm and recenter themselves. This space also allows them to practice the deep-breathing techniques they have been taught in school.

Mindfulness practice is connected to formal religious practices to make the ritual more beneficial. Students and teachers practice deep breathing before congregational prayers to find and maintain focus by placing a hand on their breath spot (wherever they can find their breath), their heart spot (from where we talk and listen to Allah), and their *sujood* spot (eyes to where the head will be on the floor during prayer). Students are reminded that all these spots travel with them through time and distances, so they are always connected to Allah even if they feel alone or sad.

Peer mediation and conflict-resolution skills from an Islamic framework paired with the practical tools of the discipline are taught to students so they understand that resolving issues is important from a religious and a mundane perspective. One reinforces the other. Restorative-justice practices in discipline also align well with Islamic concepts of equity and fairness.

Much of this awareness and resource building is used to benefit students during the school day, but it also reverberates to their families and the larger community of Muslim families as well as other faith groups and communities that find these approaches and practices adaptable to their uses.

CONCLUSION: ROLE OF SCHOOLS IN BUILDING A RELIGIOUS IDENTITY

Religious-based schools perform best when they are independent and capable of creating their own parameters for defining their purpose, values, and mission. Independent schools can also be more actively involved in civil society as incubators for developing an identity that promotes the growth of minds and mandates that students are nurtured to become contributing global citizens. But this identity cannot be created in a vacuum or through rote learning. It must be conscientiously constructed around a purposeful curriculum that considers connections and empowers young people with beneficial knowledge. And, as mentioned at the beginning of this chapter's discussion on the holistic approaches to education, identity is connected to incorporating cultural literacy, place-based learning, and an integrated subject's curriculum as critical within and as part of religious education in the context of school learning. All this while considering that love of learning and of the Divine is inherent in these young minds and should be encouraged, not drilled into them.

The more we acknowledge that children's *fitrah* (innate tendency and disposition) is toward God as a Loving, Appreciative, Merciful Protector, the more we will understand that our religious-education models only expand on this relationship. Although there needs to be a concerted effort by schools to build and maintain a religious-studies curriculum complete with standards, essential questions, objectives, assessment tools, and teacher training, religious values must be wholly embodied and modeled throughout the day across subjects, classrooms, individuals, lessons, and the personality of the school. This encompassing approach results in a living and energized practice of religion that is timeless, boundless, and inherently appreciated by young believers growing into their own understanding of who they are in this ever-changing world.

Connecting the understanding of child development and growth with pedagogy that is responsive to children's changing needs leads to more transformative teaching in schools, a well-understood principle in the field of education. What is more critical, however, is appreciating that education for the sake of imparting tools for understanding the world is transformative in itself; knowledge is then used for personal growth within the context of positive change. Children are given a basis for hope in their own lives as they grow, and educators are equipped to facilitate this process of nurturing the discourse of transformation. This is an innovative approach because children gain agency as the learner and fully appreciate the value of education as interreacting with identity formation. In turn, this approach cultivates innovation as a way of seeing the world. Children become imaginative, creative problem-solvers who use their love of learning and knowledge as a basis for building their relationship with themselves, their peers, their community, and, most fundamentally, with their own spiritual selves.

REFERENCES

Abd-Allah, U. F. (2004). *The Cultural Imperative*. Nawawi Foundation.

Anderson, S. K. (2017). *Bringing school to life: Place-based education across the curriculum*. Rowman & Littlefield.

Dewey, J. (1916). *Democracy and education: An introduction to the philosophy of education*. Free Press.

Gjelten, T. (2017). *This Islamic School helps students build their American and Muslim identity*. NPR Website. https://www.npr.org/sections/ed/2017/04/20/524510378/this-islamic-school-teaches-how-to-be-muslim-and-american

Hirsch Jr., E. D. (1988). *Cultural literacy: What every American needs to know*. Vintage.

Katz, L. G., Chard, S. C., & Kogan, Y. (2014). *Engaging children's minds: The project approach* (3rd ed.). Praeger.

Lipson, M., Valencia, S., Wixson, K., & Peters, C. (1993). Integration and thematic teaching: Integration to improve teaching and learning. *Language Arts, 70*(4), 252–264.

Liu, E. (2014, July). What every American should know: Defining common cultural literacy for an increasingly diverse nation. *The Atlantic.*

Mannion, G., Adey, C., & Lynch, J. (2010). *Intergenerational place-based education: Where schools, communities, and nature meet.* University of Stirling for Scottish Centre for Intergenerational Practice.

Memon, S. (2009). *From protest to praxis: A history of Islamic schools in North America* [Doctoral dissertation]. https://tspace.library.utoronto.ca /bitstream/1807/19154/6/Memon_Nadeem_A_200911_PhD_thesis.pdf

Merry, M. S. (2005). Advocacy and involvement: The role of parents in Western Islamic schools. *Religious Education, 100*(4), 374–385.

Miller, J. P. (2019). *The holistic curriculum* (3rd ed.). University of Toronto Press.

Niche. *Counties with the best public schools.* (2019). https://www.niche.com /places-to-live/search/counties-with-the-best-public-schools/

Pew Forum Survey. (2017). http://www.pewforum.org/dataset/2017-survey -of-u-s-muslims/

Qureshi, O. (2016). *Badr al-Dīn Ibn Jamāʿah and the highest good of Islamic education.* [Doctoral dissertation]. https://ecommons.luc.edu/luc_diss/2293

Syeed, A., & Ritchie, N. (2005). Five pillars of Islam: Practicing spirituality in daily life. In *Nurturing child and adolescent spirituality: Perspectives from the world's religious traditions.* Chapter 24. Rowman & Littlefield.

Tauhidi, D. (2001). *Towards a renewed vision of Islamic education: The Tarbiyah Project: An overview.* https://www.theisla.org/filemgmt_data/admin_files /Tarbiyah%20Overview%20-%20Dawud%20Tauhidi.pdf

Ting-Toomey, S., & Dorjee, T. (2019). *Communicating across cultures* (2nd ed.). Guilford.

Vygotsky, L. (1978). *Mind in society: The development of higher psychological processes.* Harvard University Press.

APPENDIX 1

Example of Perspective: Integrated Curriculum

The act of creating a footprint in a patch of soft earth is a teachable moment for both students and the teachers who guide them. As we think about how to teach, this simple exercise helps pull together the notion that lessons can be connected and relevant and can ultimately elevate discovery that should be the basis of education.

A footprint is a scientific fact. The forces of gravity and mass push down to create the imprint. There is no force coming from below. It is a natural reaction to an action. It is measurable and detectable through empirical tools. The reality that surrounds us works on principles, whether they have been discovered or not.

A footprint is a marker on the earth of history and geography. It gives longitudinal and latitudinal directions of where you stand on this planet, where present location is acknowledged. We live with connections to the past, as others have made their footprints at the same spot. The Iroquois Nation stood here where you are now.

A footprint reflects how to observe and use language to communicate this. We realize that something exists there that may not have before the step. There are billions of happenings to ponder and reflect on through our senses. We open our heart and our mind to witness these fully, we ask why, how, and what. Poetry, prose, and storytelling, then, are expressions of this awe and a way to share the observations and reflections of what is before us. A footprint is an acknowledgment of the Self. That is my footprint, connected to my body, my presence. My action led to it being created. I am a person, distinct and unique. My purpose is significant, my being is real. I exist, and I am.

A footprint is a realization of the power of impact. Soil was moved. An anthill may have been crushed or a patch of grass dislocated, or the print becomes a source of water as a puddle for birds. My action created a reaction, and I am responsible for the consequences, both positive and negative. The concept of caretaker of the earth is even more real when the footprint makes a change in what existed. Choosing a carbon footprint that alleviates pressures on the earth, then, is understood as a conscious effort, a true representation of a higher purpose to be mindful.

In the end, it comes together in a teachable moment from a Quranic verse about walking the earth with humility and grace. We are connected to our Self, to our Creator, and to our fellow creation in a conscientious and concerted way, through time and space. We walk the earth making footprints but keep these to a gentleness to minimize negative impact, knowing, too, that our walking is necessary and the footprints our contribution to the world. And further, we gain strength in this type of walking and connecting that gives us courage to respond positively and compassionately to those who harass or give us grief, intentionally or not.

As teachers for every age, in any context, the notion of footprints provides tools and stories to revive the spirit of learning and to give young minds reasons to explore, discover, and inhale their world so they can exhale out their love. And for teachers, it gives a chance to rediscover the meaning and significance of imprinting.

And the servants of the Most Merciful are those who walk on the earth in humility, and when the ignorant harass or disturb them, they say, "Peace!" (Quran, Surah Furqan Ayat 63).

NOTE

1. Developed in collaboration with Ismail ibn Ali, former principal of Al Fatih Academy and head of the Islamic Studies Department.

PART V

FINAL CRITICAL REFLECTIONS

TEN

TWENTY-FIRST-CENTURY PROSPECTS FOR HOPE IN TRANSFORMING EDUCATION

Advancing the Dialogue

SHELLEY WONG AND TYRONE PITTS

This hope is like a firm and steady anchor for our souls. In fact, hope reaches behind the curtain into the most holy place (Heb. 6:19, CEV).

Say, [O Prophet,] "I am only a man like you, [but] it has been revealed to me that your God is only One God. So whoever hopes for the meeting with their Lord, let them do good deeds and associate none in the worship of their Lord" (Quran, 18:110).

INTRODUCTION

In these often-quoted passages from the Bible and the Quran, hope figures as a necessary guide and a "firm and steady anchor for our souls." Moral vision, ethical values, and leadership are vitally needed in the divided and broken world of the twenty-first century, a world in which the rot of nihilism has staked a claim and threatens to stifle the dynamic energy and potentiality of youth. The situation is grave, and one powerful antidote is hope. The meaning and significance of hope are integral to understanding a common foundation for the monotheistic religions of Judaism, Christianity, and Islam. The passage from the Quran (18:110) stresses that there is One God and that if one *hopes* "for the meeting with their Lord, let them do good deeds" or *righteous work*. The monotheistic theme of "Never associate anyone with the service of his Lord" means not to include anybody in the worship of God—not to consider anyone else equal to God or worthy of worship. The goal of this volume is to present a twenty-first-century multifaceted analysis of what it means to advance hope in education in Muslim societies as well as in Muslim educational institutions and communities throughout the world. The idea of hope is used as both a *research construct* and a *value* that grounds the empirical research of the Advancing Education in Muslim Societies (AEMS) future series and guides the future orientation of educational thinking in Muslim societies today (Nasser, preface).

In this chapter, we engage—as two Christian US-based scholars—in dialogue with this volume's contributors about prospects for hope in education in Muslim societies, educational institutions, and communities of the world. We begin with Christian perspectives on hope and our own family histories as a Chinese American and American African.[1] We also discuss the US context in which Muslim places of worship, educational institutions, communities; and Muslim educators, students, and family members have faced past and current discrimination, xenophobia, and assaults on their personhood, communities, and social identities (Pew Research Center, 2017). Next, we share observations from our recent experiences of living in Palestine in the occupied West Bank, during which time Shelley Wong was a visiting Fulbright Scholar at Birzeit University (Baramki, 2010), and Rev. Tyrone Pitts was part of a South African and American African Christian delegation to Palestine (National Council of Churches of Christ in the U.S.A., 2019). We argue that the Palestinian experiences of advancing hope after seventy years of conflict are an interfaith expression. During our time in the occupied West Bank, we witnessed Christian, Muslim (including Druze), and other faiths illuminate qualities of steadfastness, moral tenacity, and boundless artistic creativity in the face of the severe challenges and restrictions of their daily struggle. We then discuss how this book contributes to advancing hope in education in Muslim societies, institutions, and communities through three broad themes:

1. **Third-space research to create spaces for hope:** We present the pathbreaking foundational work of Homi Bhabha, who has influenced the development of third-space research in ethnic and women's studies, cultural studies, and postcolonial studies (Bhabha, 2004).

2. **Socioemotional and strength-based research:** This book contributes to the growing body of research that provides hope for the most marginalized segments of society through the critique and transformation of educational models, moving from deficit-oriented to strength-based holistic paradigms.

3. **Intergenerational approaches to education across the life span:** We look at these approaches (Vygotsky, 1980) from early childhood to teacher education and advanced professional

development for educational leadership. We argue that the emerging transformative model of education advanced in this book is a framework that can be further developed in Muslim societies and educational institutions throughout the world.

Finally, we conclude with needed future research. This book, the first in the AEMS series, provides a framework for the Way Forward: A Critical Research Agenda, which incorporates Muslim diaspora, transnationalism, and interfaith efforts for advancing hope in education.

CHRISTIAN PERSPECTIVES ON HOPE

According to Palestinian Christian scholar and educator Mitri Raheb, "Hope is living the reality and yet investing in a different one. . . . Hope is faith in action in the face of empire" (Raheb, 2014, p. 130). As we engage in interfaith dialogue with the authors of this book, we experience hope in action. Hope in action is a necessary element in interfaith dialogue that is so needed in these challenging times. Individual personal narratives may provide a bridge to deepen dialogue and faith in action between Christians, Muslims, and members of other faith communities as well as nonaffiliated educators. Our formative memories as an American African and interfaith ordained minister and church administrator, and as a Chinese American professor of multilingual and multicultural education whose family was the first to break the color line in a previously all-white neighborhood in Los Angeles, California, in the 1950s (Wong, 2006) have helped us to understand at an early age the centrality of racism in US society.

Tyrone Pitts grew up in the 1940s and 1950s in Virginia in the segregated South. He attended segregated elementary, junior high, and high school, and a historic Black university and seminary until he went to a predominantly European American graduate school in the early 1970s. His understanding of hope was nurtured and developed by the stories he heard from his great-grandmother Leathia Norris, who was born during slavery. As a young girl, she witnessed the brutality and inhumanity of slavery in Virginia. She bore five children, one of them Sandy Norris, Tyrone Pitts's grandfather. Pitts remembers the system of Jim Crow (Marable & Mullings, 2009), going to American African Baptist churches with his great-aunt in a segregated community in Baileys Crossroads, Virginia. His great-grandmother survived slavery, poverty, and racial segregation to become the family matriarch, providing spiritual strength and hope for her children and her children's children.

Shelley Wong's family was the first Chinese American family to break the color line in a previously all-white neighborhood in Los Angeles, California, in the 1950s. She remembers stories from her Chinese grandparents of being chased home from work and attacked, their homes burned down, and their communities destroyed in San Francisco, California (Wong & Grant, 2016). Both of these family histories and experiences of survival are a testimony to the power of hope in action. We share our family narratives as Christians and as educators and activists who have been engaged in the struggle for peace with justice. Through our life experiences, we have witnessed firsthand the transformative power of hope for peoples in the US, Palestine, and around the world in their struggles for liberation, justice, and peace.

CHRISTIAN THEOLOGIES OF LIBERATION

The message of Jesus was a message of love, hope, and liberation exemplified by his first sermon found in Luke 4:18: "The spirit of the Lord is upon me because he has anointed me to preach the gospel to the poor; He has sent me to heal the broken-hearted, to proclaim liberty to the captives and recovery of sight to the blind, to set at liberty those who are oppressed" (NKJ).

This message of hope and liberation was central to the survival of the early underground Christian movement. However, in 312 CE, the Roman emperor Constantine converted to Christianity. In the period that followed, as Christianity became the official religion of the Roman Empire, there was a turning away from the original message of hope and liberation when Christianity was an underground church. Instead, the institutional Christian Church of Rome became the religion of the wealthy and powerful, the religion of the Roman Empire (Raheb, 2014). This history of the Christian Church as an empire, and later as European conquest and colonialism, runs counter to the meaning and significance of the life, death, and resurrection of Jesus Christ. The church of empire committed genocide and tortured and imprisoned the innocent. It initiated the Crusades against Muslims, the conquest of the Indigenous peoples of the Americas, and the enslavement of Africans through the African slave trade (Bennett, 2018). In the name of Christianity, a false theology of domination was created that justified unspeakable acts of cruelty that made life hopeless for so many. But at those times when oppression and evil seemed most powerful over the meek and the poor, there have also been theologies of liberation from prophetic Christians who opposed slavery, colonialism, and genocide; opposed exploitation and greed; and taken the side of the poor and oppressed (West, 1993). At this time, with the growth of openly anti-Muslim demagoguery emanating from the highest levels of the US government and the alarming growth of the Ku Klux Klan, Nazis, and Christian nationalist movement, prophetic voices for justice, interfaith dialogue, and demonstrations of hope in action are needed more than ever.

For one year, the authors had the unique opportunity to live in Palestine in the occupied West Bank. As US citizens committed to peace with justice, we also experienced hope in action as we witnessed Palestinian Christians and Muslims working together (Kumi Editorial Team, 2018) to embrace what Dr. Martin Luther King called the "beloved community" in their struggle for human rights (King, 2000).

MUSLIM ROOTS OF HOPE IN US HISTORY

No discussion of advancing hope in education in the Muslim community in the US is possible without a closer examination of the historical roots of Muslims in the Americas and the contributions they made as scholars, educators, and innovators that contributed to the survival and liberation of enslaved Africans in the Americas. Estimates vary from 15% to as many as one-third of all Africans brought to the Americas as enslaved people were Muslim. The Muslims that were brought to the Americas were among the most educated. They were more educated than most of their European owners and overseers, who were illiterate (Diouf, 1999). Although efforts were made to erase the language, culture, and religious traditions of African Muslims, there were Muslims who resisted and maintained their religious traditions, language, and culture despite efforts to convert them to Christianity.

Contrary to the belief that African slaves were illiterate and needed to be governed by their slavers (Woodson, 2006), there is written Arabic-language documentation that African slaves in the Americas sent letters in Arabic to loved ones in their home countries. There are also historical records of plans for revolts and religious manuscripts, such as passages of the Quran (Diouf, 1999). History is replete with African Muslim scholars and business people who made their mark through invention and economic development. One such scholar was Omar Ibn Said, a Senegalese slave in Fayetteville, North Carolina, who wrote the first definitive African history recorded during slavery in his autobiography in Arabic (Diouf, 1999). Another scholar was Mohammed Yargo, who was born a slave and bought his freedom after forty-four years of enslavement. His 1819 portrait appears in the Philadelphia Museum of Art (Gomez, 2005). The institution of slavery was maintained and reproduced by robbing African people of their ancestral wisdom and ways of knowing, their language, culture, traditions, and religious beliefs and practices. Efforts to suppress Arabic and traditional African languages by forcing English-only policies of assimilationism resulted in more power and control over the Indigenous First Nations and enslaved African people, and justified white supremacy by declaring that African descendants were not human; did not have a language, culture, or faith traditions; and were incapable of governing themselves.

The importance of education in advancing hope for Muslims in the US is intertwined with the freedom struggles of American Africans and other people of color who have challenged the systems and structures that oppress them. For Muslims, enslaved and persecuted Christians, Jews, and people of other minoritized faiths, survival throughout US history depended on their unique ability to engage in educational opportunities within their communities that protected their racial/ethnic and religious identity and heritage, while they participated in intercultural/interethnic and interfaith alliances that promoted racial justice and religious liberty for all within the broader mainstream US society.

For Muslims, American Africans, Latinx, Native Americans, Indigenous, Asian and Pacific Island Americans, and other people of color in the US, the reality of the meaning of *separate but equal* was juxtaposed—based on racism and colorism—to opposite understandings of theology and religion that were promoted by the white plantation owners. The purpose of Separate but Equal Laws (also known as Jim Crow) was to subvert unity between oppressed peoples and to destroy and erase the racial, cultural, and religious identities of non-Europeans by institutionalizing white supremacist attitudes, policies, and practices within society and its institutions—especially through education (Menkart et al., 2004). Separate but Equal Laws through White-only drinking fountains, bathrooms, restaurants, hotels, and schools engendered a racially and class-segregated political and economic hierarchy with American African and Native American Indigenous communities at the bottom. Systems and structures of exploitation were supported by a white settler and plantation owner Christian nationalist theology and ideology.

A review of the intersectionality between education, the evolution of the Muslim societies for liberation, and the American African Christian freedom movement are critical to understanding the success of the liberation struggle against slavery and segregation for Africans in America as well as the successful participation of Muslim societies in mainstream America. Although often overlooked and seemingly disconnected, these movements are inextricably interrelated (Marable, 2011; Marable & Aidi, 2009). Their history is seldom highlighted in American history textbooks or examined in educational materials. This was particularly true for Muslims of African descent in America (Gomez, 2005). Yet, Muslim and American African Christian dialogue and engagement in solidarity have for decades played a critical role in the survival of both the overlapping Muslim community and the American African community in America. Some of the greatest expressions of this solidarity are revealed by the manifestos and statements of solidarity with the Black Lives Matter movement.

For Muslim communities and American African Christians who have been attacked in their place of worship in the US, working together to oppose bigotry and forge unity is a visible sign of hope. It provides a template for Muslims, Christians, and people of faith throughout the world to explore opportunities to stand together in solidarity. No serious educational discussion of hope for Muslims in the US or the world today is complete without exploring the present-day movement of Christian Muslim dialogue within educational institutions and among ecumenical, national, international, and local church bodies and movements and Muslim mosques and societies as indicated in this book with author contributions from Palestine, South Africa, Egypt, Malaysia, and the United States. These educational institutions, Christian denominations, ecumenical movements, organizations, and local churches are engaged in dialogues of hope with Muslim educational institutions, communities, societies, and local mosques to counter the historic misconceptions that divide Muslims and Christians throughout the world.

THIRD-SPACE RESEARCH AND ADVANCING
HOPE IN EDUCATION

In response to Nasser (chapter 1) and Davids (chapter 2), who advance a research agenda and framework for advancing hope in education, we discuss the contributions of Homi Bhaba's pathbreaking construct of third-space research (Bhabha, 2004).

The authors of chapters 1 and 2, through a multifaceted and interdisciplinary investigation of hope in education, contribute to moral education and third-space research in the tradition of anticolonial (Fanon, 1963; Memmi, 2004) and postcolonial studies (Bhabha, 2004), and sociocultural literacy research (Gutiérrez et al., 2009; Lee, 2005; Vygotsky, 1980). By *third space*, Bhabha refers to an intellectual project in which former colonial subjects, at the juncture of a radical *rupture* from colonial chains of bondage and dehumanization, imagine a different social order.

For the colonized, the wretched, and the dispossessed to imagine a different social order, the opening of a third space is required. For those who have internalized the colonial master's educational values, culture, and languages at the expense of their own, a critical pedagogy of hope involves naming the systems of oppression and carving out a third space that is critical of the oppressive systems and structures. This critical pedagogy could draw on home heritage languages for greater civic leadership and engagement (Leeman et al., 2011). If the colonized intellectuals do not stand with the poor and working masses, if they continue to rule in the ways of their former colonial masters, they will continue the oppression of the past through neocolonialism but within the guise of nationalist discourses (Nkrumah et al., 1963). Therefore, educational leaders and researchers from the Global South (Pennycook & Makoni, 2019) must go beyond narrow nationalist discourses to joining internationally with other colonial subjects in solidarity through an internationalist analysis that links class, gender, and race to counter (1) the violent policies of militarism and war—what Noam Chomsky (2010) called the US "national security state," (2) the US and multinational capitalists, and (3) climate change and ecological destruction (Marciano, 2000). New political identities of international solidarity are best forged through systemic sociopolitical analysis rooted in political economy and by sharing lessons and strategies of educators who have personally engaged in the task of decolonizing research to advance hope in education.

OVERCOMING DIVISIONS

"Indeed, in the Messenger of Allah you have an excellent example for whoever has hope in Allah and the Last Day and remembers Allah often" (Quran, 33:21).

"Contexts of Hope in Higher Education" (part 2) explores the power of hope in transformative teaching through a philosophical and theological discussion of the names of Allah (Selçuk, chapter 3). Naming processes are a tool on the personal level to develop self-identity as well as an awareness of one's position and connections to others throughout the life span. Each generation must come to terms with its understanding of the meaning and significance of advancing hope in education. It is not possible to advance hope without a deconstruction or problem-posing of the hidden barriers and obstacles to the rights of all—including the most vulnerable—to quality education. Education cannot be simply transmitted from one generation to another; it involves challenging students to engage in deep reflection and analysis of their histories, cultures, values, and beliefs—to understand the past to imagine a different future. Mualla Selçuk contributes to the dialogue of *reconstructing* hope by focusing on the powerful processes of naming the Almighty. "Fusion of Horizons: A Case Study of the Pedagogy of Transformative Hope for Muslim Women's Empowerment in Malaysia" (Hussien, chapter 4) explores the power of Muslim women as they reflect on and tell their own stories. Educators of students of all ages can learn from the pedagogical insights from this study of teacher education in a small but committed class of mature women as they reflect on their leadership roles and name the systems and structures that are oppressive to girls and women of all abilities. The dialectical processes of thesis, antithesis, and synthesis require critical self-reflection, including identifying and *naming* the visible—and invisible—systems. The chapter highlights the epistemological vantage point of women who care for family members— the young and the elderly. These women contribute from their investment of labor—intellectual, physical, and especially emotional (Benesch, 2018). Greater agency through the professional development of early-childhood, elementary, and secondary teachers and higher-education faculty involves a process of analyzing one's own pedagogical practices and self-definition, conscientious attention to the education of all, and efforts to strengthen leadership of women educators.

Differences within group membership (gender, class, race, ethnicity, language, and religion) among those who should and could be allies have been used historically to divide and conquer and to maintain colonial and imperial rule. Historically, patriarchy has supported the maintenance of systems of slavery, colonialism, and capitalism. For example, women come from various classes and positions within various racial and ethnic hierarchies. Within the women's movement in the US historically, there have been divisions between those who focused on the right of white and upper-class women to vote and the right to own property and the demands of Africans—men and women—for freedom from bondage.

In the case of Palestine, there is a deep divide between Muslim education in the occupied West Bank and in Gaza. Chapter 5 (Nasser et al.), "Teacher Professional Development in Palestine: Hope Despite All," discusses a professional teacher-education effort to link professional development between educational institutions and educators in the West Bank and Gaza. Participants in this joint research project were able to provide a space for hope through sustained engagement that linked the work of transforming their classes, despite the lack of freedom and isolation of the participants in Gaza with limited resources. This study highlights the accomplishments of a well-planned teacher-education program for teachers serving the most marginalized students and families under Israeli military occupation. Through a well-designed and implemented collaboration, teachers were able to provide a moral space for educational transformation under the direst circumstances of seeming hopelessness.

Education for the oppressed requires that those workers and peasants who were deprived of an education must not only learn to read and write but also must understand that their lack of education is not because they are deficient or backward but that the political and economic systems have deprived them and their children of the right to education. The very act of learning to read is counter to the established oppressive system. Those who learn to read and write must develop a critical literacy, they must learn in community with each other how to ask. This problem-posing takes the form of a dialogue, in which the students and teachers must learn from each other (Wong, 2005).

As Freire and Macedo (2016) point out, to read the word involves reading the world (Darder, 2017; Davids, chapter 2; and Nasser, Abu Hamad, and Mleahat, chapter 5). The former oppressed, whether they be peasants, workers, or former soldiers, must enter into a dialogue of conscious awareness of the systems and structures and their individual role in transforming those oppressive systems. Freire calls this process "conscientização" (Freire, 1970, p. 19) *or conscientiza-tion.* A theme running throughout this volume is how educators become more critically conscious or aware of the inner voice of their students (chapter 4), and their own voices in the transformation of institutions, systems, and structures (chapters 8 and 9).

But how do former colonized and enslaved people understand the nature of their oppression? What pedagogy of the oppressed can they fashion to learn how to analyze their history and current realities (Freire, 1970)? And how do they learn not only to interpret but to change or *transform* those systems and structures of exploitation and domination? (Marx, 2005). The contributors to this volume ask where the hope for independence, self-rule, and freedom is when the sum of colonial discourses justifies the continued domination of Western colonial elites, rulers, educators, and missionaries (Said, 1979), requiring a counternarrative of the colonized (Au, 2018). For the colonized, the task of theory is to ask how we who have been oppressed can overcome the historic class, racial, gendered, ethnic, and religious divisions and hierarchies and injustices. For Homi Bhabha (2004), the third space opens a new cultural path "to conceptualizing an international culture, based not on the exoticism of multiculturalism or the diversity of cultures, but on the inscription and articulation of culture's *hybridity*" (p. 56).

ORGANIZING THIRD-SPACE LEARNING
THROUGH HYBRIDITY

Hybridity stands in opposition to ideologies of domination such as white settler ideologies of superiority and racial "purity" (Mamdani, 2015). We are all part of humankind or the same human species. Although race does not exist as a biological reality, many Western scientists have made false claims of a hierarchy of racial superiority, with Caucasian, Mongoloid, and Negroid in descending order falsely attributed to the size of the brain (Gould, 1996). Critical race theory (CRT) scholars point out that while there is no ontological basis to race, there is a material basis for racism—as an ideology—which is used by dominant classes to reproduce inequalities. Racism and white settler colonialism serve to justify and perpetuate domination, deep divisions of inequality, and systems of exploitation and oppression (Wong et al., 2018). CRT points to the centrality of racism as a key to understanding education and the intersectionality of race, class, gender, and other constructions of difference (chapters 1 and 2). Racism is a powerful ideology that is central to the maintenance of imperialism as the highest stage of capitalism. White supremacist ideologies under colonialism, capitalism, and patriarchy support the defense of white womanhood and simultaneously support multiple political, economic, and social systems of exploitation, oppression, and alienation.

THIRD-SPACE SOCIOCULTURAL LITERACY RESEARCH

In sociocultural literacy research, the construct of third space analyzes in-school and afterschool contexts for learning with dual language or bilingual programs (Gutiérrez et al., 2009). Hybridity is seen as both a theoretical lens and a practical method for organizing learning in which contexts for student development are diverse, conflicting, and complex: "Our analysis of third spaces has shown that learning contexts are immanently hybrid, that is polycontextual, multivocal and multiscriptal. We have examined these tensions as potential sites of rupture, innovation, and change that lead to learning" (Gutiérrez et al., 2009, p. 287).

In contrast to "purist" perspectives of language that promote only the language of the elites from the capital and look down on the language from the villages and periphery, educators who value hybridity take an additive perspective toward language, supporting a plurality of accents, and make the classroom a place where learners develop an awareness of language variation and a new cosmopolitan youth culture identity (Kromidas, 2011; Lippi-Green, 2012). Within any world language such as French or Arabic, educators can choose whether to have an additive perspective, which builds on the home language, or a subtractive approach, which replaces the home heritage language with the so-called superior language (Valenzuela, 1999, 2016).

Critical consciousness honors and embraces Indigenous people's ways of knowing and inquiry such as research as relationship and research as ceremony (Wilson, 2009). Thus, conflict, tension, and diversity are intrinsic to learning spaces. Hybridity is a feature of code-switching, mixing, and creativity, and when students work collaboratively in unofficial talk, they have a feature of improvisation (Gutierrez, 1993). The third space is the place where teachers draw from unofficial student-to-student talk. Third-space theory also provides a way to develop and transform new hybrid social identities through curricular innovation. In Malaysian secondary-classroom contexts, the addition of Malaysian authored texts to an otherwise standardized test-driven curriculum provided a point of departure for secondary students from Malay, Indian, and Chinese backgrounds to develop new hybrid shared identities (Idrus, 2015). A feature of dialogic inquiry suggested by several sociocultural researchers is the need for teachers to problem-pose concerning controversial social justice, political, and ethical issues. Several dimensions to work on hybridity and hybrid language practice include employing critical discourse analysis to see how the ideologies of racism are embedded in the language to dehumanize and blame the victims for their own genocide (using dehumanizing terms such as *half-breeds, animal nature,* and *bastards*) and property laws that support continued privilege of the propertied classes (Lewis & Naples, 2014). The Black Lives Matter movement has raised collective consciousness of the interconnections between race, class, gender, and other hierarchies of domination and privilege through intersectionality (Davis, 2011). This movement insists that the demands of the most vulnerable among us must be included in the leadership—those who face double or triple marginalization due to their race, gender, sexuality, religion, or documentation.

American African literature (Lee, 2000) and American African music from spirituals to jazz (Dixson, 2014; Ladson-Billings, 2013) have been embraced in curricular design to accentuate hybridity as opposed to white supremacist "purist" views of civilization. In traditional foreign-language instruction, the language of the elites and the city's capital is deemed the standard academic language. In this model of education, there is a subtractive (replace the Creole, working-class, or peasant variety, e.g., of language with the language of the elites) rather than an additive approach that draws on the funds of knowledge from households (González et al., 2005).

Several authors in this volume have discussed using Islamic ethics and epistemological principles and resources by drawing on holistic approaches that see the connection of mind, spirit, and body. This is in sharp contrast to Aristotelian approaches that see cognition as superior to emotions. Third-space theory reconceptualizes this binary by reflecting on ways that "we produce research by identifying how we draw on our language, culture, families, communities and the human spirit" (Castillo-Montoya & Torres Guzmán, 2012, p. 555). Once these worlds are brought together holistically, there is a new space for knowledge production in which it is possible to overcome the traditional Western dualism between thought and emotions (Dohei, 2016). Sher Afgan Tareen (chapter 8) and Afeefa Syeed (chapter 9) emphasize the importance of attending to Muslim American dual identity—a holistic approach that overcomes either/or binaries in favor of creating new third spaces to embrace a variety of creative, and nuanced multicultural, multiliterate expressions of hybridity.

SPIRITUAL AND MORAL VALUES AND THE THIRD SPACE

This volume makes a twenty-first-century contribution to the development of hope through the third space, through the Islamic theological and epistemological articulation of the spiritual and moral dimensions of education (Nasser, chapter 1). Across the monotheistic faiths of Judaism, Christianity, and Islam, hope serves theologically as a confirmation of belief in the transcendental Davids (Chapter 2) discusses three interrelated epistemological and ethical practices; namely, *tarbiyah* (socialization), *ta'lim* (deliberative engagement), and *ta'dib* (social activism). Muslim education imbues students with the idea that, through belief, prayer, charity, fasting, pilgrimage, and the exercise of morality, their actions ought to be responsive to societal demands (Selcuk, Chapter 3). Davids (chapter 2) advances the position that if Muslim education is to address the divisions and marginalization within and beyond its communities, then that education must involve hopefulness. Hope involves a reimagined account of Muslim education and advances a cosmopolitan human connection and resonance. This involves reimagining who is the community as well as transformative teaching. Tracing the historical contributions of Muslims as 30% of the African slaves is a curricular model to support thriving Muslim identities within what could otherwise be a hostile, dehumanizing, and diminishing environment (Syeed, chapter 9).

STRENGTH-BASED RESEARCH: DISCOURSES OF EMPOWERMENT

Ilham Nasser points out in chapter 1 that a major aim of this volume is to "respond to the need to shift the educational discourse in Muslim societies from deficiency to a strength-based orientation." There are many reasons for the persistence of deficiency orientations, and the very deconstruction and critical-discourse analysis of deficit educational models are an ongoing task that several authors contribute to on many levels through a project of decolonizing research (Smith, 2013; Tuck & Yang, 2012).

Pedagogies allow and celebrate code-switching and translanguaging to transform deficit orientations through an infusion of ethnic and women's studies text production. Sujin Kim and Kim H. Song (2019) point out that a multilingual family storybook project can be designed to create space for translanguaging that expands family communicative repertoires. They call their collective meaning-making *community translanguage* because it incorporates the voices of multiple social agents and multiple linguistic repertoires to go from individual competency toward collective practice in multimodal collective social space (Canagarajah, 2018). Moving from deficit- to strength-based research provides hope for the most marginalized segments of society. At the policy level, Hussien Chapter 4 discusses the Malaysian government's expansion of education to support international students as well as to democratize and dramatically expand the numbers of local Malaysian students in education.

In chapter 3, Selçuk uses the ninety-nine beautiful names of Allah to highlight the importance of authenticity, lifelong learning, and the importance of the educators. By presenting a pedagogical example of one of the ninety-nine beautiful names of Allah, Al-Fattah (the Opener, the Reliever, the Judge by whose guidance everything that is obscure is made manifest), this volume contributes to Islamic epistemology, knowledge construction, and pedagogical practices that are theologically grounded and student-centered. As students focus and meditate on the ninety-nine names of Allah, they are involved in knowledge production and meaning-making. This holistic approach connecting spirituality, cognition, and learning is a major feature of strength-based and additive approaches to education. Several contributors to this volume discuss holistic approaches in education, exploring pedagogy along the life span of the learner, from early childhood in Palestine (Nasser et al., chapter 5) to high school students in the US (Syeed, chapter 9) to teacher education of adult professional postgraduate women students in Malaysia (Hussien, chapter 4).

Chapter 9 proceeds with sociocultural strength-based and holistic approaches to education by asking the young to reflect deeply on their lived reality as children by analyzing *intentional and mindful religious studies* for developing young Muslims' identity. This is a strength-based approach, as it proceeds from the lived realities of children as young as preschool. By an *integrative or holistic approach* to religious studies, attention is drawn to cultivating (1) building on the existing love of Allah held by students, (2) nurturing the relationship of Allah as the basis for *deen* (faith), (3) emphasizing practices of faith that are integral and relevant to life experiences, and (4) teaching the importance of inclusivity and diversity of practices in worship and action.

INTERGENERATIONAL APPROACHES ACROSS THE LIFE SPAN

Hope is found through intergenerational approaches to education across the life span. Although Russian psychologist Lev Vygotsky only lived to age thirty-seven, he made substantial contributions to understanding human development through four broad lines of sociohistorical research: (1) phylogenesis, or how humans developed compared with other species, particularly through the use of tools such as calendars, (2) how humankind has developed through history (or dialectical historical materialism), (3) ontogenesis, or the study of learning and development throughout the life span, and (4) microgenesis—individual studies, often in educational settings with a particular subject matter (Cole, 1990, p. 92; Vygotsky, 1980). Intergenerational research of passing on knowledge from one generation to future generations combines the second line of research—dialectical historical materialism, which includes analysis of the political and economic systems as they develop historically within a particular epoch such as feudalism in Europe, with the fourth line of research microgenetic study. One of the strengths of this book is the contributors' attention to situating local knowledge within a global context, comparing and contrasting examples of advancing hope in education in Muslim majority societies as well as Muslim educational institutions in which the very existence of Muslim societies and institutions, communities, educators, and students is unjustly threatened, such as in the example of Palestine as well as the US.

What is the value of the intergenerational approach, and what does it mean to pass hope from one generation to the next? Several of this volume's authors have contributed to this theme, discussing advanced models and identifying policies that advance hope through education in very troubling times.

Chapter 4, "Fusion of Horizons," poses an important challenge for twenty-first-century Muslim educators. Contemporary Muslim societies are no longer at the forefront of advancing knowledge, as they were during the golden age of Islam. What does it mean to pass on knowledge to the next generation when there is a crisis of Muslim thoughts and ideas brought about by the history of colonialism? Hussien (chapter 4) suggests that an understanding of Antonio

Gramsci's (1996) concept of ideological hegemony enables us to pierce through the everyday common sense views that support the continued exploitative relations under capitalism as normative. For example, in the field of education, the construct of ideological hegemony enables us to discern the production n and (re)production of the everyday workings of unequal social relations—whether they are based on class, gendered, racial, or ethnic divisions; between the colonizer and the colonized; the exploiter and the exploited; or the oppressor and the oppressed—which are historically produced and socially constructed in the school curriculum, instruction, testing, and identification of students for various tracks and privileges bestowed through such labels as gifted and talented, or deficient and in need of remediation, or hopeless and not worthy of education.

Under capitalism, ideological hegemony works (alongside the power of the police and military) to maintain rule through the realm of ideas. The rulers can maintain their power because their subjects, rather than acting in their own interests or questioning and analyzing the relations, instead eschew a critical analysis of their own interests, out of a sense of resignation. In their false consciousness, they take these relations of abuse and domination as God-given, inherited or natural. All the institutions, policies, and practices in the superstructure are undergirded by the economic base of society. It is the moral responsibility of educators to support the development of critical consciousness and for their students to engage in the quest of ethical responsibility and justice, in all matters of their lives. Idrus (2015) discusses the example of Muslim weddings, which may be construed as Islamic but are entrenched in the culture and traditions of society rather than in Islamic principles and teachings. She also points out that the secular system of values developed through colonialism and globalization has subverted the aim of education from being "a good Muslim" to "the chase for paper qualification for better employability."

The epistemological roots of any contemporary crisis in Islamic thought and education cannot be separated from the history of Western educational thought and the need to decolonize research. We must examine the ideological roots of colonialism, capitalism—and, we might add, imperialism—as foundational to Western knowledge and education. This is consistent with Walter Rodney's (2018) insistence that Africa was not "underdeveloped" but that Europe underdeveloped Africa.

In the effort to address the loss of Muslim tradition and culture, some scholars stress the importance of adopting a dynamic rather than static and fixed view of tradition (Kazmi, 2011). Grounding a critical theory framework in an Islamic worldview entails being guided and directed by Islamic principles and values. In the case of science, Hussien (chapter 4) reminds us that in Islam's golden age, traditional Islamic knowledge incorporated medicine, botany, physics, and mathematics. The *separation* of Islamic education into *sīrah*, fiqh, and Quranic language and secular-based subjects (such as mathematics, science, and geography), which developed under Western colonialism, needs to be replaced with a holistic approach. A holistic approach has been advanced from Muslim, Christian, Jewish, and various other faith perspectives.

As each generation grapples with the significance and meaning of this division and separation of technical and scientific knowledge and spiritual growth and learning, several contributors to this book emphasize that hope lies in the integration of these separations and divisions in teacher education and professional development (El-Bilawi, Krafft, chapters 6 and 7). A key to passing wisdom and knowledge from one generation to another is to develop holistic approaches to education.

Hussien (chapter 4) further points out that a task of critical inquiry is to uncover the hidden ideologies of oppression, including colonialism, secularism, scientism, and neoliberalism. The question posed in the case study in postgraduate education directs our attention to probe the roots or the source of women's oppression. The study illustrates the value of linguistic and cultural diversity as a resource by bringing Islamic women from diverse geographical locales and from societal contexts with common and different linguistic and cultural histories and resources to engage in dialogic inquiry and learning to broaden their horizons. Each class of students brings to curriculum inquiry unique contributions, depending on the composition of the participants. Hussien's case study of a graduate education course in Malaysia of five women from different ethnic and cultural backgrounds found that they shared similar forms of oppression through a pedagogy of hope grounded in an Islamic worldview that they understood was situated. The development of new professional identities through this international educational exchange is a very exciting study, and we hope to see more of this research in the coming years. This study provides a baseline for a longitudinal project involving future collaboration between the five women participants in years to come as well as a model for other studies of women in various locations and contexts of place.

THE WAY FORWARD:
A CRITICAL RESEARCH AGENDA

This book challenge the reader to consider that through hope in education in Muslim societies we can imagine an alternative to human inhumanity, crises, divisions, and brokenness. Within these chapters, authors identify key components to propel critical scholarship and dialogic inquiry for the twenty-first century. A necessary foundation for dialogic inquiry and interfaith dialogue is to place the discussion of advancing hope in education in Muslim societies and Muslim communities within critical historical and global contexts. One cannot understand current global contexts without grounding the discussion within a historical perspective of the golden age of Islamic education and without analysis of the systems and structures of colonialism, racism, occupation, and empire (Chomsky, 2010).

A major contribution from this volume's authors is the *holistic* integration of education that infuses and integrates Muslim values, ethical and moral considerations with in lived realities, and critical self-reflections of critically conscious scholars, educational leaders, and classroom teachers. Dialogic inquiry that cultivates and nurtures Muslim values and epistemological resources for knowledge production is sorely needed in today's ruptured and broken world. More research is needed to critique deficit orientations and to contribute to strength-based pedagogical models and understandings of students' needs. Continued historical research is necessary to engage in postcolonial analysis and criticism of twenty-first-century discourse about Islam in the public sphere (Tehranian, 2008).

This entails examining and correcting bias, myths, and Orientalist stereotypes, policies, and practices in educational research, curriculum, and textbooks, the media, and the academy (Said, 1979). It also requires tracing historical roots of inequities within contemporary education as well as analyzing efforts to combat individual and collective oppression, including alienation and exploitation. This inquiry requires a deep and probing analysis of the systemic relationships between study of political economy, culture, language, and ideology. For example, in understanding women's oppression and a program of action to combat it, intersectionality has been utilized as a critical epistemological heuristic by womanists, feminists of color (Lorde, 2012), and critical theorists (Davis, 2008; Dill et al., 2007; Verma, 2017). Several authors in this volume have taken up criticality through critical theory and critical literacy (Gramsci, 1983; Luke, 2018; Marx & Engels, 2009), critical pedagogy (Freire, 1970; hooks, 1994), poststructural (Lather, 1991), and postmodernism (Harvey, 1989). Further holistic educational research that integrates social, emotional, and spiritual well-being and civic-mindedness throughout the diaspora is needed across the diversity of Muslim societies, educational institutions, and communities.

The contributors to this volume linked theory and practice through reflection. This attention to deep philosophical and ethical grounding is needed by those who are tasked with the moral education of the young. While most of the authors present research within educational institutional contexts, a much-needed area of research presented in this volume is an examination of moral education in out-of-school contexts, such as the teacher-education research project in Palestine (Nasser et al., chapter 5).

By looking at the Arabic roots for gathering (جامعة) and university, one can see through the root constructs a traditional Islamic culture of community. *Surat al-Ma'un* presents the orphan as "the paradigmatic needy figure." With the contemporary global crisis of war and occupation, the urgency of providing for orphans is of utmost importance. More research is needed to provide Muslim ethical teaching on the importance of translating prayer into action and a critical reading of sacred texts to include human rights, social justice, and liberation. More research is needed, especially in areas where Muslims are a numerical minority of the society, to dispel racist and xenophobic myths that prevent Muslims from being recognized as full citizens and contributors to that society. Part 4, "Infusing Hope in K–12 Education" provides an example of a future hope for a better life through an international model (Krafft chapter 7) and cases of Muslim education in the US where the development of Muslim social identity construction is threatened (Tareen & Syeed, chapters 8 and 9). The authors of this volume challenge an international readership of educators to probe and deepen our understanding of our identities as Muslims, Christians, and other faiths (and, we must add, as atheists, agnostics, and not affiliated) to engage in educational discourse that furthers interfaith dialogue and hope in action. In so doing, the authors begin the task of redefining community through transforming education, and reframing and reconstructing third spaces for hope, which eschew essentialism and false binaries. Finding common moral ground through creating spaces for reimagining the future is a necessary basis to link the struggle of hope in education to justice, peace, and human liberation.

Several authors are careful to point out that they have not found a single answer to very complex problems. Through problem-posing or identifying the questions to be examined from the standpoint of those who have historically been excluded from education, criticality in educational research leads to corrective steps to raise consciousness or awareness of the most disadvantaged participants. By incorporating their experiences on the margins of society they have been able to explore new innovative models and advance more democratic educational policies and practices that further hope in education for the previously marginalized and excluded. For example, El-Bilawi's (chapter 6) study of reform efforts in Egypt to incorporate multiple intelligences points out that a holistic approach into the curriculum stresses the importance of including parents, teachers, and school leadership in the educational process. She also emphasizes the need to involve teachers in the process of school reform to take their beliefs and values (and, we would add, their knowledge) into consideration rather than have a top-down model of school reform that ignores the situated knowledge of teachers and other practitioners. El-Bilawi calls for school leadership to create and maintain a comfortable and—she uses the term—harmonious relationship: "Moreover, school administration has to acknowledge teachers' needs, listen to their requests, and appreciate teachers' efforts in a sustainable and systematic manner."

We conclude with a quotation on hope from Palestinian Christian educator Mitri Raheb (2014): "Hope does not wait for vision to appear. Hope is vision in action today. Faith that makes people passive, depressive or delusional is not faith but opium. We have a great deal of that in our region and the world today. Faith is facing the empire with open eyes that allow us to analyze what is happening while, at the same time, developing the ability to see beyond our present capacities. Hope is living the reality and yet investing in a different one" (pp. 129–130).

Each contributor to this volume has presented uniquely situated accounts of historical and contemporary Muslim education from their own sociocultural, linguistic, and religious perspectives and contexts to present multifaceted, contested, and unifying definitions of hope in education of Muslims from around the world. We have appreciated the opportunity to engage with their diverse disciplinary perspectives and epistemological tools, which have provided a robust agenda for continued research for the twenty-first century.

REFERENCES

Au, W. (2018). *A Marxist education: Learning to change the world.* Haymarket.

Baramki, G. (2010). *Peaceful resistance: Building a Palestinian university under occupation.* Pluto Press.

Benesch, S. (2018). Emotions as agency: Feeling rules, emotion labor, and English language teachers' decision-making. *System, 79,* 60–69. https://doi.org/10.1016/j .system.2018.03.015

Bennett, L. (2018). *Before the Mayflower: A history of the Negro in America, 1619–1962.* Colchis.

Bhabha, H. K. (2004). *The location of culture.* Routledge.

Canagarajah, S. (2018). Translingual practice as spatial repertoires: Expanding the paradigm beyond structuralist orientations. *Applied Linguistics, 39*(1), 31–54. https://doi.org/10.1093/applin/amx041

Castillo-Montoya, M., & Torres-Guzmán, M. (2012). Thriving in our identity and in the academy: Latina epistemology as a core resource. *Harvard Educational Review, 82*(4), 540–558. https://doi.org/10.17763/haer.82.4.k483005r768821n5

Chomsky, N. (2010). *Hopes and prospects.* Haymarket.

Cole, M. (1990). Cognitive development and formal schooling: The evidence from cross-cultural research. In L. Moll (Ed.), *Vygotsky and education: Instructional implications and applications of sociohistorical psychology* (pp. 89–110). Cambridge University Press. https://doi.org/10.1017/CBO9781139173674.005

Darder, A. (2017). *Reinventing Paulo Freire: A pedagogy of love.* Taylor & Francis.

Davis, A. Y. (2011). *Women, race, & class.* Vintage.

Davis, K. (2008). Intersectionality as buzzword: A sociology of science perspective on what makes a feminist theory successful. *Feminist theory, 9*(1), 67–85. https://doi.org/10.1177/1464700108086364

Dill, B. T., McLaughlin, A. E., & Nieves, A. D. (2007). Future directions of feminist research: Intersectionality. In S. N. Hesse-Biber (Ed.), *Handbook of feminist research: Theory and praxis* (pp. 629–638). Sage.

Diouf, S. A. (1999). American slaves who were readers and writers. *The Journal of Blacks in Higher Education, 24,* 124–125.

Dixson, A. D. (2014). The fire this time: Jazz, research and critical race theory. In *Critical race theory in education* (pp. 227–244). Routledge.

Dohei, K. L. (2016). *Rethinking sexism, gender, and sexuality* (A. Butler-Wall, K. Cosier, R. Harper, J. Sapp, J. Sokolower, & M. B. Tempel, Eds.). Rethinking Schools.

Fanon, F. (1963). *The wretched of the earth.* Grove.

Freire, P. (1970). *Pedagogy of the oppressed* (Rev. ed.). Herder & Herder. (Original work in Portugese published 1968)

Freire, P., & Macedo, D. (2016). *Literacy: Reading the word and the world.* Routledge.

Gomez, M. A. (2005). *Black crescent: The experience and legacy of African Muslims in the Americas.* Cambridge University Press.

González, N., Moll, L. C., & Amanti, C. (Eds.). (2005). *Funds of knowledge: Theorizing practices in households, communities, and classrooms.* Routledge.

Gould, S. J. (1996). *The mismeasure of man.* W. W. Norton.

Gramsci, A. (1983) *The modern prince and other writings.* International Publishers.

Gramsci, A. (1996). *Prison notebooks* (Vol. 2). Columbia University Press.

Gutierrez, K. D. (1993). How talk, context, and script shape contexts for learning: A cross-case comparison of journal sharing. *Linguistics and Education, 5*(3–4), 335–365. https://doi.org/10.1016/0898-5898(93)90005-U

Gutiérrez, K. D., Baquedano-López, P., & Tejeda, C. (2009). Rethinking diversity: Hybridity and hybrid language practices in the third space. *Mind, Culture, and Activity, 6*(4), 286–303. https://doi.org/10.1080/10749039909524733

Harvey, D. (1989) *The condition of postmodernity.* Basil Blackwell.

hooks, b. (1994). *Teaching to transgress: Education as the practice of freedom.* Routledge.

Idrus, F. (2015). Examining classroom transformational spaces using the third space theory in developing students' sense of shared identity. *Theory and Practice in Language Studies, 5*(1), 28–37. https://doi.org/10.17507/tpls.0501.04

Kazmi, Y. (2011). Islamic education: Traditional education or education of tradition? In *Selected readings in Islamic critical pedagogy, Vol. 1* (pp. 23–64). IIUM Press.

Kim, S., & Song, K. H. (2019). Designing a community translanguaging space within a family literacy project. *The Reading Teacher, 73*(3), 267–279.

King, M. L. (2000). *Why we can't wait*. Penguin. https://doi.org/10.1002/trtr.1820

Kromidas, M. (2011). Elementary forms of cosmopolitanism: Blood, birth, and bodies in immigrant New York City. *Harvard Educational Review, 81*(3), 581–606. https://doi.org/10.17763/haer.81.3.n36gtv7061560v53

Kumi Now Editorial Team. (2018). *Kumi now: An inclusive call for non-violent action to achieve a just peace*. Sabeel Ecumenical Liberation Theology Center.

Ladson-Billings, G. (2013). *Critical race theory—What it is not!*. Routledge.

Lather, P. (1991). *Feminist research and pedagogy within/in the postmodern*. Routledge.

Lee, C. D. (2000). Signifying in the zone of proximal development. (pp. 191–205). In C. D. Lee & P. Smagorinsky (Eds.), *Vygotskian perspectives on literacy research: Constructing meaning through collaborative inquiry*. Cambridge University Press.

Leeman, J., Rabin, L., & Román-Mendoza, E. (2011). Critical pedagogy beyond the classroom walls: Community service-learning and Spanish heritage language education. *Heritage Language Journal, 8*(3), 1–22. https://doi.org/10.46538/hlj.8.3.1

Lewis, R. A., & Naples, N. A. (2014). Introduction: Queer migration, asylum, and displacement. *Sexualities, 17*(8), 911–918. https://doi.org/10.1177/1363460714552251

Lippi-Green, R. (2012). *English with an accent: Language, ideology and discrimination in the United States*. Routledge.

Lorde, A. (2012). *Sister outsider: Essays and speeches*. Crossing.

Luke, A. (2018). *Critical literacy, schooling, and social justice: The selected works of Allan Luke*. Routledge.

Mamdani, M. (2015). Settler colonialism: Then and now. *Critical Inquiry, 41*(3), 596–614. https://doi.org/10.1086/680088

Marable, M. (2011). *Malcolm X: A life of reinvention*. Penguin.

Marable, M., & Aidi, H. D. (Eds.). (2009). *Black routes to Islam*. Springer.

Marable, M., & Mullings, L. (Eds.). (2009) *Let nobody turn us around: An African American anthology*. (2nd ed.). Rowman & Littlefield.

Marciano, J. (2000). The need for an internationalist identity politics. *Educational Studies, 31*, 406–411.

Marx, K. (2005). *Grundrisse: Foundations of the critique of political economy*. Penguin UK. (Original work published 1857).

Marx, K., & Engels, F. (2009). *The economic and philosophic manuscripts of 1844 and the Communist Manifesto*. Prometheus.

Memmi, A. (2004). *The Colonizer and the colonized*. Routledge.

Menkart, D., Murray, A. D., & View, J. L. (2004). *Putting the movement back into civil rights teaching*. Teaching for Change.

National Council of Churches of Christ in the U.S.A. (2019, March 5). *Group Pilgrimage Statement on Israel and Palestine. Leaders of Historically African American and South African Churches February 21st–March 1st 2019. [Press release]*. https://nationalcouncilofchurches.us/group-pilgrimage -statement-on-israel-and-palestine/

Nkrumah, K., Arrigoni, R., & Napolitano, G. (1963). *Africa must unite*. Heinemann.

Pennycook, A., & Makoni, S. (2019). *Innovations and challenges in applied linguistics from the Global South*. Routledge.

Pew Research Center. (2017, July 26). *U.S. Muslims concerned about their place in society, but continue to believe in the American Dream*. https://www.pewforum .org/2017/07/26/findings-from-pew-research-centers-2017-survey-of-us -muslims/

Raheb, M. (2014). *Faith in the face of empire: The Bible through Palestinian eyes*. Orbis.

Rodney, W. (2018). *How Europe underdeveloped Africa*. Verso.

Said, E. W. (1979). *Orientalism*. Vintage.

Smith, L. T. (2013). *Decolonizing methodologies: Research and indigenous peoples*. Zed.

Tehranian, J. (2008). The last minstrel show? Racial profiling, the war on terrorism and the mass media. *Connecticut Law Review, 41*, 781. https://ssrn.com /abstract=1312941

Tuck, E., & Yang, K. W. (2012). Decolonization is not a metaphor. *Decolonization: Indigeneity, Education & Society, 1*(1). https://resolver.scholarsportal.info /resolve/19298692/v01i0001/nfp_dinam.xml

Valenzuela, A. (1999). *Subtractive schooling: US-Mexican youth and the politics of caring*. SUNY Press.

Valenzuela, A. (2016). *Growing critically conscious teachers: Social justice curriculum for educators of Latino/a youth*. Teachers College Press.

Verma, R. (2017). *Critical peace education and global citizenship: Narrative from the unofficial curriculum*. Routledge/Taylor & Francis.

Vygotsky, L. S. (1980). *Mind in society: The development of higher psychological processes*. Harvard University Press.

West, C. (1993). *Prophetic fragments*. William B. Eerdmans.

Wilson, S. (2009). *Research is ceremony: Indigenous research methods*. Fernwood.

Wong, S. (2005, 2011) *Dialogic approaches to TESOL: Where the ginkgo tree grows*. Taylor & Francis/Routledge (formerly 2006 Lawrence Erlbaum).

Wong, S. (2006). Perpetual foreigners: Can an American be an American? In A.
Curtis & M. Romney (Eds.), *Color, race, and English language teaching: Shades of
meaning* (pp. 81–92). Lawrence Erlbaum.

Wong, S., Eng, S. C., & Von Esch, K. S. (2018). Critical race pedagogy. In J. Liontas
(Ed.), *Current trends in ELT and future directions. TESOL encyclopedia of English
language teaching.* Wiley/Blackwell Publishers.

Wong, S., & Grant, R. (2016). Racializing justice in TESOL: Embracing the
burden of double consciousness. In L. Jacobs & C. Hastings (Eds.), *Social
justice and English language teaching* (pp. 165–176). Information Age & TESOL
International.

Woodson, C. G. (2006). *The mis-education of the Negro.* Book Tree. (Original work
published 1933)

NOTE

1. Instead of "African American," Tyrone Pitts self-identifies as "American African." We
use this term throughout the chapter as a description of his core identity as a member of the
international African diaspora and his lived experiences and family history as a descendant of
enslaved African people in the United States.

AUTHORS' BIOGRAPHIES

ILHAM NASSER is Director of Empirical Research in Human Development, part of the International Institute of Islamic Thought's Advancing Education in Muslim Societies (AEMS) initiative. She has spent over twenty-five years in research addressing children's development, teacher education, and professional development, and is the author of peer-reviewed books, journal articles, and book chapters. She holds a PhD in Human Development and Child Study from the University of Maryland–College Park and was a faculty member in teacher education (promoted to associate professor) at George Mason University. Her research focuses on teaching and learning as well as curriculum development in sociocultural and political contexts and ways these influence children's development.

NURAAN DAVIDS is Professor of Philosophy of Education in the Department of Education Policy Studies in the Faculty of Education at Stellenbosch University. Her research interests include democratic citizenship education, Islamic philosophy of education, and philosophy of higher education. She is a fellow of the Center for Advanced Study in the Behavioral Sciences at Stanford University (2020–2021). She is coeditor of the Routledge series *World Issues in the Philosophy and Theory of Higher Education*, associate editor of the *South African Journal of Higher Education*, and an editorial board member of *Ethics and Education*. Her most recent publications include works coauthored with Y. Waghid: *Teaching, Friendship and Humanity*; *Teachers Matter: Educational Philosophy and Authentic Learning*; *The Thinking University Expanded: On Profanation, Play and Education*; and *Democratic Education and Muslim Philosophy: Interfacing Muslim and Communitarian Thought*.

MUALLA SELÇUK is Professor of Philosophy and Religious Sciences in the field of religious education at Ankara University, Turkey. Her research focuses on teaching Islam in diverse societies and contemporary ways of teaching Islam. She served as the first Muslim president of the Religious Education Association (2018) and recently received the Order of Merit of Germany (2020) for her religious and interreligious works. She has worked on many international projects, including Islamic Worldview, Dictionary of Encounter, and Interreligious Anthropology. Her most recent book is *Teaching Islam within a Diverse Society*.

SUHAILAH HUSSIEN is Associate Professor in the Department of Social Foundations and Educational Leadership in the Kulliyyah of Education at International Islamic University Malaysia. She holds a PhD in Education (Philosophy) from the University of Sheffield and has been teaching for more than twenty years at different levels of education. She is an editorial board member of the *IIUM Journal of Educational Studies* and the *Journal of Education and Educational Development*. Her research interests include critical pedagogy, sociology of education, and multicultural education.

DR. BASSAM ABU HAMAD is a faculty of Public Health at Al-Quds University in Gaza, Palestine, holding a PhD in Human Resource Management from Sheffield Hallam University in the UK.

SULIEMAN MLEAHAT is a specialist in early-childhood development with over twenty-five years of experience in international education development. He has worked with five international nongovernmental organizations, successfully planning and implementing numerous preschool education projects in Palestine, Lebanon, and Sudan. He is currently the education director for the American Near East Refugee Aid and is based in Ramallah overseeing the upgrading and construction of over two hundred kindergartens and the training of hundreds of teachers. Sulieman has a BA (East Anglia) and an MSc (Bristol) in international development.

NORA EL-BILAWI is Assistant Professor of Education, a researcher, and an education consultant with over twelve years of experience in academia and research writing, as well as six years of experience in adult and K–12 ESOL teaching. Areas of expertise include teacher education, international education, and multicultural education. El-Bilawi has published many papers and conference presentations in the fields of international education, crosscultural education, teacher training and professional development, Teaching English to Speakers of Other Languages (TESOL), education reform, and the role of policies in educational and social change. One of her projects (with professor Ilham Nasser) was designing and conducting professional development trainings for practicing teachers in diverse contexts.

ANDREAS M. KRAFFT holds a doctoral degree in management sciences at the University of St. Gallen with special focus on organizational psychology, culture, and development. He has academic specializations in social psychology of organizations, work and health psychology as well as positive psychology from the University of Zürich. Dr. Krafft is an associate researcher at the Institute of Systemic Management and Public Governance at the University of St. Gallen. He teaches at the University of Zürich in the field of work and health; the Master of Applied Positive Psychology at the University of Lisbon, Portugal; and the Freie Universität Berlin Social-Psychology of Hope. He is copresident of swissfuture, the Swiss Society of Futures Studies; board member at the Swiss Positive Psychology Association; and head of the International Research Network of the Hope-Barometer since 2010.

SHER AFGAN TAREEN is a postdoctoral fellow at the Center for the Study of Religion and the City, Morgan State University. He studies religion as a social determinant of health, with a particular focus on Islam. His research and teaching focus on the conjoining between humans, machines, and the environment; in other words, artificial intelligence, with women fomenting this exchange to exercise authority as healers.

AFEEFA SYEED is Founder and Board Member of Al Fatih Academy, a nonprofit independent school whose curriculum integrates peace and civic education while nurturing an American Muslim identity grounded in cultural and religious literacy. Here, she develops model educational resources and tools reflecting an integrated approach that nurtures spiritual and learning connections. A cultural anthropologist, Afeefa has for the past thirty years worked with government and nonprofit organizations in the areas of educational innovation; religion; identity; gender inclusion; countering extremism; and integrating cultural and religious context into policy, programming, and diplomacy. She served as senior advisor at the US Agency for International Development, has been a scholar consultant for the Carter Center, is currently a research associate with Cambridge University's Institute on Religion & International Studies, and is a senior fellow and advisory council member at the Institute for Global Engagement Center for Women, Faith & Leadership. Afeefa also serves on the Ghazali Children's Project Advisory Committee.

SHELLEY WONG is Associate Professor at George Mason University, Fairfax, Virginia. She is author of *Dialogic Approaches to TESOL: Where the Ginkgo Tree Grows* (Taylor & Francis), coeditor of *Examining Education, Media, and Dialogue under Occupation: The Case of Palestine and Israel* (Multilingual Matters), and coeditor of *Teachers as Allies: Transformative Practices for Teaching Dreamers and Undocumented Students* (Teachers College Press). A former president of TESOL International, Shelley received a BA in Sociology at the University of California at Santa Cruz, an MA in TESL at UCLA, and an EdD in Applied Linguistics at Columbia Teachers College.

TYRONE PITTS is general secretary emeritus for the Progressive National Baptist Convention Inc. and cochair of the Interfaith Working Group of the Coalition to Transform Advanced Care. He serves on the Central Committee of the World Council of Churches. He previously served as Director of Racial Justice for the National Council of Churches of Christ and was chair of the board of directors of the Morehouse School of Religion. Dr. Pitts is an ordained minister, having earned his Doctor of Ministry degree from the United Theological Seminary in Dayton, Ohio, his MDiv from Colgate Rochester Crozer Divinity School, and his BA in Fine Arts Education and Philosophy from Virginia State University.

INDEX

Lightning Source UK Ltd.
Milton Keynes UK
UKHW041218080922
408480UK00002B/87